Praise for

Me Life Story

'Told in her funny, down-to-earth style, like she's
sitting at your kitchen table sipping a cuppa'
Heat

Llyfrgelloedd Caerdydd
www.caerdydd.gov.uk/llyfrgelloedd
Cardiff Libraries
www.cardiff.gov.uk/libraries

CAERDYDD
CARDIFF

'Incredibly honest'
Best

'Funny... moving'
Irish Sun

'Warm, funny and honest'
Kentish Express

'A heartwarming, honest, modest, inspirational and
totally hilarious life story… Absolutely loved it from the
first page to the last and highly recommend to everyone!'
Chat About Books blog

ACC. No: 05109602

'I read this in one sitting as I was enjoying it so much that I just didn't want to put it down. I highly recommend this book – it's such an honest, funny and all-round lovely memoir!'
Rather Too Fond of Books blog

'The perfect book to curl up with... I genuinely loved this book from start to finish. Filled with wit and warmth, this book is an inspirational story that shows dreams can come true'
Handwritten Girl blog

'*Me Life Story* is peppered with humour [and] is written in a friendly, down-to-earth manner... An interesting, entertaining chat in book form'
From First Page To Last blog

'This book! It is incredible! This is an incredibly honest, moving and funny look into Scarlett's life up to now. 11/10'
Tishylou blog

'This book is hilarious, honest and just so fun to read. I read the whole thing over the course of a day because I genuinely couldn't put it down. It felt like a chat with your best mate, it was definitely a brilliant read! Highly recommended'
Bibliophile Book Club blog

SCARLETT MOFFATT

Me Life Story
Sofa, So Good!

BLINK
bringing you closer

Published by Blink Publishing
3.08, The Plaza,
535 Kings Road,
Chelsea Harbour,
London, SW10 0SZ

www.blinkpublishing.co.uk

facebook.com/blinkpublishing
twitter.com/blinkpublishing

Hardback – 978-1-911-600-46-6
Trade paperback – 978-1-911-600-49-7
Paperback – 978-1-788-700-24-5
Ebook – 978-1-911-600-50-3

All rights reserved. No part of the publication may be reproduced, stored in
a retrieval system, transmitted or circulated in any form or by any means,
electronic, mechanical, photocopying, recording or otherwise, without prior
permission in writing of the publisher.

A CIP catalogue of this book is available from the British Library.

Typeset by EnvyDesign Ltd
Printed and bound by Clays Ltd, St. Ives Plc

3 5 7 9 10 8 6 4 2

Copyright © Scarlett Moffatt, 2017
First published by Blink Publishing in 2017
First published in paperback by Blink Publishing in 2018
All photos courtesy of the author unless otherwise specified
All illustrations © Shutterstock

Scarlett Moffatt has asserted her moral right to be identified as the author of
this Work in accordance with the Copyright, Designs and Patents Act 1988.

FSC
www.fsc.org
MIX
Paper from
responsible sources
FSC® C018072

Every reasonable effort has been made to trace copyright holders of material
reproduced in this book, but if any have been inadvertently overlooked the
publishers would be glad to hear from them.

Blink Publishing is an imprint of the Bonnier Publishing Group
www.bonnierpublishing.co.uk

*To my mam and dad (for all your love and support), to
Ava (for making me laugh everyday), to my auntie Kirsty,
nanny and pappy (for always being there and for all
those sleepovers where I got to watch* Carry On *movies as
a kid), and to the future generation of the family parties
Joshua and Noah xx*

CONTENTS

AMOFFZON

Top customer reviews

★★★★★ **Love the book. Love the girl.**
By Elisabeth Moffatt
Format: Hardback | Verified Purchase

Absolutely loved this book from start to finish – it made me laugh out loud. And I'm shocked at just how truthful Scarlett has been. Some very emotional pages which I must admit brought a tear to my eye. An added note: Scarlett's mother sounds like a hoot. 10/10!

★★★★★ **My sister is a LEGEND!**
By Ava Moffatt
Format: Hardback | Verified Purchase

Eleven out of ten. Best book I've ever read! I loved reading it, I feel like I almost know Scarlett lol.

★★★★★ **One word: canny.**

By Mark Moffatt

Format: Hardback | Verified Purchase

Could not put this book down. Read it in a day.
Nice one kid.

INTRODUCTION:
Sofa, So Good!

★ Ant always stands on the left and Dec on the right. They call it the 180-degree rule.

★ Over its lifespan, your sofa will be witness to roughly 293 arguments and 1,369 cuddles.

★ We find on average £1.80 hidden in our sofas every month. That equates to nearly £180 over the sofa's lifetime (champion: that'll buy 211 sausage rolls from Gregg's).

As I stand there shaking like a shitting dog and smelling of mealworms, I clench Joel Dommett's hand. Ant and Dec are about to announce who has won *I'm a Celebrity … Get Me Out of Here!* And to be perfectly honest I have no idea how I even made it onto the show, never mind made the final two.

I was all ready to say, 'Well done Joel, mate, you've done it, you've won!' But when Dec announced, 'And the new … *Queen* of the Jungle is …', it actually took me brain at least five seconds to process what the words actually meant. 'Queen? Hang on, that must mean I have won, because, well, Joel has a penis and the Queen doesn't have a penis.'

I could barely contain my emotions as I was ushered to the throne by Geordie royalty Ant and Dec. Wow! The show I had watched since I was eleven years old, the show that for the past two years people had watched me watch on *Gogglebox*. Nothing felt real as I was crowned the Queen of the Jungle.

Being on the *I'm a Celeb* throne is my most celebrated sit thus far. This book tells me life story through a whole series of seats. I'm always happiest sitting down. I think there is nothing better than simply sitting around with your family. The comfort and security of the family sofa is where you can truly be yourself, where you can sob your heart out and not be judged, where you can laugh so hard your belly aches.

We all love being a couch potato watching the television from time to time and I personally see it as a hobby. If you want to get into the technicalities of it, I know you're not physically doing much, but your eyes are getting a good workout, aren't they? I mean, really you're practically doing bicep curls – reaching into the packet of crisps, bringing them up to your mouth and repeat. Your legs get some exercise too, as you've got to do a Usain Bolt to the kitchen and make a brew during the ad breaks.

We also all love diving into a good book now and then. When I was little I used to always choose the same three books to read (or for my parents to read to me). It would either be a children's illustrated Bible (although I'm not particularly religious), anything by Dr Seuss and *Aesop's Fables*. That's because I love how the stories in these books always have a motivational quote, a life lesson or a moral at the end. So that's what I've done in this book for you. As well as this, I have started each chapter with one of my true loves in life: facts. This is because I was one of those weird children that actually enjoyed learning. Hopefully, you can take away a few snippets of information from this book and shock your friends with some new-found knowledge. So, say your friend briefly mentions the fact there seems to be a lot of pigeons in town today, you can add, 'Did you know birds cannot urinate?'

So I want you to take a seat, whether it be in the comfort of your own sofa, on the top deck of the bus, the Tube (so you don't have to make eye contact with anybody) or on the throne of the house (the toilet). I want you to get comfortable and get ready to laugh, cry and maybe even learn as I chat to you about some of the highs and lows of my life.

So yeah, so far, sitting on my arse has worked out pretty well for me. That's why I always think:

'Sofa,
so good!'

4

EVERYONE STARTS OUT
AS AN ARSEHOLE

✯ Everyone starts out as an arsehole (we form
around it in the womb).

✯ Down the sides of sofas, underneath carpets,
eaten by children and pets alike ... somewhere
in the world there are over a million missing
Scrabble tiles.

✯ The first nativity scene didn't appear until 1223.
It is a re-enactment of Jesus's birthday (which
was not actually 25 December, it was more
likely 17 June, scientists now think).

It all started with a game of Scrabble (as most good tales do). The year 1990, me mam Elisabeth, known to her friends as Betty, then aged twenty, had black Tina Turner-inspired permed hair and stood pretty and petite at five foot two. My mam has always had golden sun-kissed skin, which she normally hides under layers and layers of black clothes. With Disney princess features of a button nose, little round face and blue eyes she is just beautiful. Now we all get a mix of our parents and from my mam I took my monobrow, my coarse hair and little sticky-out ears. But I would also like to think I get my intelligence from her. She can digest a whole book in one day, she can do a Sudoku faster than anyone I know and can complete a Rubik's cube in less than ten minutes. Despite this she still loves trash TV like *Mob Wives* and *Toddlers and Tiaras*. She is such a fussy eater and eats nothing but beige food (chips, rice, bread – even her condiments like salad cream and mayo are beige). I definitely get my sarcasm from her; her tongue is so sharp she can cut glass with it.

My dad, Mark, who everyone knows as Toffo, was then twenty-four with an Alan Shearer haircut (that's what he asks for when he goes to the barbers). Standing at five foot seven he has the cheekiest chappy smile you have ever seen. My dad isn't really a sun worshipper and has what I like to call ginger skin, translucently pale with freckles (I can say this because I love gingers and I inherited this skin from him). He loves historical documentaries and football and I get my passion for museums and conspiracy theories from him. He eats nothing beige and instead eats anything that has once had a pulse (he also doesn't believe in sell-by dates; he thinks it's a conspiracy against consumers).

They are the complete opposites in every aspect but that's why they work so well together. They had no idea that when they first laid eyes on each other in 1988, as their eyes met across the Queen's pub dance floor and the sound of 'The Only Way Is Up' by Yazz and the Plastic Population filled their ears, they had found their soulmate. And that just two years later, on this day, 'the Scrabble day', the pair of them would have just found out they were both expecting a little baby girl (me).

Undecided on names, they did what every couple does – made a brew, sat themselves down on their very nineties brown floral sofa and played a game of Scrabble to determine who would pick the order of the names of their firstborn precious child. They had both already chosen names from their favourite movies to narrow the search down.

My mam had chosen *Gone with the Wind*, more specifically Scarlett O'Hara; the insecure, spoilt, intelligent heroine who is hopeless around men and who made a smashing dress out of a pair of curtains (I feel like this namesake explains a lot about how I ended up, especially the A* I got in GCSE textiles for making a corset).

My dad had chosen his favourite movie too. I know what you're thinking: did he choose a classic dad film, like *The Godfather* – did he want to name me after Diane Keaton? Or maybe Bonnie from *Bonnie and Clyde*? Oh no, not my dad, because that would be far too normal. Nope, my dad is a huge sci-fi fan and his favourite movie involves a woman giving birth through her stomach to a freaky, phlegm-covered creature from God knows what planet. That's right, Sigourney Weaver in *Alien*. (I feel like this other namesake explains my love of

UFOs and why I have never been brave enough to give birth.)

Thank God my mam knew the word quixotism (eighty-one points on a triple word score). So now as I'm about to start school as a five-year-old child, I have to learn how to spell my full name (which in all honesty I couldn't properly spell until I was about ten).

Scarlett Sigourney Moffatt.

Being named after stars from the big screen, it isn't surprising that one of my favourite things to do was to sit down and get engrossed in watching the TV.

That and reading; I have always loved to read and to be read to. When I was little I remember sometimes wishing the day away as I'd love it when 8.30 p.m. would come round. 'What do you want for your supper, little one?' my dad would shout through from the kitchen (because clearly it's easier to shout than to walk ten steps into the living room). 'Two crumpets please, with the edges cut off.' Nine out of ten times it would be crumpets with a ridiculous amount of butter on (almost more butter than actual crumpet) then my mam or dad would take me to my bedroom, tuck me in and read me a story.

I realise now just how blessed I am to have had such an amazing upbringing with loving parents because I understand that not everybody has a childhood like this. But I don't take the relationship I have with them for granted. Don't get me wrong, me and my mam argue like cat and dog as we are so similar (she would never admit this). But they are my best friends. It might sound sad to some, but we are the County Durham Von Trapps, the Bishop Auckland Brady Bunch; we even sing together in the house. Sickening, I know.

So when I wasn't being a geek obsessing over *Aesop's Fables* or Dr Seuss I was watching the good old telly box. My earliest memory of this is when I'm about five years old and I'm sat on my nanny's comfy sofa propped up on a big V-shaped pregnancy pillow. Now my nanny (my mam's mam), Christine Smiles – I know, great name! – is one of those amazing stereotypical nannies. She has a cute little brown pixie crop which sits on top of her four-foot-eleven-inch body (she claims she should be given free wedged shoes from the government) and she is always wearing an olive-green dressing gown and knitting. When she isn't knitting she likes to moan about the weather, and she gives the greatest hugs and always has a freezer full of goodies like screwballs, choc ices and Arctic rolls. And she has always, for as long as I can remember, had strange little sayings and songs like this little tune:

'No, you cannit push your nanny off the bus
No, you cannit push your nanny off the bus
You cannit push your nanny, coz she's your mammy's mammy
Don't push your nanny off the bus.'

However, there is one thing about her that's a little different to a typical nan: she was only thirty-seven when she became a nanny. Looking back now, it's crazy to think I saw her as my old nanny when I'm only a decade away from being that age myself.

We would sit together for hours on her grass-green leather recliner couch (you cannot ever decline a recline) as she brought me endless supplies of Horlicks and peanut-butter sandwiches. Sometimes she would even let me eat the peanut butter straight from the jar with a little silver teaspoon. If it was a hot summer's night we would share a big bowl of tinned fruit with squirty cream. My favourite thing to watch with my nanny was Norman Wisdom. A lot of the jokes (as I was only five) would go straight over my head, but there's one episode where he loses his trousers out of the train window that made me laugh so hard I would cry. I'd annoy my nanny by asking her to rewind that bit over and over again. The living room would literally shake because of the vibrations from rewinding the VHS player. I would shush the inanimate object telling him (yes, the VHS player was male) to be quiet in case he woke up my Grandad Tommy who was always napping.

I used to love it when I got to have a sleepover on a Saturday at my nanny and grandad's. I'd lie in bed with my Noddy toy (I have had this plush Noddy since I was three years old; he has faded over the years and has had his bell in his hat changed about twenty times and he smells like damp, but he is a safety blanket to me) and I would watch the same two films that I'd watched the last time I slept over. *Carry On Screaming!* and *Willy Wonka and the Chocolate Factory*. Always in that order so I could go to sleep dreaming of a chocolate river. I'd raid my nanny's knitting cupboard when I watched *Willy Wonka* as it was full of family-sized chocolate bars, normally fruit and nut (so I would pick the fruit out as no one wants one of their five a day in a chocolate bar). It's like the unwritten law that you have to eat sweets and chocolate whilst watching this movie; it creates a sweet ambience – that and the fact my mouth always waters when Augustus falls in all that chocolate, the lucky guy. Growing up on Norman Wisdom and *Carry On* movies from the age of five, it's not surprising that I have an unusual sense of humour.

As a family we all have quite a warped sense of humour so I can't pinpoint directly whose genes I get it from. We have never been one of those families that sit down formally at a table for Sunday roast and make pleasantries. I mean when I was a kid we would go to my nanny's every Sunday and Grandad would make a cracking dinner, but we would all sit on the couch with the television on. That said, it was switched on purely for background noise so we weren't really watching it properly. Normally it would be an *EastEnders* omnibus so I'd just get a glimpse of Phil Mitchell and his egghead or hear Peggy screaming, 'Get out of my pub!'

Sundays are some of my favourite ever family memories. There would be a constant whistle in my nanny's house on a Sunday: the kettle would permanently be on the go as there was always at least nine of us wanting a brew. Drinking strong cups of Yorkshire tea from the age of five must be a northern thing; I think all that caffeine does something to your brain and makes you instantly friendlier. Me and my cousin Keegan (who is two years younger than me) would be asking for our Sunday dinner to be put in a bowl because the dogs would be trying to get to our plates and the gravy was that watery it would be spilling all over the carpet. We didn't want to risk spillage because we didn't want to get in trouble and not be allowed a slice of Arctic roll.

Ah, the joy of all of us sat around, winding each other up. Ever since I can remember, my family have always been brutal. Slating each other, character building as my mother would say. In our family, the more you love someone the more you insult them. A loving conversation and a sign of affection on a classic Moffatt Sunday would go like this:

Uncle Danny: 'You alreet like, dick lips?'

Dad: 'Aye, sound, shitty arse, how's work gannin'?'

Auntie Kirsty: 'Toffo, pass me the salt from the side of the couch, lizard neck.'

It has always been this way in the Moffatt household. I learnt from a very young age that no one is realer than your family. They compliment you behind your back, but criticise you to your face. That is real love! In all honesty we are just like the Royle family when we are all gathered together. Now I don't mean Her Majesty, Prince Philip and the other lovely lot. I mean the TV show where they would all sit around the telly and natter – Jim Royle, Denise Royle and Antony (the lazy streak of piss). My mam reminds me of Barbara; she's the glue that holds the family together, and bless her she always seemed to be running around like a blue-arsed fly when I was a kid.

However, our work ethic is completely different to TV's Royle family. It's crazy, as a kid I actually remember being annoyed about my mam and dad always being at work. Other kids in my class got picked up by their parents. Some of my friends whose parents had split up got to see their dads for a whole weekend. But my dad got up when only owls should be awake: 5:30 a.m. his alarm would go off, and still does go off at that time to this day, as he needed to go off on his shift as a welder. My dad would leave home when it was dark and come back home when it was dark, six days a week. I felt like I'd only see him for an hour a day.

My mam and me would wake up at about seven in the morning. I would sit up in my cosy bed while my mam, without fail, would be singing tunefully, 'Good morning, good morning, here's your mam to wake you up. Good morning, good morning to you!' I would rearrange all of my Beanie Babies that I'd got free as a toy from my McDonald's Happy Meals (1996 Maccy D toys were the best) before skipping down the stairs. Me mam would get ready for work; she worked in retail at a shop called Etam. My school uniform would be laid out nicely pressed for me and I would wave my mam off as she jumped on the 1B bus and go to my friend Kyle's house where his mam would take me to school.

'It's not fair,' I'd shout at Mam and Dad later, as I'd storm up the stairs at home, wishing they would lose their jobs so they could spend all their hours with me. It's only now as an adult that I realise I was the one who wasn't being fair. I didn't give my mam and dad the credit they deserved for how hard they grafted. That's why every day I just try and make them proud; it's my way of saying thank you.

If I ever was 'naughty' as a kid, like when I'd storm upstairs, I had a system that would always get me back in their good books. I've actually passed this knowledge down to my little sister Ava (there's a fifteen-year age gap between us but don't worry, I'll be chatting lots about this little tinker later). What I'd do is I would write my parents a heartfelt letter complete with illustrations of love hearts, and I'd sometimes – if I had done something really bad – lick the paper so it looked like my tears had fallen on it.

The letter would normally read:

> To the greatest mam and dad in the world,
> I am so so so sorry for what I have done.
> I think it would be best for all of the Moffatt
> family (Mam, Dad and the dog Glen) if you
> took me back to the shop you bought me at and
> swapped me for a better kid. I am packing my
> bag right now.
>   Love you and miss you already
>   Scarlett xXxXx

I would then quickly run down the stairs, shove the letter underneath the living-room door, give three loud knocks and run back upstairs. I normally had to only wait by my bag on the landing – packed with the essentials of my Noddy toy, a spare pair of pants, some Roald Dahl books and a coat – for about three to four minutes. Then I would hear the footsteps of my loving parents coming up to comfort me. They had bought into the letter. Hooray! I wouldn't be swapped for another kid; they forgave me. So then I'd go downstairs, sit on the couch and my dad would ask me what I wanted to watch on the TV.

I'm sure if you asked my family they wouldn't say I was a 'bad kid'. I always said my pleases and thank-yous. I never liked upsetting anyone or seeing anyone upset. In fact, on a few occasions I remember my mam telling me not to be so sensitive as I would see an old person sat eating by themselves and instantly burst into tears. I don't like the thought of anyone being alone, so I'd daydream about adopting the old person and them coming to live in our spare bedroom. I'd bring them a bowl of Werther's Originals every morning, and let them watch old documentaries about the war. They would never ever have to be alone again.

However, despite not being a 'bad kid' I did have a couple of slip-ups where I would have to be sent to my least favourite seat. The naughty seat. I remember being about six and being told I was only allowed one KitKat from the tin. So I snuck to the kitchen and shoved a whole multipack down my pyjama leggings. I walked to the couch bold as brass with misshapen legs, crackling when I walked from all the tin-foil wrapping, and sitting there watching *Changing Rooms* on the TV, just waiting for my mam to tell me it was bedtime so I could feast upon all forty KitKat fingers. However, the gas fire was on three bars and all the chocolate soon melted to the point where it started to come through my pyjamas and looked like I had violent diarrhoea. No one won that day: I lost my favourite pair of PJs and my dad had no KitKat for his bait box for work the next morning.

Like I said, I wasn't a bad kid, in fact I was a bit of a hermit so I didn't ever get into trouble outside of home. I mostly just read. I'd sit in my rocking chair (I know I sound about eighty) and read endless pages of Roald Dahl, Dr Seuss, C. S. Lewis, Jacqueline Wilson and Terry Deary. The characters were my friends – although I did have a Friday ritual with an actual

Me and Rosie lounging around with our fab fringes.

human being friend. Every Friday, without fail, I would go to my best friend Rosie's house.

Rosie was beautiful inside and out. Confidence oozed from her, she had the most beautiful auburn hair that went right down to her elbows (everybody complimented her on it), porcelain skin and little rosy red cheeks to match her name. We would get given 50p after school to go to Steve and Suki's shop which would buy us a 20p mix-up bag, a gobstopper, a packet of Space Raiders crisps, a Taz chocolate bar and a juice drink that had been frozen (bloody inflation eh, you couldn't buy a packet of crisps these days for 50p). Then we would make the walk up Busty Bank and her dad would make us pancakes for tea. Didn't matter what the weather was – every week it would be pancakes.

Rosie's dad had rhubarb in his garden, so he'd give us a cup of sugar and a stick of rhubarb and we'd sit and watch *Bernard's Watch* and we'd eat our rhubarb, dipping it in the sugar. Then he'd come on through with the pancakes (I had mine with golden syrup on – to be honest it was always more golden syrup than pancake) and we'd watch *The Queen's Nose*.

The only drawback was that Rosie's was the first place I'd ever watched a programme with clowns in it, and ever since I was a bairn, I've hated clowns. Where does that come from? My mam said that when I was four, Darlington, a town that I live near, opened its first McDonald's. We went along to it as soon as it opened as I was so excited for a Happy Meal. I mean, a meal that literally makes you happy. Well, imagine my disappointment when we rock up to find Ronald McDonald was there. I hated him on sight. I was petrified and closed my eyes for so long, I fell asleep.

So I don't know whose bright idea it was, but one time when I went round Rosie's – it must have been around Christmas 1999 as the tree was up – we decided to watch *It*, the Stephen King horror story about a demonic clown (getting into the festive spirit). We were literally nine years old. Oh my God, I didn't sleep for a week.

I didn't dare tell my mam, because I knew that she would go mad. But I kept saying, 'Can I just sleep in your bedroom tonight?'

She'd be like, 'No, you've got to sleep in your own bed.' I'd just be lying there thinking every shadow or noise was 'It'. Absolutely terrifying.

Here is another random fact: did you know that Johnny

Depp is terrified of clowns? Not being funny but he is best mates with Tim Burton and played a man who had scissors for hands. So if even Captain Jack Sparrow doesn't like clowns, I don't feel like I'm being such a wimp after all.

Me and Rosie never discussed *It* or clowns ever again. We focused on the joy of Christmas and pretended the clown night never happened. Anyway we had bigger things to worry about; it was the Timothy Hackworth Primary School Nativity Play. Me and Rosie and the rest of the class all sat down cross-legged on the cold, hard assembly floor (how we all didn't have piles from sitting there for hours on end I do not know), with our fingers on lips to stop us chatting (which was stupid as you could still talk), all nervously awaiting the most important news of the year: who was going to play who in the school nativity play (big news when you are nine). I was crossing my fingers and toes tight and muttering to myself, 'Please not a narrator, please not a narrator'. Followed by, 'Please not a barnyard animal, not the barnyard animal.' Hallelujah! I hadn't been given my role yet and there was only the role I'd been waiting to play my whole life left … Mary.

'Sorry, Scarlett, I forgot about you there, you will play … Angel number two,' announced Mrs Henderson cheerfully.

'Holy Santa Claus shit! Is this real life? I don't even have a part with a name, I'm not even Angel number one.'

Scarlett's monobrow strikes yet again; after all, we can't have an ugly child play the Virgin Mary. That's what I imagined all the teachers had discussed in the staff room, anyway. For the third year in a row the teacher's pet, Stacey Vaughn, was given the part of Mary and I was gutted. If only

I had perfectly straight hair like Stacey Vaughn instead of looking like Winnie the Witch crossed with Crystal Tipps. If only I had nice delicate eyebrows that looked like little worms rather than one huge bushy slug across my forehead. If only I could have been given the part of Mary.

I was not going back home and telling my mam and dad to get ready to get the old bed sheet, pipe cleaners and tinsel out yet again to make another angel costume. Nope, not happening. So what I did was I slightly manipulated the truth. 'Sit down, family, I have very exciting news. I am going to be the mam of baby Jesus. That's right, I got the part of Mary!' They were buzzing. My mam called my nanny up to tell her the great news.

So a few weeks pass and I've helped my mam make the Mary outfit by dyeing an old bed sheet blue and I've learnt my Mary lines with the help of my dad. The big night arrives. The curtains open and there I am. Angel number two – you can spot me as I'm the only angel in Bethlehem with cerulean blue undertones to my garment. Stacey came out and gave a performance that Dame Judi Dench would be proud of. As the curtain closed and everyone's family was allowed into the class for orange dilute and biscuits, I didn't even dare look at me mam and dad.

'Sorry,' I whispered, thinking I was going to get in trouble, but my mam and dad just looked at me. 'We are proud of you whatever you do, you don't ever have to pretend to be something you're not.' Then the words no child ever wants to hear: 'We are more disappointed than angry.'

No, not the 'd' word, anything but that. This was honestly the biggest lie I have ever told to date – I mean we laugh about this story now, but to be honest it did teach me a valuable lesson. Just be yourself; you should never have to lie to impress people. In the words of Dr Seuss, as read by Mam and Dad during my childhood bedtimes:

> *'Those who mind don't matter and those*
> *who matter don't mind.'*

Chapter Two

HOW IS EVAPORATED MILK THERE IF IT'S ALREADY EVAPORATED?

★ During World War II, British soldiers got a ration of three sheets of toilet paper a day. Americans got twenty-two (they must have bigger arses).

★ The average worker bee produces about one-twelfth of a teaspoon of honey in her lifetime (remember that when you're smothering it all over your toast).

★ The original Encyclopaedia Britannica written in 1768 described our solar system as having only six planets. Uranus, Neptune and Pluto (now known as a dwarf planet) were yet to be discovered.

I loved primary school. I genuinely looked forward to sitting on my little, cheap blue plastic classroom chair, constantly knocking my knees on the tray underneath my desk, ready to learn. As I mentioned earlier, I loved learning and being able to fill my brain with facts. My passion for facts is just part of my character. My dad knows loads of facts about history. He always says if you don't know your history, you can't know your future. So we've always been into history and we'd watch documentaries together. Wherever they were in the programme, we'd actually have to have an encyclopaedia open to find out about that place.

We went old-school because we couldn't use Wikipedia. We only had dial-up internet, and that would take ages, especially if my mam was on the phone to my nanny. Then we couldn't get on the internet at all, so we'd be looking through the encyclopaedia. My dad would take me to the library too. We actually liked going to the library. Can you believe that?

This could be where my love of Professor Stephen Hawking stems from. He is my crush. I just love Hawking. He is the cleverest man on the planet – and he adores random facts! I know, of all the men I could have had a crush on – Brad Pitt, say, or George Clooney – but nope, I am all about the Hawking.

I am a huge question asker, much to the annoyance of everyone I know really. My Google search history legitimately looks like an eight-year-old child has pinched an iPhone. Examples of my recent searches:

How do worms eat if they haven't got a face?

How do I know if I'm real and not just a dream of somebody else?

Are eyebrows facial hair?

Who wrote the Bible?

How is evaporated milk there if it's already evaporated?

It was 1996 when I first started Timothy Hackworth Primary School, I was five and enjoyed watching *Brum* or *Chuckle Vision* on a morning with my Lucky Charms (before they banned the cereal for having more sugar than a bucket of blue Smarties), Coco Pops or a dunk (a dunk is basically a cup of tea with a whole packet of biscuits; bourbons or chocolate digestives were my favourite. Never really seen the point in malted milks or plain digestive biccies).

Although I kept myself to myself and didn't really have a close set of friends, I enjoyed Timothy Hackworth Primary. I flitted from group to group at playtime and never really sat with the same person at dinner. Even though Rosie was my best friend we didn't actually hang around together much in the playground. I also never had someone I could instantly run to when the teacher would say, 'OK class, everybody get into pairs.' Sometimes I would water all the plants in the junior building for the teachers during break and I would have a little chat in my head to the plants. It's statements like that, when I look back, that make me now see why I didn't have a squad.

I'd love to just sit in and read a book. Why would I want to be outside when it's spitting with rain, playing bulldog, stick-in-the-mud, kiss, cuddle and torture or making daisy chains? I would much rather be reading about what trouble Tracy Beaker was getting herself into at the Dumping Ground. Jacqueline Wilson was who I wanted to be when I was older;

I would read her books – *The Illustrated Mum*, *The Suitcase Kid* – over and over again. 'Goosebumps' books were my favourites on rainy days, like *How I Got My Shrunken Head* or *Say Cheese and Die*. Books and the characters in them were always my friends. I'd be transported into another world and for that half an hour I could be anybody I wanted to be. I could be beautiful, popular, confident, even a famous movie star.

Imagine my delight when at the age of six our school is introduced to this brand new event: World Book Day. Reading out the newsletter to my mam and dad over my shepherd's pie at teatime, I explained that the whole school, even the teacher, was going to dress as any character from a book that we wanted. This wasn't a mufti day where you would pay 50p and wear your own clothes; oh no, this was going to be so much better.

'Dorothy from *The Wizard of Oz*?' my mam suggested. Then my dad piped up, 'Or she could go as a Disney princess?' I just couldn't decide. The date of World Book Day arrived and in true Moffatt form we were lastminute.com. I had no outfit and I was stressing out. Me mam had an idea. She came from the kitchen with a pair of black tights, some newspaper, my black school headband, a roll of black bin bags and some yellow gaffer tape. 'You'll go as a bee,' she announced.

I was fuming. I know the expression 'she could wear a bin bag and look good', but come on mother, this was social suicide. Surely I couldn't pull this off? Sweating I was, all padded out with newspaper tucked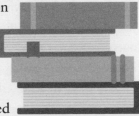

into a bin bag, held together by strips of yellow gaffer tape. Off to school I trotted with my character's book in my hand: R. L. Stine's Goosebumps' *Why I'm Afraid of Bees*. I even came second and won a certificate for best dressed. See, old-school costumes are the best, none of this store-bought princess dress with matching head-dress malarkey.

Despite loving to learn, my favourite part of the day was still dinnertime. I bloody loved school dinners. Those handy little blue trays with a compartment for your drink, cutlery, main and dessert. Turkey Twizzlers, the cheapest baked beans they could find in tins the size of wheelie bins and potato smiley faces were my favourite. Followed by that chocolate cake that's covered in sugar with the texture of a brick, with lashings of green minty custard. Jamie Oliver, eat your heart out. Kids these days don't know what they're missing now they have this Pasta King and salad bar shit going on. Just give them some of those 9p sausages and chunky chips, builds the immune system up. Never did any of us nineties kids any harm.

Remember school trips? I never went on any of the extravagant ones, but I did love a school trip. I remember being in Year 6 when it was the year of the millennium, 2000. The majority of the class were going to Paris. When it was announced, all the other girls, even at eleven years old, were talking about trying to sneak a glass of wine when the teachers weren't looking and how they couldn't wait to try authentic Paris pizza. I quickly pointed out that Paris wasn't known for its pizza, it originated in Italy, and mentioned how I couldn't wait to try their local delicacy of snails. After that conversation it seemed like everyone had already worked out the sleeping arrangements at the hostel (without me). So I decided it would be best if I didn't go.

There was me and about eight others out of a year of sixty kids that didn't go to Paris. So what did the school make us do while everyone else was enjoying the Arc de Triomphe and eating freshly baked pain au chocolat? We had to create a sixty-page project on France. Bit cruel when I look back now, sitting there in class with worksheets, having to cut out pictures of the Eiffel Tower and Pritt-Stick them onto the page while the pissed-off teacher who didn't get to go on the trip moaned about how the other kids and teachers will now be on top of the real Eiffel Tower taking in breathtakingly beautiful 360-degree panorama views of all Paris. I honestly didn't mind; my mam every night that week made me and my dad meals like mince and dumplings but with a French twist (baguette and butter on the side) while we watched reruns of Crystal Maze and Gladiators. She'd even got some croissants in for my breakfast. So I didn't feel like I was missing out.

The greatest school trip I ever went on was when I was ten years old and we went to Eden Camp. Now Eden Camp occupies a former Second World War prisoner-of-war camp of thirty-three huts. This camp is full to the brim of old war memorabilia, ration books, Nazi uniforms and images of Hitler. Scarlett, how is this your favourite school trip? Well, it was at Eden Camp, surrounded by all the horror of the Nazis, where I had my first ever kiss. How romantic, I hear you cry.

The teacher had forced the class to sit girl/boy on the coach to stop us all from messing around. I was put next to Christopher Minns. He wasn't the coolest of kids but he was still quite popular. He was well liked due to his vast collection of shiny Pokémon cards that he would swap. It's my first ever recollection of actually sitting and chatting to a boy for more than five minutes, and even if it was forced, I felt like it was fate. Christopher was just lovely; he had shaved brown hair, a tan and everybody said he looked like a young Mr Bean (not Sean Bean, the actual Mr Bean as portrayed by Rowan Atkinson).

We chatted for the full hour and a half of the journey about the important stuff in life – what we liked to watch on TV, our favourite takeaway, etc. We even shared a dislike of a couple of people in our class (nothing brings people closer together than the shared dislike of another human). I found out he loved Goosebumps as much as me, and he had been to see Steps in concert too with his little sister. He showed me this trick where he turned his eyelids inside out and I showed him my trick of saying the alphabet backwards really fast. This was my first experience of a date and I was loving it. At one point I remember I found myself laughing at jokes he was telling, even though they weren't funny. What had I become?

The coach pulled up to Eden Camp and I knew that was our relationship over; he would scoot off to his friends and I'd tag along with Rosie and her mates again. But no, he asked if he could be my partner around Eden Camp. I'd never felt this feeling before. I could hear my heart beat and had a sudden urge to give him a cuddle. But I didn't, I kept my cool. 'Sure, I'll be your partner.'

As we walked around I gave Christopher Minns some insightful extra facts that weren't on the leaflet we had been handed. I was trying to be cute. 'Did you know, Christopher, that during rationing, adults weren't even allowed a real-life egg, just one packet of dried eggs every month?'

'You are so clever, Scarlett,' he said, then he mumbled these beautiful words that I shall never forget: 'I love how you have your hair like Pippi Longstocking in those plaits.' With that, in bunker number three, surrounded by old newspaper clippings with the creepy ambience of wartime music playing in the background, he kissed me on the cheek. I wanted to scream, I couldn't believe it. A boy liked me, for me. My face flushed crimson and we held hands (well at least whenever the teacher wasn't looking) for the rest of the day.

That night at home, lying in bed, I started planning our wedding and wondering if I'd miss being a Moffatt now I was going to be Scarlett Minns. On the plus, at least I'd get to keep the same initials – SM. I named the three dogs that Christopher and I would have: Rosie, Jim and Rag Doll. I imagined our mansion (we could afford this as Christopher would find a rare shiny Pokémon card and it would be worth millions).

Sadly that illusion was shattered the next day at school when he completely ignored me. It was just a school trip romance, apparently. I was gutted but it did give me that confidence boost I needed to keep on just being me. About a week later he had a new relationship (the dickhead). In fact, he started going out with none other than Stacey Vaughn (yep, the bitch that stole the role of Mary away from me) but I'm not bitter. In the words of RuPaul:

'Don't get bitter, just get better.'

Chapter Three

IF YOU LIKE PIÑA COLADAS AND GETTING CAUGHT IN THE RAIN

★ There's no tooth fairy in Spain – when Spanish children lose a tooth, they put it under their pillow and a small mouse called Ratoncito Pérez comes to collect it and leaves a small gift or money in its place.

★ Dolphins and whales have belly buttons (weird I know, but not weirder than the fact that goldfish have teeth in their throats).

★ James Blunt recorded his first album while living with Carrie Fisher. 'Goodbye My Lover' was recorded in her bathroom!

E ven though I loved school, I loved the six weeks off even more, because it meant me and the family would be going on our jolly holidays. These have varied through the years from camping out, to caravan parks, to bathing on the sunny beaches of Europe. Wherever we would go, despite being slightly shy, I would partake in whatever kids' club was on offer. I would make a new best friend, adopt whatever accent they had (Liverpudlian, Cockney, even Swiss) and pack my case at the end of the holiday with endless certificates and bits of shite arts and crafts I had made.

The first ever holiday I can properly remember snippets of was a week in Spain – Salou to be exact. I got my new passport with a photo that made me look like I had an abnormally large head. The date of issue was July 1998, so I was only seven. My mam told me to pack a little backpack as she packed the big cases for the plane (when you're seven, a two-and-a-half-hour flight sounds like forever). Of course I packed my Noddy toy, my Tamagotchi (otherwise she would die and to me she was my child), a pack of Pokémon cards in case I bumped into anyone who wanted to do some swaps and give me a shiny, my *Aesop's Fables* book and a colouring book and pencils my mam had bought for me at WHSmith.

'Should we take the crocodile-shaped lilo this year? I can go in the attic and bring it down!' my dad shouted down the stairs.

'No, they're only about ten pesetas, Mark, stop being tight. What did you even bring it back for anyway? We haven't got space for a bloody crocodile in the case, we can only just fit the bloody toiletries in here.'

35

'It was just an idea. 'Ere, don't forget that little list of people that want fags bringing back. Right, Scarlett, I'll take you up to bed in a little bit, kid, when you've finished packing your boot bag.'

'Dad, I'm not being funny but the street lights aren't even on. *The Bill* hasn't even been on the telly yet.'

'We all need to go to sleep super early because the taxi is booked for three in the morning to get to the airport. You don't want to be tired on the first day of your holidays, do you?'

I lay there awake, just staring at the animal wallpaper on my walls with the same feeling I had on Christmas Eve. I kept picturing all the things I would be doing on my jollies. Paddling around the sea with my little mermaid armbands on (I've never been a strong swimmer, as some of you would have seen when I was in *I'm a Celebrity* and I had to be rescued by Larry Lamb – but I'll come back to that disaster later). Trying to beat all the other kids' sandcastles with my dad and digging a hole big enough for me to stand in. Getting up super early so we could save a sun lounger before all the Germans got the best ones. Being allowed to eat a whole share bag of Cheetos to myself in one sitting. I couldn't wait.

The morning came and I put on the outfit that was laid out, having been specifically bought for travelling purposes: new Tammy Girl T-shirt, leggings and Daz white trainers. I was ready! At the airport we bought tubes of Pringles, chocolates and sweets in fear that we wouldn't see English food for another week. I also managed to persuade my mam to get me an *Art Attack* magazine at duty free because it had a free little notepad with it.

'Have we definitely got everything, Mark?'

'Yep.'

'Money, tickets, house keys and passports?'

'Here's the passports. You have the money and everything.'

'Bloody Nora, look at my passport picture. Do I really look like that, Mark? Like is that my actual face? I hope border control at least do a double-take, I look like a criminal on that.'

Sitting on the plane (and thanking the Lord I was short as it meant I actually had leg room), I was ready for the adventure ahead, trying to listen to the safety information – although there's always that one family who are chatting so loud, all in matching tracksuits. I don't know why I brought loads of stuff to do on the plane because as soon as we were in the air I fell straight asleep until touchdown when that same family woke me up by clapping and cheering because we had landed safely.

'Phew, the heat hits you like a brick wall. It's too hot for me, this, far too hot, I'm melting, I think the soles of my shoes are actually melting,' I said as soon as we got off the plane. 'Dad, do you think you could fry eggs on this floor?'

'Woah, deffo kid.'

'Behave, you two. We have only just got off the plane. It's 29 degrees, we're hardly at boiling point.'

We had a whole fortnight of the Spanish sun ahead of us and my nanny and grandad were meeting us there on the second week, which I was super excited for. This all-inclusive thing was pretty new and we all wanted to take advantage of it. To be honest, me and my dad saw it as more of a challenge than a benefit and over the course of the holiday my dad

*Being a beach babe and having a little
cheeky wee in the sea.*

sickened himself with about twenty tubs of the 'free' ice cream that tasted more like mousse.

When I wasn't eating ice cream I would be having fun in the kids' club, which was run by a woman called Grace who had skin like leather and always had a fag in her hand. We would be let loose on the karaoke, have ping-pong championships and make pictures using lots of glue and pipe cleaners. I had a little friendship gang at kids' club. There were two Swedish brothers who could speak a little English: Douglas, which I pronounced as 'Dog-less', and Dennis, which I pronounced as 'Dean-ish'. There was also Rebecca who was a Yam Yam from the Black Country near Birmingham and Clare from

Glasgow (whose name I insisted was pronounced 'Clear'). So by the end of the day I had a very mixed accent.

'Where am yam gewwin tonight, Scarlett?' asked Rebecca.

'Din-er, think we are staying in the hotel, Rebecca, coz we don't have to pay for stuff here and there's gonna be the mini disco and a man who comes and you can have a picture took with his big snake and flamenco dancers.'

'Gonnae no dae that, I don't like snakes,' said Clare.

'Oh I love snakes, the bigger the better, Clear. Oh well, if I don't see you all later I'll see you tomorrow. Bye.' I smiled.

As I skipped back to the sun loungers where my mam was baking and my dad, despite being sat in the shade all day, was slowly going crimson, I was so excited for our first night out. We went back to our room to get ready. Now me and my mam have naturally curly hair anyway but on holiday it is something else. We are like bloody Crystal Tipps. Doesn't matter how many times you go on holiday you never get used to using a hair dryer in blazing heat – it is sickening, like I actually have a mini sick while I do it. But I managed to do it then I popped one of my new dresses on and sprayed myself with my mam's Angel perfume.

The mini disco always started the same, with some Spanish song which no one understood and which probably meant something very inappropriate as the one word you could understand in it was 'sexy', but it had a kiddy dance to go with it so it's all good. Then the competitions would start where you could win a certificate and a cocktail for your parent, even though all the cocktails were free anyway as it was all-inclusive (they'd get round this by bunging a sparkler and a fancy straw in it and pretending they'd used the top-shelf spirits). The host – whose stage name was Mario – explained the first event. Mario was tantastic and super shiny, his hair gelled into spikes, and he always had his shirt undone to his belly button. In a nutshell he resembled a really basic value Ricky Martin, always smiling and hanging around all the mams, especially the single mams.

'Ladies and gentlemen, boys and girls, give us a cheer if it's your first night joining us for the mini disco. Right, for those who cheered let me explain, I am going to go around the children and ask their name, where they come from, what they want to be when they're older and their funniest joke. They all get a certificate for taking part and the winner wins a cocktail for their mummy.'

I still remember the look on everybody's face when the first little boy went up to the mic. 'My name's Robert, I'm from England. I want to be a footie player when I grow up and play for Man United.' I mean some people cheered and some people actually booed a six-year-old child because he mentioned Man U.

'And can you tell us your funniest joke, Robert?'

'What did the big dog say to the little dog?'

'I don't know, what did the big dog say to the little dog?' The audience waited in anticipation and Rob's parents started winding the disposable camera up ready to take a picture.

'FUCK OFF!'

'Right, someone come and collect Robert from the stage please and wash his mouth out with soap and water.'

I wasn't as nervous about telling my joke now. 'Hi, I'm Scarlett Moffatt, I live in County Durham and I want to be a bus driver when I'm older, but only the double-decker ones.' I was actually obsessed with wanting to be a bus driver, which is ironic as I've taken my driving test four times now and have failed every time. I once failed because I stopped that close to a school bus we had to wait ten minutes for all the kids to get on the bus because I couldn't go around it.

'And can you tell us your funniest joke, Charlotte?'

'It's Scarlett!' I always get called Charlotte even though it's not my name at all. It's like calling someone Shaniqua when their name is Siân.

'Two cannibals start eating a clown. One of the cannibals says to the other, "Does this taste funny to you?"' I mean none of the kids laughed but the host loved it.

'Good one, Charlotte, can you tell us another?' I was put on the spot and didn't want to waste my thinking space on correcting him about my name. So I did what most kids do and just made up a joke.

'What did the pirate say on his hundredth birthday? Aye Matey.' And that was the joke that won my mam and dad two Sex on the Beaches. I don't know how my dad kept it down to be honest, as he was drinking pint glasses of Baileys – well, the Spanish version which is called Willies. I think he was only drinking them so my mam had to ask for a large Willy every time she went to the bar.

Eventually the day arrived when my nanny and grandad were getting to our hotel. They were getting in at 7 p.m. that night so my mam and dad decided we should spend the day at the beach as nanny isn't keen on beaches (she says they're too sandy). After eating my own bodyweight in cakes and random meats from the breakfast buffet we decided to head to the beach. The hotel staff were so cute and gave us packed lunches to take with us (not to be confused with a lunch box, which is a noun meaning a container used to help fruit get out of the house for the day and return safely for the afternoon). No, this was a brown paper bag containing a ham-and-cheese baguette, packet of crisps and a bottle of tepid water.

There was a huge bouncy castle on the beach. 'Dad, please can I go on it? It's only five potato peasant things.'

'Aye, go on then.'

Now we should have noticed it was mostly Spanish kids on the castle, Spanish kids who had the sense to have socks on. I was crying through the fun, the plastic was that hot. I ended up blistering my feet and couldn't even wear jelly shoes without wincing. So after that I just lay on my sun lounger in the shade looking after my Tamagotchi.

My dad went off on one of his walks while my mam sunbathed and he came back with some brochures about a glass-bottom boat experience. Not just any glass-bottom boat but one that takes you to see a shipwreck. This instantly cheered me and my sore feet up but Mam took a bit of persuading.

'Mark, what shipwrecks have there been here really?'

'Ah, come on Betty, even if we don't see that we will see some beautiful fish, it'll be amazing.'

'I can't stand fish and it's perfect tan weather. There's not a cloud in the sky. I haven't just got boob sweat, I've got "humidititties". Is there a place I can sunbathe on there?'

'Probably, come on, life is for experiencing new things.'

'What will I be able to see on this glass boat thing?'

'Dolphins, maybe even a whale, come on.'

'All right then, it could be fun, you've won.'

We must have only been on the boat for five minutes and my dad turned green. I don't mean a hint of green, I mean Hulk's second cousin once removed green. 'I genuinely think I'm having a heart attack, I'm going to be sick,' my dad cried.

Me and my mam rushed to get the captain. 'He has a touch of sea sickness, tell him to hang his head over the side if he feels like he is going to be sick,' he said.

'It is not sea sickness. I'm a bloke, I don't get sea sickness, I'm having an actual heart attack.' We stayed by my dad's side while he swayed side to side moaning about what a shit idea it was to come on a glass-bottom boat, whilst everyone else marvelled at the beautiful fish and children as young as three skipped along the deck. When we finally arrived to land, suddenly my dad's 'heart attack' stopped. We still have a laugh about this and when he goes to have a bath we tell him to be careful he doesn't get sea sickness.

I was so happy for 7p.m. to come. Nanny and Pappy were there and we made our way down to the disco.

'Can I have a mocktail, Grandad?' I asked. 'That girl's got one over there and it comes with a big straw that looks like a parrot.'

'Is it on the all-inclusive drinks list, like?'

'Yeah, Grandad. Look, it's called a virgin piña colada, it just sounds like a pineapple milkshake.'

So my grandad Tommy came back with a tray of drinks and we enjoyed the hotel entertainment. It was a magician who was making doves in birdcages disappear. I had nearly sipped my way through a quarter of my drink and I honestly couldn't stomach any more. 'It tastes too funky, this drink, I don't like it,' I moaned.

Some things don't change... My smile is still this big now when I see a piña colada.

'Is it too milky?' My mam grabbed my drink to have a try of it. 'Bloody hell, Tommy, it's got alcohol in this!'

'Has it? I asked for a piña colada like she said.'

'No, a virgin piña colada, that's the one with no alcohol in it,' she giggled. Luckily I didn't drink too much of it otherwise I'd have been the only pissed nine-year-old in the resort. But hey, what a way to have your first ever alcoholic drink.

Me and my dad would also like to go and watch either *Only Fools and Horses* or *The X-Files* in a sports bar next to the beach. We would sit there for hours watching it. Apart from the *X-Files* introduction ('do le do le do'), where an eye would zoom in. That is when I'd have to close my eyes at that part and my dad would tell us when it was over. That would freak me out.

My mam would moan, 'Come on, we need to go back to the hotel now, there's another cabaret show!'

'Just one more episode and we will, Mam, pleeeease.' Me and my dad had flown all the way to Spain just to sit in the shade and watch a show you could watch back at home.

I just loved that there was always a twist in *The X-Files*. I think part of me believed it was real as a kid, because my dad used to say that it's a documentary. So I did for a good year think that it was based on true events. I did think, 'Oh God, I can't believe that we're living in a world where this happens and no one is even talking about it!' I used to get really caught up in it. No wonder I've turned out the way I am!

The X-Files was my guilty pleasure back then. Do you know what it is now? *Love Island*. Me and my mam binge-watch it. She'll kill me for saying this, and I know it's a weird thing to watch with your mam because it is very rude, but we record them all and watch three or four off the trot. We love it.

We all giggled so much on that holiday. I made friends who I said I would be pen pals with forever and that we would all meet up again. One letter later (as yes, I was slightly odd as a child and didn't do the whole email thing, I'm traditional and like the feeling of licking an envelope shut. If they still had them I'd probably have a carrier pigeon to be honest) and we never spoke again. My dad's sunburn might have faded but the memories will last forever.

I loved our family holidays. If we didn't go somewhere in Spain or Greece we would go away to a caravan park and stay in a static, and one year we thought we would be really adventurous and stay in a tent. Now I love a caravan, especially when it's raining and you can hear the raindrops bouncing off the roof. Me and my dad had a hilarious trick: when my mam went to the toilet, we would run out with loads of bread, throw it on the roof and then it's like a scene from an Alfred Hitchcock movie – seagulls literally take over. You think they're going to lift the caravan off the ground. My mam is petrified of birds, you see, it's a sickening sense of humour I know but it makes us laugh.

I love getting in from a day of metal detecting and crabbing and sticking on all the bars on the gas fire whilst watching *Countdown*, chilling while my dad makes jacket potatoes for everyone. Caravan holidays have a special place in my heart. Camping holidays in a tent though, they can fuck off. I went on one when I was fourteen in August 2005 and never ever again.

We went to Blue Dolphin in Scarborough and although we didn't need any basic survival skills as we had an electric hook-up, it still didn't make life easier. Firstly it took about two hours to put up a four-man tent, as it had rained the night before so we had to put plastic sheets underneath the tent so we didn't slide away. There was that much plastic all you had to do was move slightly or even breathe heavily and the whole tent sounded like a crisp packet rustling. On the first night it was so cold me and my mam had all our layers of clothes on, plus a sleeping bag and a sheet, and even then we had to put the hairdryer on and use it as central heating.

If this wasn't bad enough, this was the night that in my family we refer to as Bluntgate. We were woken up (as tents are wafer thin) by a family of ten singing their lungs out.

'You're beautiful, you're beautiful, you're beautiful it's true. I saw your face in a crowded place, I don't know what to do ...'

James Blunt's 'You're Beautiful', repeatedly from one in the morning for a full hour. As much as I love that song and it was huge at the time it now makes my heart hurt with anger when I hear it. If that also wasn't bad enough, we all bunched together in the one compartment of the tent and Robert and Yazymn (my mam's godchildren and my good friends) decided they wanted to squeeze in too. So now we were cold, tired and squashed. When I finally drifted to sleep I heard my dad let out a scream. It was still dark outside and we were all annoyed to be woken up. Turns out little Robert didn't want to wake anyone to ask if someone would take him to the toilet so he just wet himself (he was only five so we let him off). But he had accidentally leaked all over my dad's only coat. Which meant my dad was walking around for the rest of the holiday in polo shirts with no jacket on when everyone else had coats, scarves, hats and gloves on.

Despite all this it was still a hilarious holiday where we laughed from start to finish. Even though I was fourteen years old, every night in the club house I danced to all the classics: 'Chocolate', 'Superman', 'YMCA'. It was even funny when things didn't go to plan, like when we went to Scarborough Fair and it started raining cats and dogs so we all got soaked and ate fish and chips followed by a lemon-top ice cream in the rain on the beach.

See if you sit and really think about the last five items you bought, I bet you're like me and you can't off the top of your head. Yet I can almost relive every moment of that camping trip. As I have got older I've realised that your time is the most valuable gift you can give to anybody. Whether it's a holiday abroad, a day on the beach or a weekend camping trip, it's good to make memories away. As I was drifting off to sleep thinking about my old favourite book, *Aesop's Fables*, a few of the quotes would stick in my mind. One that always did was:

'Adventure is always worthwhile.'

Chapter Four

STRICTLY SCARLETT

★ During each BBC series of *Strictly Come Dancing*, approximately 57 litres of fake tan are used (my idea of heaven).

★ Conspiracy theorists say there are secret underground tunnels running from Blackpool Tower to the Winter Gardens that were once used by performers. Reports that Tupac and Elvis are currently held down there are unconfirmed.

★ Bruce Forsyth (who will sadly be missed, he really was the king of *Strictly*) was actually older than sliced bread. His own mother would have had to slice her own bread until Baby Bruce was four months old.

I remember my tummy feeling the same as it did on my first day of school. I didn't just have butterflies in my stomach, I had the whole fucking zoo. I was sitting in the hallway on a bottle-green pleather (plastic leather) chair at Dianne White's dance school with my mam. It was a clammy day and my bum was sticking to the seat. I was wearing a little white sparkly dress and silver sparkly dance shoes all ready for my first ever dance medal test. I felt like a princess, like a really nervous princess.

It was Sunday 31 August 1997 and I was only six. There were so many of us crammed in the hallway, packed in like a tin of sardines, as everyone was crowding round the little TV. They all gasped in horror and some even wept as they watched the horrific images on the BBC. The banner across

*Loving the sky background —
I'm like a floating princess.*

the screen read: 'Princess Diana dies in Paris crash'. We can all remember where we were on that day and that's where I was. I remember feeling guilty that I was there dressed as a princess when the real princess would never get to wear dresses like that again. Such a sad day.

I can hear you say it, why ballroom and Latin dancing? Well, my mam had a love of *Come Dancing*, the original. The huge dresses, the old-time music, the grandeur of it all. My mam would have loved to have learnt to dance so she took me along to her dream hobby. I thought it was the greatest thing since sliced bread. Yes, it was not the coolest of hobbies to have at that time as the kids at school often taunted me, 'You do old-fogey dancing, granny dancing.' But I didn't care; I couldn't wait to get this medal test over and done with so I could start going to competitions. I'd show them kids at school when I'd waltz into the classroom and paso-doble past everyone to the front of the class to show the teacher my huge first-place trophy (at least that was the dream anyway).

The medal test was as terrifying as I thought it would be. There was one sole judge sat behind a pine desk at the bottom of the dance floor; she was sipping black coffee which smelt so strong I felt like I was getting high from the caffeine. She had sparkly glasses on, red lipstick that bled into her creases and her face looked like she had just smelt dog shite. She had an 'I'm it, you're shit' sort of look. You know the type of woman I mean – mid fifties, wears nothing but beige cardigans and white trousers. Miserable she was. I remember thinking a woman with such an angry face should not be allowed to wear nice sparkly glasses. With trembling tot fingers I handed over my dance sheet and I danced a cha cha cha and a foxtrot, smiling through gritted teeth all the way through and trying to forget I felt as if I was going to throw up. 'Highly commended' I was awarded. Not quite a distinction but I was on my way.

Now I am not meaning to sound a bighead; as you know I am not one to boast. Saying that, I must admit I got canny good at dancing. I won lots of regional competitions so I got to represent the Tyne Tees at nationals. I got into quite a lot of national finals and I did pretty well. I have around 600 trophies and shields. And where do you keep them, Scarlett? Pride of place on the mantelpiece? Maybe a few in that drawer everyone has that's full of old batteries and mystery keys? Nope, they are all collecting dust in the attic. There is no trace of my dancing days in my mam and dad's house, what with my mam's love of minimalism.

When I was younger, my dad put up some varnished

UNI-TED Congratulates
his Club Member on passing
another test in his
Award Scheme

Scarlett Moffatt
Maroon Ballroom Badge
October 1997

WELL DONE !

HIGHLY
COMMENDED

Nicholas Baird
Club Secretary

wooden shelves above my bed to display some of my more impressive trophies, so until I was about eleven my bedroom was like a little dancing shrine. Sometimes paranoia would kick in on a night and I'd lie awake staring at the trophies thinking, God, if these shelves broke all of a sudden I'd be disfigured or even killed by a mountain of my own trophies. I'd literally be a victim of my own success.

My first ever memory of a dance competition was when we had a fun competition at Redcar Bowl (by fun competition I mean it wasn't for a title, but believe me what with all the dance mams it was never particularly fun – it was more friendly competitiveness). My mam spent the whole of the night before the big comp sewing red sequins onto a black skirt. Bless her, she had plasters on her fingers from where she had pricked herself but she knew it was worth it as I was so excited to wear the outfit. However, nothing is ever plain sailing for the Moffatt family and once we got there we were told it was regulation dresses only and no one could dance with sequins or crystals on a dress. I had to borrow Debbie Brown's dress which was far too big for me and I just look back now and feel so bad that my mam's efforts were never seen on the dance floor. I do remember coming fourth that day though and standing in the line-up and seeing my mam's smiley face, it made me so happy inside.

As time went on and I got older, I realised that winning at competitions wasn't just about how passionate you were about dancing, or your efforts, technique or your presence on the floor, but you also were judged on how you looked (similar to life really). So when I was about twelve or thirteen I told my mam I didn't want to look washed out under the glaring lights of Blackpool's Winter Gardens ballroom. So I was ready to try a product that is now one of my best friends: fake tan.

The first time I properly fake-tanned, I'm not talking about a bit of bronzer, I'm talking full-on spray tan. Me mam bought a spray tan machine and the solution, and I stood in the bath while I was sprayed to within an inch of my life. I remember going to bed and feeling like a professional with my little golden glow. However, the horrific sight that greeted me in the mirror when I woke up on the morning was not golden. I was glowing all right. A radioactive glow. I was luminous. I wasn't even orange, I had literally invented a new colour. A cross between David Dickinson's mahogany tan and a jar of piccalilli. (That said, it wasn't as bad as the time I used moisturiser before getting a spray tan and it went green. I was dancing around the dance floor like Princess Fiona from *Shrek*.)

If you're reading this and you've danced before or still dance you will understand the importance of making sure that everything is stoned (this is a dancing term for spending hours sticking diamonds or crystals on everything), from the handle on your shoe brush to your dress bag. Everything must be stoned for a dance competition, especially nationals. The man-hours that went into stoning, my house was like a bloody sweatshop.

The IDTA Nationals was a weekend-long competition that would determine who was the best dancer in the United Kingdom. There would be around 2,000 spectators, over 100 dancers in each category, six judges and a panel of adjudicators on stage. Each dancer would be given a number to wear on their back which is what the judges mark down, and you could check who was in your category and if your arch-nemesis was in your round by consulting the dance programme. This competition is a huge deal. Some dance mams take nationals too far. Like there's a line and they're so far over the line it's just a dot to them. They would get their child's face printed on a T-shirt and wear it for the whole weekend. Banners would be made. There would always be one dickhead who would rock up with a foghorn. Some dancers even had custom-made dressing gowns to protect their dance dresses or suits.

My mam and dad were never that obsessive. Yes, they wanted me to do well, but they would sit quietly at the back and just shout my number and name occasionally as I danced past. My mam would sit with a constant smile on her face, not because she was so happy, but to remind me to smile when I came past as I did not have a pretty concentration face. The feeling you would get when you danced past your dance school and everyone would cheer just makes you feel invincible. My mam would eyeball the judges and try and count how many times I got marked down.

When they did callbacks and they call out the numbers chronologically, oh my days. You get a feeling that can only be described as a 'situation', you know that situation where you leave the house and about twenty minutes later you get that awful feeling of 'did I leave the iron on, am I going to have to go back and be late for work or risk it and come back to find my home in ashes?'

That's just reminded me of something. One time me and my mam got back from a weekend in Blackpool and the house nearly had come down into ashes. My dad had gone out on the Saturday night, had a few jars and got a bit tipsy. Then decided that rather than ordering a takeaway he would put a frozen pizza in the oven. Of course he forgot about that pizza, didn't wake up to the fire alarm (although the rest of the street did) and was instead awoken by two firemen. I didn't know people's faces could turn purple from rage until that day when my dad explained to my mam why we needed a new kitchen.

My favourite part of the Blackpool dance competition experience as a kid was having a whole weekend with just me and my mam. The fun we had going to Coral Island, spending £20 on the donkey derby to win a stuffed toy you could get from the pound shop, and eating nothing but fish and chips and rock the whole weekend. I just loved it. Blackpool as a kid was so magical. I would get so excited about the illuminations (later, when we took my little sister Ava, thinking she would find it as spellbinding as I once did, she said it was a waste of electricity). But the highlight of the weekend was the Blackpool Tower ballroom. Ah the lights, the smell of scones, the old people shuffling round the dance floor and their look of astonishment as an eight-year-old got up to jive … I loved it all, but the pièce de résistance for me was the Wurlitzer. Now, if you've never had the good fortune of seeing this in action, it's a cross between a Dynamo trick and a *Britain's Got Talent* act. The organist rises as if by magic through the stage whilst playing the huge theatre organ. It is just hypnotic. Again spoiled by the reaction of my little sister who said, 'Well yeah, Scarlett, he's coming up from a trap door, it's not rocket science.' She absolutely ruined the illusion for me.

I always enjoyed staying in a traditional Blackpool B&B. The floral carpet that stuck to your feet clashing with the patterned wallpaper that looked like some sort of optical illusion. The chants of the hen and stag dos outside your window as they paraded the streets with inflatable penises and T-shirts that said 'Saucy Suzy' or 'Drink till you shit yourself'. The buffet-style breakfast where you would help yourself to as many rashers of bacons as your heart desired. The cute glasses you would get for your orange juice that were the size of a thimble. Some of my greatest memories were made here. I know Blackpool gets some stick, especially recently, but I hate that people slag it off. I will never hear anybody slag Blackpool off; if they do I will defend it all day. I love Blackpool, it's the Vegas of England.

I remember one time at Blackpool, the night before a big competition, we went to see the circus in the Tower. Now they had no lights on during the performance and I needed the toilet midway through, so my mam came with me. This was way before mobiles had proper torches so we were trying to find our way down the stairs with nothing but the glare from a Nokia 3310 screen. BAM. I fell from top to bottom. My mam carried me to the toilet to check how injured I was, worried whether I'd be able to perform the next day. But as soon as she saw me in the light she started howling with laughter. The reason my bum hurt so much was because a couple of false nails (they get everywhere) had somehow ended up being embedded into my arse cheek from the fall. She had to literally prise them out.

Saturday would come, first day of the competition weekend. We'd had our fun on the Friday and now it was time to put everything we had practised in the last year into these two days. My competition ritual would begin with me eating my own bodyweight in breakfast (I'd buzz if there was black pudding) at the hotel, knowing I'd not be able to eat anything else for the rest of the day as I'd be so nervous. This would be followed shortly after by a dance poo – a nervous poo that can only be described as shitting through the eye of a needle. We all may look glamorous in our beautiful gowns and 1950s Hollywood glamour make-up and hair but let me tell you, every dance competition's toilet absolutely stinks and is stained with dancing skid marks.

I'd also love to buy or find a lucky charm: a penny, a stone, a hair clip, which if I didn't come first would be quickly thrown away as that would be the reason I didn't win – I'd found a jinxed charm, just my luck. Blackpool Nationwide weekend was the biggest competition of the year (although it felt like the biggest weekend of your entire life). Me and me mam would laugh at what we would call the Blackpool bun brigade. At about 7.30 a.m., the Winter Gardens was just swarmed with an army of girls with buns in their hair and you could literally smell the Elnett hairspray before you could see them. Everyone was the colour of antique mahogany furniture with their hair slicked down (a little trick we would do is use black shoe polish to make your hair shinier), and you'd see kids as young as five with more make-up on than Lily Savage. It truly is a spectacular sight.

It's only as I've got older that I have realised just how many sacrifices were made in order for me to dance. My mam would work her arse off in Etam for a whole month and a half and that wage would go on a dance dress that I would wear twice. My dad would work overtime to pay for private lessons and trips to competitions. I mean I sacrificed my skin – my skin is literally stained orange from all the tan. But to me, winning or getting in a final was my way of saying thank you to my mam and dad, because if it wasn't for them I wouldn't have been able to do the sport that brought me so much happiness, and has given me such great memories and lifelong friends.

My favourite memory of a dance competition was when I had just turned fifteen and we were at the nationals. This is the day I remember changing how I presented myself to the world – not just the dance world but school too. It's the day I grew in confidence. I was tanned up to my eyeballs as per usual. I had a beautiful monochrome dress covered in Swarovski crystals (a second-hand dress but no one needed to know). My make-up was inches thick. I had gone for the theatrical look and admittedly I was looking more like Marilyn

Manson than Marilyn Monroe, but I wanted to stand out. There were just under a hundred people in my section and we were whittled down throughout the day. When they called my number for the final six I was overwhelmed. I had never made a national final before, only ever the semi-finals.

I waltzed, foxtrotted, tangoed and quickstepped around the dance floor. I was in my element. Then it came to the Viennese waltz – this dance is basically spinning on a constant loop for three minutes. The speed we danced I thought at one point my actual head was going to come off, we were literally going about 90 mph and I feared my head was going to spin right off and roll off the dance floor. Luckily for me, necks are quite sturdy and as you know my head is still intact to date.

When the dancing was over and all 2,000 spectators were on their feet ready to find out who had won, I grabbed my mam and dad's hands. 'I'm not bothered where I place, I just can't believe I got in the final,' I told them. When they announced sixth place and it wasn't my name and number I remember squeezing my mam and dad's hands. 'This will be me next.' But it wasn't. They announced fifth, fourth, third and now it was time to find out who was runner-up. Now I always say in dancing I would rather come third than second. The reason being, you get the applause of the person's family and dance school who have just found out they have won. Also rather than people congratulate you they are almost sympathetic: 'Aahh, next time maybe,' or 'Oh, you were so close.' It's like, HELLO! I just came second!

They announced second place and I couldn't even hear who they announced for the thunderous noise of clapping from my dance school. My dad, who never gets emotional, definitely had a little tear in his eye (either that or a sudden case of conjunctivitis). I had won! It's been the only time I have ever won the nationals but I don't care. I feel so lucky that I got to have that feeling of picking up that trophy.

Dancing was my escape. When times were hard, when the bullying started, when I felt alone, I would dance. It's like I would plunge into a fantasy world, escaping everyday worries and stress. I didn't become a different character or an alter ego like Beyoncé and Sasha Fierce when I danced, I became the real Scarlett. Well, the Scarlett I wanted to be. The one who didn't give one flying fuck about what other people would say about me, the Scarlett who didn't care about the bullies or people saying I was weird. Dancing gave me a lot of confidence, it was the one thing I knew I was good at. It helped me not to care what other people said; so what if I was a bit different? I could dance. It's where my true friends were, it's what made me the happiest and where I was most able to truly be myself.

We all have that one thing we are good at. Whether it be a skill, humour, or simply being caring. Focus on your positives. Remember what Einstein said:

'Everybody is a genius. But if you judge a fish by its ability to climb a tree, it will live its whole life believing that it is stupid.'

Chapter Five

BIKES AND BELLS

★ The largest rideable bicycle has a wheel diameter of 3.3 metres (10 feet 10 inches) and was built by Didi Senft from Germany. *Gut gemacht!*

★ Forcing yourself to smile when you're sad will actually elevate your mood. Thanks to endorphins from smiling, 'fake it till you make it' actually works.

★ The classic Disney character Goofy is not a cow, nor a human, he is an anthropomorphic dog who wears a snazzy orange turtleneck.

I once read somewhere that your teenage years were meant to be the greatest years of your life. They're having a laugh, aren't they? It was the six-week holiday before starting secondary school and one thing after another went wrong. The year 2001 was a difficult one for me. One day in particular changed my life.

I remember the whole thing like it was yesterday. My mam was going round my auntie's house for a cup of tea. 'Can I come with you, Mam? I'll ride round on my bike,' I said.

'Course you can but make sure you wear your helmet,' Mam requested.

'Come on, Mam, I start big school soon. I don't need a helmet.'

She gave me that look, that look that every mam possesses; her eyes were telling me you better put that bloody helmet on or there will be hell to pay.

Perching myself on the black foam seat of my bike and wearing my gherkin-green helmet, I rode up and down the quiet street, ringing my little bell like I had done so many times before, humming Aqua's 'I'm a Barbie Girl'. I was loving life. I have always been a cautious character so I was riding around slow enough for kids to brisk-walk next to me.

Then I heard a screech of tyres as a car came speeding round the corner. I swerved, making sure I was at the side of the road. Everything suddenly went into slow motion. What could have only been thirty seconds of my life felt like I was stuck in a time loop that was never going to end. The car bumped the back of my bike and I could see it speed off through tear-filled eyes. As I flew over my handlebars I remember squeezing my eyes closed. Screaming on the inside, please don't hurt, please don't hurt! Knowing I couldn't stop the inevitable fall.

I felt the impact on my chin first as it smashed onto the concrete floor, followed by my teeth. I didn't know what had happened but I just remember wanting the pain to stop. I thought my teeth had gone through my gums. I had shattered my front two teeth on the gravelled road. My once favourite white Tammy Girl top was now crimson. Some girl called Kayleigh screamed so loud my mam and auntie came out of the house to see what was going on.

My mam was screaming, 'Oh, help! I don't know what to do!' I remember some of the kids in the street trying to pick up the shards of my teeth to help me while my mam was in hysterics calling the dental surgery for an emergency appointment on my auntie's landline.

My mam grasped my hand in the taxi on the way to the dentist. 'It's going to be OK. It could have been so much worse if you hadn't had that helmet on, Scarlett. We have to focus on the positive, sweetheart.'

I sat back on the black leather dentist chair wishing I were sitting anywhere but there. 'How many injections am I going to need?' I could barely even make out what I was bleating out myself.

The dentist, as most adults do when you're younger, directed all of his answers to my mam. 'Scarlett is going to need eight injections, and the nerves in her front right tooth are going to have to be removed. This will result in this front tooth quickly turning black as the tooth is technically dead. Due to the gums and teeth having so much trauma she will probably have to wait until she is around eighteen to twenty-one before she can get veneers. I would start saving now as they're very expensive.'

I looked at my mam who appeared as a blur because of all my tears. I endured the pain of the injections. Wishing so loud in my brain, if only I could quickly turn back the clock and not go round the street on my bike. I knew that once I sat up from that dentist chair I would probably not have the confidence to smile for a very long time.

In fact it was a whole decade of my life before I smiled again. Even when I wanted to, I didn't. I haven't got one photo with my grandma (my nanny's mam) Frieda (God rest her soul) where I am smiling. I haven't even got photos with my little sister when she was a baby or a toddler where I am smiling showing my teeth. I would talk with my hand over my mouth in the hope no one would notice my horrendous teeth. I would look down when people spoke to me, probably looking like such an ill-mannered teenager. I had no confidence with boys for years – I mean, who would want to kiss me? The only rare occasions I did smile in front of others was when I was dancing at competitions. But that was me playing the most confident version of me.

Not being able to walk into secondary school on my first day and smile at the other kids was hard. If the monobrow eyebrow slapped across my face wasn't enough, I had now been blessed with black goofy teeth that looked like they were having a party without me. I had a pale, freckled, chubby-cheeked face that emphasised the fact puberty had hit and I had a faint black tash. I honestly looked like a brunette Helga Pataki from *Hey Arnold!* (I was watching beautiful blondes like Christina Aguilera in 'Lady Marmalade' music videos and that's what I aspired to look like at the time.)

For the first year of secondary school my front teeth were half the size they had been. When I was finally given caps on my teeth they were very bulky and the right tooth was still black. This gave the bullies a lot of leverage for nicknames. Some of them were actually quite inventive, I was impressed: Polystyrene Teeth, Cap-tooth Scarlett, Chessboard Teeth, Black Tooth, Scruffy Teeth – and the most original one of all, Goofy.

I remember daydreaming that one day I would wake up like they do in the movies and I'd be beautiful. My teeth would be as white as Simon Cowell's in *Pop Idol*. My hair would be silky and poker-straight, I'd have perfectly groomed eyebrows, the tash would be gone and my tan would look like I'd been dipped in liquidised gold.

But even my 'ugly duckling turning into a swan' daydreaming came down with a crash. Not long after the accident I was diagnosed with Bell's palsy, a type of facial paralysis. The doctors said it could be because of the trauma of smashing my teeth. Now I am under no illusions that there are worse afflictions to have but at the time, being eleven years old and starting secondary school where it is so looks-orientated, it was just soul-destroying. I couldn't even dream about being pretty because it was just one thing after another.

When the Bell's palsy struck I remember staring in the living room mirror, screaming and screaming. 'Mam! Dad! Help, help!' One minute I was fine and the next minute I felt my whole face collapse. I could barely open my left eye; it drooped so much that it looked like I was winking. My mouth slouched and I could barely string a sentence together. It's like I was fighting with my own face, my own tongue, to get my words out. No matter how hard I tried I couldn't get my face to go straight again. I couldn't even force my eye open. I was utterly petrified. I honestly, at that moment in time, thought I was dying. I remember feeling like I was having an out-of-body experience; I could hear the blood rushing around my body. I stood grabbing my face with both hands, trying to manipulate it back to how it looked before it slouched. Literally pulling at my face, pinching it so hard I was making it red. 'Go straight, go straight!' I screamed. There was nothing I could do, I felt like I wasn't even in control of my own muscles.

My mam thought at first that I was playing a prank; she honestly thought I was joking. 'Stop it now, Scarlett, it's not funny,' she snapped. I couldn't even speak. I was inconsolable. She then realised I was not putting it on. My dad grabbed my coat and my parents took me to the hospital where the doctor diagnosed me with Bell's palsy. This condition has the symptoms of a stroke but it causes temporary weakness or paralysis of the muscles in one side of the face.

After my initial diagnosis we all had to sit back in the waiting room of the paediatrics department surrounded by paintings of clowns and smiling faces on the wall. The doctor entered the waiting area. 'If you'd like to follow me ...' We were now all crammed in a very small hospital room. I can't remember details about the room, just that it was very small and stuffy, but I do still remember what the doctor looked like. He was my dad's height (five foot seven), his clean-shaven skin was as smooth as a baby's arse and he had kind eyes. (You know what I mean, sometimes you can meet people and their eyes look right through you. Like Katie Hopkins, for example, if you look closely at her eyes they look sad, like she just needs a good cuddle. But this doctor, he had the eyes of a gentle man, he had David Attenborough kind of eyes.)

'If you can take your socks and shoes off, Miss Scarlett O'Hara, I'll pop you on the scales. I just need to explain something to your parents about why we need to do some blood tests. Now it is nothing to be scared of, I promise it will only feel like a scratch.'

I smiled, without showing my teeth. I was so relieved that the doctor was so kind.

The doctor continued calmly talking to my parents as he prepared me for the blood test. 'We need to do these tests as on rare occasions Bell's palsy can be an early manifestation of acute lymphoblastic leukaemia,' he said.

I had no idea what any of the words meant and I'm so pleased I didn't. It's only now I look back I understand why my parents got so upset. My dad had just recovered from a rare skin cancer just four years before. So I know the thought of his little girl having to have tests for that awful C-word – cancer – was heartbreaking. My dad picked up my sock, held it to his eye and started to cry.

'Come on, Dad, my socks don't smell that bad.' I smiled weakly, trying to cheer him up. Even though I was nervous and confused at what was happening I just wanted to hear my dad laugh, not cry.

I remember when my dad got diagnosed with cancer, although now it feels like that part of our life was just a distant nightmare. It started when I was nearly eight years old and we were all sat on the sofa eating sausage casserole and watching *Gladiators* (it's so weird how you remember minor details). My mam saw a small lump on my dad's back as he was just chilling in his joggers. There was no freckle or mole around it so my mam tried squeezing it, thinking it was a spot. But a few weeks passed and it started getting bigger and my mam got worried and forced my dad to go to the doctor's about it.

That evening when my dad got back from the doctor's he seemed really relaxed. 'The doctor said it was a cyst and to just keep an eye on it,' he said. But my mam kept checking it constantly as she just had a bad feeling about it. She made him go to the doctor's again a month later as it had got even bigger. 'It's just a cyst, Betty, stop worrying. They're going to remove it, I've got an appointment for two weeks.'

I now get so angry – if the problem had been properly diagnosed when my dad had originally gone to the doctor's, he wouldn't have had to go through all the agony he went through later. By the time he went to have it removed at the surgery, the doctor said it was too big and it needed to be taken out at hospital. 'We are just going to cut a piece of the lump now and send it for a biopsy, Mr Moffatt. This will take around ten days and hopefully we will be in touch with good news,' the doctor told him.

A few days later, me and my mam were sat on the back seat of the 1B bus, being rebels. I can't remember where we had been, but my mam got a call from my dad at work. 'This isn't going to be good news, I can feel it,' I remember her saying when she saw it was his number.

'Betty, can you come to Darlington Hospital now? I'm

about to set off from work. The doctor has called and told me I need to go to the hospital immediately.'

Mam cried the whole journey on the bus.

'What's wrong, Mam?' I asked.

'It's Dad, he has to go to hospital, we are going to meet him there. It's just a few bus stops away.'

'Don't worry, Mam, Dad is Dad. He is super strong, he will be fine.' To me my dad was my superhero; he could lift me on his shoulders like I weighed nothing.

When we arrived he was already shut away in a little room with the doctor. 'I'm afraid you have a malignant melanoma, Mr Moffatt.'

'Does that mean I have cancer?'

'It does.'

'But half an hour ago I was welding at work, how is this happening?' It didn't sink in and I remember him coming out of the room with an expression I can only describe as defeated. He just looked blank.

They said they'd be in touch when they had an appointment for him as he would have to have X-rays and a CT scan.

My dad sat in the front seat of the taxi on the way home, crying quietly. Mam said later she'd only ever seen him cry once before, and that was when I was born. He wasn't even crying for himself, it was for me and Mam. At the time, my mam was my age now, twenty-seven, and my dad was just thirty-two. But my dad was lucky and the day after his diagnosis he got a bed at James Cook Hospital and had all the necessary scans and X-rays over the next week.

The surgeon was called Dr Viva. He told my mam there was a strong possibility the tumour was wrapped around his spine and if it was they wouldn't be able to operate. I don't know how my dad coped or slept over the next few days waiting for his operation.

He had a room on his own and I remember every day when we went to visit him we drove past a factory just beyond Stockton that displayed the time and temperature and we knew then we were just ten minutes away. I would get excited when I saw it, knowing I'd soon be able to give my dad a cuddle. I remember my mam telling me in the car, 'We have to be brave, we can't cry even if Dad looks poorly. If we cry it will worry Dad and it's like saying God, this is serious, this is cancer.' As soon as we left the room we would cry together, we sobbed our hearts out, but as long as we were in that room with my dad we were strong, stronger than Wonder Woman.

I slept in my mam and dad's bed while my dad was in hospital and we cuddled and cried and every night we would say lots of prayers. It's strange because my mam wasn't a big believer but she said that even a non-believer can change their minds when you think maybe someone is listening and maybe can help you. When I think of what my mam must have been going through, she was dealing with all of this and she was just my age. I get stressed if the hairdresser cuts too much of my hair, and there she was dealing with a kid and the worry of losing her one true love.

I remember the man in the room next to Dad's, he used to proper cheer my dad up by telling him funny stories. I sometimes have a little think about him and wonder if he is OK. When my dad was feeling down, this man – who had been in an accident at work and lost both his legs – used to tell my dad off and tell him to stop being so bloody soft as he's got a family to think about.

When Dad had his op he was so lucky. Yes, the tumour was huge, leaving a scar the size of a dinner plate and an indentation a couple of inches long, and he had to have skin grafts on the backs of both his thighs, but they managed to remove the whole tumour. He was allowed to come home on Christmas Eve and that was the greatest Christmas any of my family ever had. I only got a few presents to open as obviously my mam had other priorities than present-buying that year, but I didn't care at all. I had my dad; I had him there on Christmas Day to cuddle, to pull a cracker with, to eat the middle parts of his puddings with (I wouldn't let him have the crusty edges).

My dad made a speedy recovery. A nurse came out every day for a couple of weeks to clean and cover his skin grafts and he was advised to take six months off work, but Dad being Dad he was back at work grafting away just eight weeks later.

Me dad has had a few little lumps removed since then but nothing serious. He was told by the doctor at the time it was a rare form of skin cancer. I think once you have been through something like that it makes you appreciate people and life more. We all moan about shit sometimes, really unimportant things, but life is the most precious gift we have. He was so lucky to beat cancer's arse. I know so many friends and family that haven't been that lucky and it's just devastating. But we cannot let that bloody C-word win – one day we will find a cure, and in the meantime we just have to keep donating and doing our bit. We can help beat it by going to the doctor's as soon as we see a potential problem, we need to check for lumps, any changes in moles, go for that prostate exam and us women have to go for our smear as soon as we get that letter. Doctors these days are on the ball but you have to help yourself. It is still a terrifying illness.

So I know for Dad the thought of his little girl having to have tests for that bloody C-word was heartbreaking. But only three hours or so after my dad was crying into my sock the doctor came back in to tell us some amazing news.

'The tests have come back and your daughter is fit and healthy – other than the unfortunate case of Bell's palsy, of course. I'm going to give her a strong case of steroids and she will have regular check-ups, but it should have cleared within three months.'

I'm so grateful the doctor was right. The worst of it lasted around three months and then to my great delight I was starting to look like the old Scarlett again.

And yes, that's the Scarlett that I once stared at in the mirror and ripped to shreds. The Scarlett whose face I would rearrange in my head to have longer hair, flawless skin and perfect teeth. The Scarlett who once wished she looked like the girls in *Smash Hits* magazine. It's crazy: before the Bell's palsy I was so self-critical but once the steroids worked I was so happy. It made me appreciate what I had.

I wasn't completely the old me; the condition does still affect me to this day. I normally sleep with an eye mask at home as I still can't close my left eye properly, and it's also caused a droop with my left eyebrow. So in photos it constantly looks like I'm doing the Elvis Presley eyebrow. I do get some trolls on my social media commenting on my face and how unsymmetrical it is, or saying that my teeth are ridiculous. But do you know what? I really don't care. Because having that palsy made me wish so hard to be the old me. Looks are only skin-deep. I'm here, I'm alive. The outcome could have been so much worse when I came smashing down off my bike or when I went to the hospital that day and had those tests done. Who gives a shit if my face is a bit wonky and my teeth are a bit goofy?

Remember to always love yourself for what you are, not hate yourself for what you're not. As the American author Regina Brett once said:

'If we all threw our problems in a pile and saw everyone else's, we'd grab ours back.'

Chapter Six

DO YOU WANT TO GO TO THE PROM WITH ME?

★ The Nokia 3310 has a 55- to 245-hour battery life, even on standby. Talk about long lasting. It was chosen as one of the three national emojis to represent Finland and is known as 'the brick'.

★ One in ten British parents admit to paying £500 for their daughters to attend their school prom (tan, make-up, hair, outfit, shoes, travel and of course the corsage).

★ A new grading scale of 9–1 will be used for GCSEs in the UK, instead of the old A–U grading.

I remember sitting on the top deck of the 5A bus pretending to read my *Sabrina the Teenage Witch* magazine so I didn't have to make eye contact with anyone else. The anxious little Scarlett in my head kept repeating the same two lines: 'You are not ready for this, pretend to fail everything so they put you back into primary.' The thought of secondary school terrified me. The horror stories you'd hear – one kid at primary said, 'One of the first years got their head flushed down the toilet just for looking at a Year 11 in the eye.' I later found out this wasn't true, but that still didn't make me feel any more excited for the day ahead.

I sat there in my aubergine purple jumper, crisp white Fruit of the Loom polo shirt, and trousers that I promise were fashionable at the time – they were half trousers, half skirt. They were that tight they were marking every part of my body they touched, all set off nicely with my orange tan from a dance competition I'd attended two days prior.

A high-pitched electronic noise entered my consciousness. My polyphonic Mozart 40 ringtone was going off in the front-zip compartment of my McKenzie backpack. The backpack that was bigger than my entire torso so I could fit in all the essentials – which I would later learn I did not need. The words 'MAMMA BEAR' pixelated across the illuminated Nokia 3310 screen.

'Hello. You OK, Mam? I only just left five minutes ago.'

'Yes, I'm fine. God, can I not just ring ya to say I'm so excited for you? Ya will remember this day for the rest of your life. Nanny and Auntie Kirsty say good luck. I just wanted to check that you've definitely got everything you need for your first day at big school.'

'It's called secondary school, Mam, and yes.'

To be honest I didn't even know what half the stuff was that was in my bag.

'Have you got your scientific calculator?' (This is misleading as you never ever use it in science.)

'Yes, Mam. Can I go now? I'm really busy, you interrupted my game of Snake on my phone there. Bye, love you.'

'Hang on, I'll go through the list the school sent. I've got it in front of me. You check you have everything in your bag, OK? Compass … highlighters … multiple packs of ballpoint pens both black and blue … HB pencils …'

'Yes, I've got all of them, Mam, along with the glittery gel pens you bought me, a bendy shatterproof ruler and a novelty eraser that's shaped like a hot dog.' (I really thought the hot dog rubber would score me some cool kid points.)

'Brill, have a great day. I'll make you your fave for tea: fish finger sandwich, beans and chips with loads of vinegar on for you. Bye sweetheart, love you.'

After the phone call and the promise of a smashing tea, I arrived at my new secondary school in Bishop Auckland. I was meeting my cousin Demi at the old metal gates. We heard the bell go off so we rushed inside, following the big posters with arrows on them. There we found all the first years huddled together in the assembly room, rounded up like cattle. We were given shiny new planners and a whole load of information that no one was listening to about fire safety.

'I wonder whose form we will be put in? It's so exciting,'

Demi whispered. With that, the headteacher started reeling off names and what room we would need to shuffle to. Luckily me and Demi were put in the same form class. I walked into 7TR, Miss Tyron's room, and to my surprise everyone was smiling. I breathed a heavy sigh of relief and kept reminding myself that everyone else was feeling as apprehensive about this new environment as me. I was pleased me and Demi were put into the same form class; to be fair we were both thick as thieves. I remember the first term in Year 7 we both didn't get great grades and got in trouble for chatting at the back of the classroom a lot so we both decided to pretend parents' evening wasn't happening on the date that was in the newsletter. We came up with a plan. We both Tipp-Exed information about the evening on the newsletter. Technically, I wouldn't class this as a lie, it's just not giving away all of the facts.

Obviously my mam was slightly suspicious. 'Why is this part blanked out, Scarlett?'

'Because it was meant to be parents' evening but it's been cancelled for some reason.'

Now me and Demi both knew our parents would call each other. 'Janine, it's Betty. Do you know when parents' evening is?'

'It's been cancelled, our Demi said it's probably going to be rearranged again in a couple of weeks.'

I mean some would say that was deceitful but I would say it was genius. How we both didn't end up working for MI5 I do not know.

I quite enjoyed the first term of school. I even had my first crush. Seamus he was called, I knew he was way out of my league as a lot of girls fancied him and he was in the sporty cool crew during PE but I could still fantasise about him and read his horoscope in my *Mizz* magazine (not creepy at all).

However, something changed after the first term. I came back after the week's holiday (what we call up north 'potato-picking week') and the gaggle – what I called the group of popular girls – decided I was now the chosen one. The one who was going to be bullied. Now as I've mentioned, due to the bike accident I had only half of my two front teeth when I started school and the right one was black. This was enough to make me the brunt of all their jokes.

It lasted three years, just constant shit from these idiots.

'Scarlett, who's your favourite Disney character? Is it Goofy? Because that's who you look like.'

'Why are you so orange, Scarlett? Did your mam shag a carrot?'

'Do you ever brush your teeth, Black Teeth?'

'Errr, Scruffy Mouth, buy some mouthwash will you?'

'Monobrow Moffatt sitting in a tree, K-I-S-S-I-N-G with rotten teeth.'

It got so bad with them shouting stuff out during class that the teachers decided it would be best to put me in isolation. Yes, that's right, I was just trying to do my work but I was the one being punished by being isolated even more. So I had to sit in a room with five other kids and do worksheets, so now my education was suffering because I wasn't getting the same lessons as that gaggle of bitches.

They even created a website all about me (which now when I look back, I'm pretty flattered about). It was pretty shit graphics, like I don't think Mark Zuckerberg will be calling them up asking about their layout plans any time soon. But it was a site saying I loved Digimon and that I had no friends and it included a little poem about my teeth. Sounds silly now but at the time I was devastated. I cried so much. Because I was separated from the gaggle during lessons they came at me during breaks and threatened to kick my head in after school. Again the solution was to reduce my education: they let me out of school ten minutes early, so I would wander round Asda car park for an extra ten minutes and contemplate what the fuck was my life.

I loved getting into my house, it was a safety blanket. I found TV very helpful then. It's an escape really. I remember watching a lot of Victoria Wood, and she always seemed to take the mick out of herself. I thought, 'Well, she seems happy enough' so then I started doing the same really. It was nice as well because at the time on the telly all of the girls were just beautiful. They were either sidekicks or news presenters and they were all very well groomed. Even in cartoons, there was never someone that was average-looking. You were either a geek or you were in the cool group.

Whereas Victoria Wood broke that mould because she took the mick out of herself. She would do these sketch shows where she looked stupid and she'd wear a swimming cap or a beret, but people were laughing with her, not at her. That was a breakthrough moment for me. I realised, 'Oh right, so you don't have to be either beautiful or geeky. You can just be average-looking and funny.'

I think I really learnt from that. It's weird because you don't even think at the time that you really are learning from it, but Victoria Wood definitely taught me a lesson.

She showed me that making myself the butt of jokes could help me at school. I think that is why my mam and dad joked a lot with me as well, just to show it doesn't mean that people hate you if they're joking. You've just got to take it on the chin. But I also remember my dad saying, 'Just ignore those girls because it's jealousy.' I was like, 'Dad, what are they jealous of? I don't understand. I think they're just being evil. Are they jealous that I turn up looking like a mahogany door every Monday because I've been to a dance competition? I don't get it.'

Inspired by Victoria Wood, I decided in Year 9 to start taking the piss out of myself. I mean, can words really hurt if you're giggling at them yourself? I made friends with a few of the girls who were also always on their period every week when we went to the swimming baths for P.E. Every week: 'Sorry Sir, we are on our periods so we can't go in the water.' No male teacher is going to argue with a bunch of thirteen-year-olds about menstrual cycles.

I started to enjoy school more; the bullying never stopped but it had almost become bearable. One day all of the Year 9 classes were called to a surprise assembly. We were all speculating at what we thought it was going to be about. 'Oh my God, has someone died?' 'Maybe one of the teachers has won the lottery and is leaving one of their favourite pupils loads of dosh?' 'Maybe Mr Green has been outed as a pervert, he is a bit odd.'

It was none of these things.

'Stacey Dixon has won a competition in *Mizz* magazine for writing a short story,' the head announced. 'She has come first, and her prize is that our school is going to hold the 2004 *Mizz* prom!'

It was amazing. There were going to be celebrities like Paul Danan from *Hollyoaks*, who went on to appear in the first ever *Celebrity Love Island*, and some blonde woman from *Big Brother* called Shell would be making an appearance. There would be chocolate fountains, mocktail makers and of course someone was going to be crowned prom king and queen.

The whole assembly started to buzz like an old fridge. It was so exciting, nothing like this ever happened in Bishop Auckland. Everyone started chatting about dresses and dates. Shit, I thought, I need to get a date.

Now I literally had nothing to lose at school, it's not like I could ruin my street cred by getting rejected. So I thought sod it, I've got to ask Seamus if he'll go to the prom with me. What's the worst that can happen? He can say no and I'm in the same position I'm in now. I was thirteen, and despite fancying the lad for two years I'd probably said about ten words to him in my whole life. So I just went up to him at breaktime, bold as brass.

'Hiya, you OK?'

'Yeah, you feeling OK? Not like you to be chatty.'

'I know, I think it's the excitement of this prom thing. Do you think you will go?'

'Yeah, defo, me and all the lads are going to get a stretch limo like pimps.'

'You going as a pimp, ha, can I be your ho?'

And yes, that's exactly how I asked him. I wanted the ground to swallow me up and spit me back out.

'I don't mean an actual ho, I just meant a date, that's not ho'ish in the slightest.'

'Why not? Aye, I'll be your prom date.'

Now I was just as surprised as the rest of the year. Part

of me did wonder whether it was a dare, like is it going to turn into a scene from *Carrie* and he's going to throw pig's blood and guts on me when we rock up there, but he was actually just a really lovely lad. We started spending more time together in school and he even complimented me on occasion. Now I have never taken compliments very well. Someone will say, 'Your hair looks lush today,' and I'm like, 'Happy birthday'. I never know what to say. But with him it was different. I would tell him Victoria Wood jokes and make observations around the playground. He would tell me all the secrets about the cool PE group and how his mate Greg always wore tracksuit bottoms rather than shorts during football because he couldn't grow leg hair.

The week before the prom came around quick and because my mam now worked at Burton's, she helped Seamus get a suit for the prom. His mam came along, and we got a suit and a tie that matched my dress – it was so amazing.

That was the highlight of my time at that school. I don't think Seamus realised just how much it meant to me. We danced, we drank mocktails, we giggled and then a week or so after prom me and Seamus never really spoke again. Not even a smile on the playground.

Around the same time, the mother of one of the only friends I had at school, Helen Race, decided to open a B&B in the Lake District. So Helen left and I was back to being in isolation and finishing school ten minutes early again. I had lost all interest in studies and I just couldn't cope with school any more. I would pretend to be poorly constantly so I didn't have to go in. That's when my mam and dad sat me down.

'We have always taught you that running away is not the

When the monobrow is starting to creep in and your dad's cut your fringe too short to hide it.

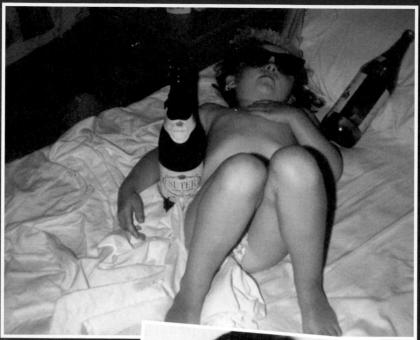

Always been a party
animal. Joke. My parents
have photos of me like
this on every holiday
we've been on. They
think they're so funny.

The men I can always
rely on – my dad and
Noddy.

From the age of 7, I've always tried to plan what transportation I could use to meet some aliens.

ME

The infamous bee outfit. Second place for a bin bag, a pair of tights and some yellow gaffer tape. My mam's like Gok Wan.

Facebook friends for life. I love how three of the girls are now dance teachers. (I'm the one who has more fringe than face.)

When you tan your head, arms and legs... but forget your torso is going to be on show.

Me and my beautiful little sister, Ava, looking pretty in pink.

First week of freshers and look at our fashion choices. I especially love my Pussycat Doll leather gloves (fingerless, may I add).

We love hockey, but we also love fresher's week and cheap wine... and I apparently love teeny tiny shorts.

Ready to graduate at York Minster with a 2:1 BA Honours degree (not sure I have a head for a hat).

Can you spot which one I am? (The only one who got fake tan stains on her graduation gown.)

answer but in this case, Scarlett, it is. Your work is going to suffer; you're not reading any more like you used to. You don't even want to go dancing. All you want to do is sit in your bedroom and pretend you're poorly so you don't have to go to school. Me and your dad have really thought about this so ... how would you feel about moving schools?'

I didn't know what to say. I thought I'd managed to hide how miserable I was.

'Why don't you switch schools, kid? You aren't happy there,' my dad said gently.

Even though I had tried to play things down my mam and dad knew. It's like a superpower that parents have. They have the ability to know when you're lying, if something's wrong and also the ability to make carrying very heavy shopping bags look effortless.

So I went for a meeting at my school. I sat down on a black swivel office chair in the headteacher's office, resisting the temptation to spin round on the chair and ready to pour my heart out. I explained how I just needed to be somewhere I could feel safe so I could concentrate on my studies. I was met with sour faces but I ploughed on. 'Mrs Wood,' I said. 'There's another school that I want to finish my GCSEs at. Sunnydale in Shildon.'

The reply I got was not what I was expecting. 'If you go to Sunnydale, it will come to the summer of 2006 and you will end up having no qualifications to your name. It hasn't got the greatest reputation and it's too late to be changing schools and subjects when you are about to go into Year 10.'

That response made me more determined than ever. 'You are not telling me that I won't get one GCSE. If you want to learn and do well, you will. It doesn't matter what school you go to!'

I knew if I wanted to achieve anything I had to leave. See, sometimes withdrawing and leaving has nothing to do with being weak, it has everything to do with strength. In the words of *Don Quixote* author, Cervantes:

> 'To *withdraw is not to run away, and to stay*
> *is no wise action when there's more reason to*
> *fear than to hope.'*

Chapter Seven

QUARTER LITRE OF VODKA AND A BLUE PANDA POP, PLEASE

✶ One of the first people known to have invented the modern office chair was naturalist Charles Darwin, who put wheels on the chair in his study so he could get to his specimens more quickly.

✶ The record number of fish and chip portions sold in a chip shop in one day is 12,406 at Marini's in Glasgow, set in 1999.

✶ Vodka is popularly believed to soothe jellyfish stings. It helps disinfect the wound and some say it alleviates the pain - though other studies say it might aggravate it. (I say you should always keep a little bottle handy if you're by the seaside, just in case.)

So aged fourteen, I was due to go to this new school, Sunnydale, after the six-weeks' holidays. Now over the summer holiday, puberty hit. And I started to change in other ways too. My mam took me to get my eyebrows waxed, the caps on my teeth looked a lot less like polystyrene, and yes, my tooth was still black but it wasn't as noticeable. I just felt like everything was finally starting to come along nicely; even my face was starting to look more symmetrical which was something I was always conscious of because of the Bell's palsy. I just all of a sudden wasn't as ugly as I had been. I'm not saying I was a stunner or anything but I felt so much more confident in my own skin. I went to this new school and I just thought, right, be the dancer version of you, Scarlett, be confident.

I have to add, the school has since closed down (due to a few bad Ofsted reports) but honestly these were the happiest two years of my teenage life. Yes, it was a bit rough; yes, its nickname was Scummy Jail; yes, it didn't have the best facilities, but I didn't care. And why didn't I care? Because everybody was nice. I had friends. The teachers were encouraging.

The other really mint aspect of the new school was that you could go out for your dinner, which you couldn't at the other school. We'd go to Beedle's Chip Shop and get a free bag of scraps and half a bag of chips, which cost 50p. How I wasn't fat in school, I don't know! I literally would just eat that and then on the way home, because the shop was right next to the bus stop, I would get another bag of chips. Or I'd say, 'Have you got any of the fish ends?' And you'd get a bag of fish ends for £1.50. And then I'd go home and say, 'Oh, what's for tea, Mam?'

The only problem was that the new school was miles away. I had to get a bus at seven in the morning to a place called Shildon. It was where I went to my old primary school, but we moved after then. It was a bit of a ballache, if I'm honest.

But, even though I had to get up so early to get on the bus to the new school, it was worth it. And my old friend Rosie – who I used to eat pancakes with every Friday – was there. So I already had a friend, and I soon made friends with her group. To be honest I just got on with everyone in my classes. We would sit on the green during breaks and chat about *Sabrina the Teenage Witch*, who we fancied in class (everyone liked Gillan, the school player) and me and Rosie chatted about old times, making the rest of the group giggle.

'Remember that time we Sellotaped each other into cardboard boxes and fed each other digestive biscuits covered in butter through the holes?'

But we did also have the kind of sensible and meaningful conversations that you have when you're fifteen years old in the year 2005.

'Would you rather go on a date with Duncan from Blue if he had arms for legs and legs for arms, or if he had eyes for nipples and nipples for eyes so he had to wear really low-cut vests everywhere so he could see?'

'Would you rather be stuck in a room for a full seventy-two hours with Peter Kay's 'Is This the Way to Amarillo?' on repeat or Black Lace's 'Agadoo'.

Now I must admit I did slightly alter the real Scarlett while I was at Sunnydale. Only a little, though, and it was just because everyone at that school was a bit chavvy (in a good way) and I wanted to fit in. I said to my mam, 'I need to stop wearing cowboy boots and skinny jeans. I definitely need to stop wearing tops with lots of sequins and unicorns on, as no one else is wearing them. I need to get some "chavvy" clothes.'

So we went out into Darlington town and bought me a new wardrobe. My mam must have spent a fortune, bless her, on loads of Fred Perry hoodies and Nike Air Maxes; I even got some pink Timberlands and loopy earrings. My mam just wanted me to fit in too. I got a pretend gold chain and started going to raves called Power House and listening to MCing.

'PC Liddle, policeman on the fiddle, sold all his drugs to the man in the middle, who put it on a plane, Newcastle Airport, picked up by a dealer in a light blue Escort.'

'Scarlett, seriously, do you have to have that music so loud? Anyone going past the house will think you've got a bloody ASBO singing along to that shite.'

'Mam, man, it's not singing, it's MCing, this is a classic.'

'It's classically shite.'

'It's MC Scotty J. This is real-life stuff, it's what kids are going through these days.'

'Right, you tell me who do you know who has even been to Newcastle Airport let alone sold drugs and drove away in a frikkin' Ford Escort?'

She had a point and it was just a phase. I forced myself to fit in. All the while, I was like, this is not me at all, but for once I thought, well, I can still be me listening to shite music and be dressed in this attire. It just meant I didn't stand out as much as the fifteen-year-old who was wearing cowboy boots, watching *Red Dwarf* and listening to Wham! Fitting in is really important. It's everything when you're a teenager.

I also turned into a little bit of a rebel at school. Well, I never really got in that much trouble (only for chatting or asking way too many questions) but I did wear trainers for school. I'd wear my Clarks shoes to go out the house but then put them in my bag once I got on the bus. That was me being a rebel. If the teacher noticed they'd give you a big yellow sticker and put it on your jumper. The yellow sticker meant that you were wearing incorrect uniform.

'Come on, Scarlett, trainers again.'

And I'd be like, 'I can't wear normal shoes, my tendons are shorter than an average person's. Trainers help me, Miss – you don't want me to walk around school in pain all day, do you?'

It was stupid because the teachers thought it made you look silly wearing a big yellow sticker, but actually it was a badge of honour. You were walking around and you'd see another yellow sticker and you'd be like, 'Yeah, a fellow rebel!' I think it did the opposite to making you look stupid, because all the cool kids wore yellow stickers. It was almost like we were in a gang.

Now I was never cool enough to be in the smoking crew. (I've never actually tried a cigarette, as my dad drummed it into my head that they're poisonous. When my mam used to smoke we would snap some of her fags in half and put them back in the packet, or we would write little messages on them like 'cancer stick', 'don't do it, Mam' or 'ashtray breath', much to her annoyance when she would dish out her fags on a night out with all these obscene messages on – although it obviously worked as she hasn't smoked in over ten years.) However, now apparently I was cool enough to get invited to drink down the rec.

'My sister's boyfriend said he can get us some booze from the corner shop on Friday night. We're gonna get a few bottles of Lambrini and vodka if you're up for it,' a girl from my English class said.

'Erm, how many people are going to be there? Will we not get caught out?'

'No, Scarlett, honestly it's fine, plus everyone will be there. Just bring three quid in tomorrow so I can give him the money to buy the booze. We're all chipping in.'

I handed her over five quid there and then and she gave me the two-pound change she was going to use for her dinner. I felt slightly anxious as I had never drank before but equally excited that I'd been invited to the rec on a Friday night.

My alarm went off on the Friday morning. 'Good morning, good morning, Scarletto,' my mam greeted me. 'Toast and peanut butter or Coco Pops?'

'Coco Pops please, Mam.' Every spoonful of cereal was harder to swallow as I knew what was about to come out of my mouth was lies. My brain started going crazy. What if she can tell I'm lying? What happens if she finds out what I'm really up to? What happens if she grounds me, stops me from going dancing? What happens if she never talks to me again?

'Mam, is it OK if I stop at Rosie's tonight? I know it's last minute but her dad said we can get a takeaway and watch the new *Harry Potter and the Goblet of Fire*, he's got it on copy.' Technically I was going to be doing some wizarding skills myself; I was going to do a disappearance spell. 'Evanesco' and the quarter-litre of vodka has gone.

'Yeah, of course it is OK, just give me a bit of notice next time – you could have told me last night. Make sure you take your phone so I can get in touch with you. Shove some pyjamas and that in your PE bag.'

'I will. Have a good day at work, Mam, love ya.'

All day we passed notes around the class about the 'wrecky' (definition: cross between getting wrecked from alcohol whilst sitting in a rec). We were buzzing. This was my first ever time having a drink (apart from that pina colada I had when I was nine that my grandad bought me). Me and Rosie organised to go to Libby's house to get ready beforehand and Rosie brought over some Lambrini she had stored in her bedroom that her sister had left over from the previous week. Now, note to self: if there is one thing I've learnt from this experience it is DO NOT drink Lambrini that has been sat in a warm bedroom with no cap on for a week. Normally I love a little glass of Lambrini but room temperature and flat as a fart, it's not good.

'I'm going to get so drunk I won't even remember my own name, me.' Libby was known for always slightly exaggerating. We walked down to the rec wearing our light blue skinny jeans and me with my black pleather fringed jacket. I was ready to sit on a swing, listen to some MCing through a speaker and enjoy my first alcoholic experience.

Turns out my £3 not only got me a quarter bottle of vodka but an added bonus of a blueberry Panda Pop to mix it with.

'Down half of the vodka so you can put the mixer in the bottle, Scarlett,' said one of the girls. Before I had a chance to say no, peer pressure kicked in and six others had joined in with the chanting.

'We like to drink with Scarlett coz Scarlett is our mate, and when we drink with Scarlett she downs her drink in: ten, nine, eight, seven, six, five ...'

Half of the bottle was gone. Why the fuck do adults do this every weekend, I thought. My breath smelt like the ethanol we used in science class. My throat and insides were on fire and that £3 could have bought me two bags of fish bites from the chippy.

As the night went on and everyone had played the usual Truth or Dare, which involved telling the whole group who you fancied, necking on with someone or making a dodgy phone call to the local pizza shop, I started to feel seriously sick. I remember the sudden numb feeling of not being able to control my own body. I felt like my legs were made of jelly and I was trying to walk on a waterbed. However, I also suddenly had a boost in confidence and started running round the rec like a demented spider monkey, hanging from the bars and shooting down the slide. I even threw a chip at Chelsea Lowland's head (something you just do not do).

Then the word-vomit started. I was telling my friends things that I was only going to regret in the morning. 'I know you fancy Dylan, mate, but to be honest he told me he just does not like you at all. Seriously, you're wasting your time. He said he would rather get with Mrs Coleman than you and she wears jumpers that have pictures of wolves on them.'

Then the actual vomit started, all over my white Nike Air Maxes. I called the house phone, begging my mam to pick me up. 'It's not ya mam, it's ya dad,' said the voice at the other end of the line. 'She's already on her way and will be there in two minutes.'

'How though, is she in a rocket, is she Mystic Meg? How did she know to come?'

'Because she's your mam and someone spotted you running around being a little idiot pissed as a fart in Shildon Park.'

When my mam arrived she didn't speak to me for the whole car journey back. Instead I got home and drank lots of water while they finished their Chinese takeaway (the smell of which didn't help my current condition: rat-arsed-itis). I spent the whole night throwing up in a washing-up bowl and crying. I was ill for the whole weekend. Not saying it put me off but I didn't drink again until I was eighteen. I still went down the rec but I just drank the Panda Pop mixer minus the vodka.

I loved everything I learnt at Sunnydale. Including not drinking week-old warm alcohol, the skill of boning a corset in Textiles and of course how to MC. Now I understand that to some it might have looked like I was running away from the bullies and giving them what they wanted when I decided to change schools. I remember fearing that I had actually let them win. But the day I got my GCSE results was the day I knew I had beat the bullies. Not with violence or name-calling, but by being happy and succeeding. I ended up getting the second-highest grades for GCSEs in the whole school. I got fourteen GCSEs in total; yep, I took extra ones on just to prove a point. I got four A*s, and the rest were As, Bs and Cs (except maths which I had to redo three times at college before I got a C – but we won't get into that).

See, I actually learnt a lot from my bullies. I learnt to grow a thicker skin. I learnt that words hurt so to try to always be kind, because blowing out someone else's candles doesn't make yours shine any brighter.

I actually bumped into one of the main bullies when I was out doing a weekly food shop recently. I hadn't seen her in a decade yet I still felt nervous when I saw her face. I even went to go down a different aisle to avoid her, then I thought no, why should I run and hide? I'm not the one who did anything wrong. To my absolute surprise she approached me when she saw me. Full of smiles. 'Hiya, Scarlett. Wow, I did not expect to bump into you today. You're doing great. I was laughing the other week actually with my two little girls because thanks to you they think they have the coolest mam ever now they know their mam was friends with you at school.'

Now usually I would just smile, say 'tell the girls I said hi' and walk away. But she used the F-word, 'friend'. I'll be honest, I felt like ramming my basket into her shins (and I am not a violent person). How dare she use the word 'friend'? Was she a friend when she came into the school with fake plastic teeth pretending to be me, shouting 'Goofy' at the top of her lungs in English class? Was she my friend when she and her crew would stare at me and laugh during lunch to the point where I ate my lunch in the toilets?

And then it just came out, before I could even stop myself: word-vomit. I told her what I was really thinking. 'Why would your daughters think we were friends? We have never been friends. You bullied me for three years, you destroyed my confidence. I moved schools because of you and your gang.'

'Oh, Scarlett, we were just kids then, it's just kids' craic.'

'It might have just been kids' craic to you, but let me tell you this. I pray and hope your two daughters never have to go through or deal with what I went through, because I wouldn't wish it upon anyone.'

And I meant that, I really wouldn't want my worst enemy to feel that way. Before she even got a chance to reply I put down my basket in the middle of the aisle, walked out of the supermarket and felt like cheering.

I know some might think, well, you shouldn't have gave her the satisfaction, but for me it was closure. See there's an inspirational quote I like:

> 'When people hurt you over and over, think of them like sandpaper. They may scratch and hurt you a bit, but in the end, you end up polished.'

Chapter Eight

DAD SAID I'M HIS FAVOURITE, SORRY

*   A Pennsylvania State University study revealed that by the time children turn eleven, they spend about 33 per cent of their spare time with their siblings.

*   Research revealed that 65 per cent of mothers and 70 per cent of fathers show a preference for one child over another (although no parents ever would admit to this).

*   Ava Gardner was married three times, to Frank Sinatra, Artie Shaw, and Mickey Rooney. Grace Kelly was the first ever actress to have her name on a US postage stamp, which appeared in 1993.

My little sister Ava Grace is my favourite person in the whole world and was born the same week I got my GCSE mock results. Without even realising it she makes me want to be the best I can ever be just so I know I do her proud.

Up until the moment she was born, I was an only child. If you've been an only child and the centre of attention of your family for fifteen years, it's hard when all of a sudden you're told, 'There's going to be a new little Moffatt.' If I am going to be totally honest, although I had always wanted a little sister I never imagined it would be happening at an age where I was almost old enough to have children myself. It was mixed feelings: part of me was very excited but the other part was apprehensive about sharing my parents with somebody else.

I actually found out my mam was pregnant by accident. I heard my mam chatting away to my nanny on the phone and saying, 'Well, how do I tell her?'

So as a joke, I came waltzing into the living room: 'Oh, come on then, are you going to tell me about this new baby?' My mam, now thirty-six and still this sarcastic amazing woman, looked at me with a face I've never seen her make. She hung up on Nanny and burst into a fit of tears. 'What's the matter?' I said. And then I thought, 'Oh God, what is the matter?'

'I didn't want you to find out this way!' she wailed.

'Find out what? What are you on about?'

'I'm pregnant!'

'Are you really? I don't understand. How? Oh my God, I hope I wasn't in the house when it … happened.'

'When what happened?'

'The baby-making, Mam! Oh, I don't know whether to be happy or throw up.'

'Oh Scarlett, don't, I really didn't know how to tell you. Well, you know a couple of weeks ago when we were at the Blackpool dance competition and I kept being sick?'

'And we just thought it was nerves?'

'And then your dance shoes absolutely stank of sweat after the comp and I got them out of the box, and I immediately ran to the toilet and was sick? Well, that wasn't dancing sweat that made me ill, that was your little brother or sister.'

I had to keep it a secret for a month (which felt like a bloody lifetime). The rest of the family found out because my Uncle Daniel started singing 'Daddy, daddy cool' to my dad at a family tea party. It didn't take people long to put my mam's weight gain and that song together before they guessed it.

My mam's pregnancy was so lovely because my auntie Kirsty also fell pregnant just two months after my mam so they got to experience it together. I went shopping with them both and as the months went on and we got baby clothes and pushchairs and cots I was so excited. When we found out my auntie Kirsty was having a little boy (my cousin Joshua) and my mam was having a little girl I cried and cried. I couldn't believe there was going to be a mini-me running around.

The day came, 23 June 2006. My sister was born. She is as cute as a button, is covered in little freckles, has that hair colour that isn't quite brown or blonde (mousey colour we call it) and has beautiful blue eyes. Ava Elisabeth Grace Moffatt. She was named after the beautiful actress Ava Gardner, my mam (of course) and Grace Kelly. She actually wants to do

West End shows when she's older so I am hoping she takes after her namesakes.

Because I was moving to university by the time Ava was her own little character, I did make a huge effort to come home every weekend. I didn't want to miss out on her growing up.

I remember I came home one weekend when Ava had just turned five and went to go and put my stuff in my room and it was now baby blue with dinosaur and fossil prints all over the walls and about ten Build-a-Bears piled up on the bed.

'Where's all my stuff?'

'Ava needed a bigger bedroom.'

'Hey!'

'Well, yes, but all your stuff's at uni now.'

'I've still got to come back eventually, and then I'll be bringing my stuff back.'

I couldn't believe I had been downgraded. She got the biggest bedroom in the house, and I got the littlest room: the Harry Potter room. In fact it was worse than sleeping under the stairs. I was like Alice in Wonderland. You know the scene where she grows and her arms are out the windows and her legs are out the doors after she's downed the bottled labelled 'Drink Me'? That's what that room's like. You can't even open the door fully. You've just got to half-open the door and then jump on the bed. When I go back now, I'm still in the closet room. That room used to be my chill room with a little couch in the bay. Now I've got to fit all my stuff in there.

Everything did all change quickly, and it was hard at first because my family life was completely different. It was really bizarre, but I would not change it for the world. It really altered the dynamic of our family when Ava arrived, but in a good way. I can't even remember now what life was like without her.

What's funny is that me and Ava still argue! Despite there being fifteen years between us, we still wind each other up. So if there were only a couple of years between us, it would not be good news because we're both so sarcastic and we're both really stubborn.

I'm going to sound evil here, but she winds me up all the time. She'll say things like, 'Oh, you always get your own way because you're on the telly.'

So my parents would ask, 'Do you want a cup of tea?' And Ava will say, 'Why? Because she's on the telly?'

'No, because me dad's asking if I want a cup of tea.'

Or she'll go, 'Someone was talking about you at school today.'

'What were they saying?'

'Oh, you don't want to know.'

'Well, what are you mentioning it for?'

'You really don't want to know.'

So she's purposefully winding me up. Or because she knows it gets to me, she'll go, 'I love you – I don't care what people say.'

'What are people saying?'

'Nothing.'

She's only eleven. I know I've got to cool it a bit, but I'm like, 'Ava!'

When I wind her up, she runs upstairs and says, 'I'm not talking to you any more.' Until five minutes later she will come back down and go, 'Mam and Dad love me more' – especially if they're out of the room.

I say, 'Will you stop saying that, Ava?'

'They tell me all the time when you're not here. Dad said that I'm his favourite, sorry.'

'Really?'

'Yeah, he loves me more.'

'The thing is, he might love you more, but he's had fifteen more years with me.'

'What?'

'I mean, that's OK. You've only been in his life eleven years, but I've been in it twenty-seven. We had a full fifteen years without you.'

'Why do you always say that?' And she'll storm out.

'Come on, Ava, I'm only joking.'

Then she retaliates by shouting from the top of the stairs: 'Yes, but he said it was the worst fifteen years of his life before I came along.'

She's hilarious. Honestly, she's the funniest person I know. But she still manages to wind all of us up. For instance, as soon as he's finished with a cup of tea, my dad will just put it down on the floor. She'll go, 'Finished with that, Dad?'

'Yes.'

'Oh, does this look like the kitchen?'

'I just finished it.'

'Go and put it away in the dishwasher then.' She's like a little mam.

My mam rang us yesterday and said, 'I've been laughing at Ava all day.'

'Why?'

'Because I was telling her that I am the funniest person in the world and Ava was going, "No, Mam, you're not funny at all.

Anthony in our class is funnier than you. He has never told a joke in his life, and he is still funnier than you."'

Because Ava is so angelic and smiley, she just gets away with it. I'll go in the house, and she'll say, 'You look different, don't you?'

'Oh, in what way?'

'Just in certain ways.'

'Don't prolong this, Ava, just say it.'

'No, no, Mam always tells me that if I haven't got anything nice to say, then don't say anything at all.'

Or my mam will ask, 'Do I look fat?'

And Ava will reply, 'I wouldn't say you're "not" fat, but you're definitely not a fatty. No honestly, Mam, you're not fat – you are just ... easier to see.'

'Oh.'

Some of my friends have got kids of their own, and I always feel like I've got the best of having a child. I get to spend time with her and do loads of fun things. But then I also get to give her back and say to my parents, 'There you are. I've had her for a full weekend.'

She comes down to stay with me in London quite a bit. When I lived in Newcastle, she used to come over for sleepovers all the time. She's always told Mam that she needs to buy her a big suitcase for her fourteenth birthday. Mam was like, 'Why?'

'Because I'm going to live with Scarlett.'

She says that all the time. I don't know where she's got fourteen from, but she always says, 'Remember, for my fourteenth birthday, I want a big suitcase, so I can put all my things in because I'll be moving in with Scarlett.'

Of course, a big suitcase isn't going to be enough for all her stuff from her *massive* bedroom, but she doesn't care. She's got two bedrooms now. That's right, I don't even get a Harry Potter cupboard now I'm officially an adult. So she's got her chill-out zone room now.

When I went back home recently, Ava had got loads of these dog stickers and she had stuck them all over the wall of her chill room. She's got posters of the 'fluffiest dogs' top ten. So there are pugs and chihuahuas everywhere. I was like, 'What is this? I can't bring the girls round here for pre-drinks when we've got these pug stickers staring at us. Jesus.'

So she's now colonised my room as well. And every time I go home now, she always stops in the bed with me, and we top and tail. So now I can't even go home and sleep in the bed by myself. You're made to feel guilty because she'll knock on the door and say, 'I'm going to bed now. Can we—?'

'No, Ava. I just want to sleep by myself.'

'OK, then. I mean I hardly get to see you, but it's fine.'

'It's just you're eleven now.'

'Yeah, it's fine, I just missed you.'

'All right then.' I always give in because she's such a good guilt-tripper.

On other occasions, Ava will be so dramatic and start coughing and grabbing her throat as if she's choking.

'What's the matter?' I ask.

'Nothing.'

'What are you doing that voice for?'

'I just feel really dehydrated. My mouth is like a desert.'

'What do you want to drink then?' Because she won't go and get herself one – she'll just moan and moan and moan.

'Oh, just get me an orange juice. Two ice cubes.'

And we do it. I mean, we've only got ourselves to blame because we do it.

My mam messaged me just this morning about Ava. This is what I mean about my little sister. Mam said, 'Oh my God, your sister is being a rebel.' Mam had got an email, saying: 'Attention, Dear Animal Jam Parent. This email is being sent in regards to your child's account, Funny Wolf. This email is to inform you that the Funny Wolf account has been suspended for twenty-four hours because of inappropriate behaviour that violated the Animal Jam rules.'

It was something about gifting. You're not allowed to just ask someone, 'Can you please give us an animal?' They've just got to give you it. But Ava writes in code. So she will write her request in coded numbers. She's so good. She learnt from the best.

Animal Jam have sussed her out, though, and suspended her. She is that clever she was creating code words by using a mixture of letters and numbers to get ahead of the game. (For those who don't know, Animal Jam is like an online outdoors, so for kids who want to learn about adventure and make friends, but virtually.)

She'll be like, 'Scarlett, I've been so unfairly suspended. Can you sort it?'

'You shouldn't disobey the law.'

'Oh come on, Scarlett, it's not the real law, it's Animal Jam law! Send them an email please.'

She is such a little character and she is like me in so many ways. She is quiet and shy until you get to know her properly and then she opens up. She loves facts and conspiracy theories, she strongly believes in time travel and she loves drag queens. Some of my best friends are drag queens – Tess Tickle (Mr Tickle), Emma Royd and Cara O'Iara – so she has grown up around drag. When we have our sister nights we binge-watch Disney, Goosebumps and RuPaul's *Drag Race*. I recently got a little bit of stick because for her eleventh birthday I bought her a life-size cut-out of RuPaul, a Michelle Visage book and T-shirts and hoodies that say things like 'Sashay away', 'RuPaul for President' and 'May the best woman win'. People said it was inappropriate that Ava even watched drag queens. My reply to that? 'What, you've never seen a pantomime at a young age?' We all encourage Ava to never judge anyone. She loves the glitter, glamour and how fun drag is. I love that she understands that it is OK to be the real you. Whether that's drag queen, lesbian, gay, transgender or just a kid who loves conspiracy theories like her sister.

Every day I tell her, 'Be a colourful Fruit Loop in a world full of Cheerios.' In the words of RuPaul:

> *'If you can't love yourself, how the hell you gonna love somebody else?'*

Chapter Nine

DO YOU NEED A BAG WITH THAT?

★ Asda's Merthyr Tydfil store sells the most white socks in the whole of the UK – one pair every six minutes. (Maybe there's a lot of people who dress up as Michael Jackson in town, who knows?)

★ In 1644, Oliver Cromwell's parliament 'banned' Christmas – or at least celebrating it – saying that the day should be spent in fasting and remembering the sins of those who had previously turned the day into a feast. (Bet yule never knew that.)

★ Coronation Street villain Richard Hillman drove his wife Gail into a canal right outside Asda's Ashton-under-Lyne store, sparking an inflatable of visitors.

I have had a lot of jobs. From putting the penny sweets into mix-up bags, to retail, to watching the television, to selling mobile phones, to working nine to five in an office. One of the best jobs I had, which I loved, was being a checkout operator at Asda. I got to sit in the swivel grey chair behind my own little counter. I was eighteen and I got £7.80 an hour, which is amazing. Also we lived opposite – actually across the road, literally thirty-two seconds away exactly – from Asda. Plus I suit the colour green.

That's the main reason why I went for the job – that and the fact that I got 5 per cent off all the shopping for me mam and dad, so I scored extra Brownie points with them, especially at Christmas. If you're doing a big shop, that's quite a lot of money, that is.

You had to be eighteen for the job as I wanted to have the power to serve people alcohol. I never really fancied working on stacking shelves or the meat counter; I prefer sitting down to standing up. Plus I'd be nibbling at the pork pies all day. So on my eighteenth birthday I handed my CV in. They sent me an application form a couple of days later. I filled that out and made the next stage: the team interview. We were split into teams and got to talk a bit about ourselves. All the time there are officials there with their Asda badges on, making notes and stuff. It's soooo nerve-wracking!

Then they put loads of spaghetti and marshmallows in the middle of the table. They said, 'Right, in teams of four, you've got to make a structure with these materials.'

And I was like, 'How is this going to show them if I'm good at the job or not?' I thought it was going to be like how fast can you put ten tins of beans in a carrier bag and stuff, but it wasn't. They must have been looking to see who was a good listener and who was good at leading a team. I passed that stage as well.

Then I had to go for a solo interview. Honestly, it was like they were picking someone to be their new chief executive rather than a checkout girl, the amount of interviews I had to do. My mam would be like, 'How's it going?'

'Well, I'm through to the next stage.'

'Jesus, it's like *The X Factor*! It's like you're through to boot camp or judges' houses!'

Then they'd ask you to sell them a pen at the interview. They put a pen on the table, and they went, 'Right, can you sell me this pen?'

I'd watched a lot of TV in my time, so immediately I knew what to say. I went, 'Right, can you just sign here?'

They couldn't because I'd already picked up the pen.

'Ah, course you can't ... What you need is this pen!'

It was like a scene from *Wolf of Wall Street*. I thought I'd definitely got the job. From there, I was just on a high from the interview. I went home, and I was really confident. I was like, 'I've nailed it, Mam, honestly, this time next week I'll be filling those carrier bags.' And I was right, a week later I started.

Despite all the great things about working in a supermarket I take my hat off to anyone who does it now. It was different back in the year 2008 when I worked there. How do you cope with the carrier bag charge? When I worked there you didn't have to pay for a carrier bag. Back then you didn't have this problem of five pence for a bag, you just had to ask people, 'Do you want a bag for life? No, that's fine, have as many free carrier bags as you want. You ruin the world – that's fine! Yeah, you tell those dolphins choking on plastic that you couldn't be arsed to carry two items to your car so you needed a bag. Go tell them as they go extinct! You lazy bastard.' Honestly, some people. Just because they were free they'd be doubling up, I mean that is taking the piss. Just pay ten pence for a bloody bag for life, man, you're killing the eco system.

I couldn't do it now with that trauma of people arguing about paying for a bag. When the charge was first brought in, I wouldn't pay for one ever. I'd carry stuff home because we only lived across the road from Asda. My mam was like, 'Why don't you just get a bag?'

'No, I'm not paying five pence for a bag!'

And then I'd get angry with myself if I forgot my bags. I'd be like, 'I've got a bag for life, but I left it at home.' So then I refused to buy another bag for life because now I've got that many, I've got a bag for life for every day of my life, and that defeats the object of a bag for life!

People would also complain to me about the produce, saying things like, 'This tin's got a dent in it.'

'So what?'

'Well, can I get any money off?'

'It hasn't ruined the contents inside. It's beans, what's it matter if the tin's a bit dented?'

'Why are you putting them on display?'

'They're only going in your food cupboard. No one will see them!'

I just don't care about things like that at all.

The customers could certainly be tricky. Someone once threw a box of paracetamols at my head. You're only allowed two boxes because of the suicide risk. So the till doesn't let you scan more than two boxes. The customer started ranting and raving. 'I'm going on holiday. I'll just have to go to another shop.'

'Well, you'll have to do that. I'm sorry.'

'OK then, I'll just go to another person in here.'

'You can't now because you've just told us. So I'll have to tell the manager.'

At that point, she just threw the paracetamols at my head. Luckily, it wasn't a tin of beans, but it's still assault. I was like, 'You can't do that!'

I was just in shock. So I rang the little buzzer, and then got security to take the customer out. I was like, 'You need to remove this woman – she's just thrown a box of paracetamols at my actual cranium!'

On another occasion, I had someone scream at me, literally calling me all the names under the sun. I mean the situation was stupid, but I don't make the rules – I was just trying to do my job. There's this mixer that's in the alcohol aisle, but it doesn't have any alcohol in it. It's cranberry juice and orange juice. It's a cocktail mixer, but my till was flagging up that you've got to be eighteen to buy it, and obviously the customer wasn't eighteen.

I was saying to her, 'I'm afraid I can't serve you.'

'But I can go and get cranberry juice and orange juice and mix them together.'

'You'll have to do that because I can't sell you it. The till is not letting me. I'd love to, but I can't – I'd lose my job.'

She went mental and started screaming, 'Checkout girls? More like fucking Nazis!'

And then I had another woman who was with her kids. She didn't have her ID and she looked very young. She could have had her kids when she was fourteen for all I knew. She was trying to buy plastic cutlery. You had to be eighteen to buy plastic cutlery, so I couldn't let her without ID.

She really kicked off. 'Who am I gonna stab with this? It's not even strong enough to butter fucking bread, never mind stab someone!'

'I know, but I've got to ID you, otherwise I'll get in trouble.' The policy is 'Challenge 25'. I took my job very seriously. I mean, at times I did think I was the police. ID, ID, ID: the power does go to your head. It's that green uniform and that badge!

When I got my little badge for working there more than one year, I felt like Lord Sugar. Honestly, I felt invincible. I remember getting that and strutting through Asda and being like, 'She's here, she's arrived' with my little green gilet on. I loved Asda.

Everyone was so friendly – except for the people that threw paracetamol at us, obviously! You got to meet loads of interesting people. Ahh, there was this old man who would come in every Wednesday. I think I was the only person he saw during the week. Sometimes he'd literally just come in for a couple of items and a chat.

He'd want to chat about life in general. He'd be like, 'Hiya, Scarlett, what are you up to?'

I'd just tell him about my day until the next customer came along, and I'd be like, 'Aww, see ya later.'

There was another man – oh my God! – who would come in and no one would want to serve him, God bless him. So I'd always end up serving him because I'm like, 'Come oooon.' I love interesting people. Some people say weird, I say interesting.

He would have this radio thing with him all the time, like a big, massive walkie-talkie. He'd have the same crack every time. He'd come in and you'd go, 'You all right?'

'Yeah, been listening to the ambulances.'

'Right …'

'And I've been listening to the police as well.'

'You know that's illegal. You know you're not supposed to do that.'

'Yeah, I know, but I've just heard there's two lorries that collided out there.'

'Ooh, right. Have a good day, then.'

And the next day, he would come in and tell literally the same story about the lorries. Every day, every single day he would come in and I'd be like, 'What's been happening?'

'There's two lorries that collided out there.'

'Ooooh, God. Have a nice day.' Every day!

He was harmless really, but everyone in the store would be like, 'Oh God, I got lumbered with him today.'

'Don't say it like that,' I'd reply. 'He's just a bit nutty, do you know what I mean? He's not hurting anyone, he's not really listening to the police. He just wants attention, and then he's on his way again.' He'd literally just come in to buy a can of pop, I think just to talk to people.

I used to love him. He was one of the reasons I was so upset when I finally had to stop working there. I was starting university and it would have been too much travelling home. I would miss the little old lady Margaret too; she would always be so excited for her trip with her carer to the store. She used to chat to all of us checkout girls, telling us about what she had been knitting or watching on the television. It's so nice to cheer people up and put a smile on someone's face if you can.

This may be overstating it, but in a way working in stores or retail is a sort of social service. I just think honestly sometimes you were the only person that those people would speak to all day, sometimes all week. You don't know what's going on in someone's life so if you can give a little smile and be kind you don't know the difference you will make to that person's day. As a tale in *Aesop's Fables* once said:

> *'No act of kindness, no matter how small,
> is ever wasted.'*

Chapter Ten

IRONY: GETTING BURGLED DRESSED AS A BURGLAR

✴ In 2011, a crowd of 3,872 people in Dublin, Ireland, broke the record for the largest gathering of people dressed as 'Where's Wally?'. The feat took place at the Street Performance World Championship in the city.

✴ In 2010, York University fined its hockey club £200 after it made students drink a concoction of dog food, anchovies, raw eggs and goldfish.

✴ The University of York has a higher density of ducks than any other university.

I wanted to become a dance teacher originally and own my own dance school. That was what I had always dreamed of. The summer after I'd done my A levels at Queen Elisabeth Sixth Form (where I had received three qualifications including an A in Dance), I sat on my sofa at home with my huge, heavy Dell laptop, refreshing the page to UCAS for about two hours when I finally got the confirmation through. 'You have been accepted into York St John's University.'

I was eighteen and was going be a YSJ student, class of 2009. I was the first person in my family to go to university. I was so excited. I enrolled in the dance degree; although nowhere in Britain covered ballroom and Latin, York St Johns did do 'contemporary dance'. Now this is an art I can appreciate and love watching – however, actually dancing in a room full of strangers, pretending to interpret a tree swaying in the wind or a mole-rat burrowing to safety, I can positively say it wasn't for me.

After eight weeks of the degree, everyone's parents were invited down to see our Christmas dance show. My nanny Christine and Mam came down and they said afterwards the best bit was the mulled wine and mince pies. I came out dressed as a giant panda wearing a red jacket and a black leather briefcase, swinging my arms and walking in straight lines. Even through the panda eyes I could see my mam and nanny crying, not with pride but with laughter. To be honest I felt like joining in.

'What was all that about?' my nanny asked.

'I was meant to represent a human who felt enclosed and caged by society. Work was my life and just like a panda in a zoo I was being watched constantly by CCTV.' Deadly serious, I looked at them both, waiting for the expressions on their faces to change to understanding.

'Load of bloody shite.'

I had to agree with my nanny, it really wasn't me at all. The other girls were so passionate and I loved them for it. But I was just going through the motions. I am not one to give up but I knew over the Christmas holidays I needed to look into changing my course.

I knew I wanted to teach children but all the courses for early years were taken. But that didn't stop me. I kept looking, and one day, when I was out with all the family for Sunday dinner – me mam, dad and little Ava – I was ready to make an announcement. 'I've looked into it and I'm going to have to do a three-year course with subjects that are on the curriculum, like English, maths and physical education, and then do a PGCE to become a teacher. There's a course that looks really good: it's physical education and sports coaching, I get to do placements with special educational needs children and it also includes dance. What do you think?'

'Go for it, kid. You are great with children and they always seem to love you,' said Mam.

'Aw thanks, I will then. I'll do it.'

So I enrolled on a physical education and sports coaching degree and I started in January. Now one thing I lack is common sense and you would have thought I would have got the memo about going to the first lecture in sportswear but sadly I didn't. I rocked up with pillarbox red hair, false eyelashes and a leopard print maxi-dress on.

I sat on the wooden benches of the lecture hall and looked around at the people I was going to be spending the next three years with. Yep, I was the only one not wearing Jack Wills or a tracksuit. But unlike school I instantly had a positive feeling about my time at York St John's. I wanted to embrace every aspect of being a student. From doing all-nighters in the library, to eating nothing but nine-pence Super Noodles, to being involved with a society and of course Freshers' Week.

I loved all the placements, which involved going into schools and teaching dance and gymnastics, and I sometimes brought drama into the sessions to help build the children's confidence up. I even spent one of my summers off in America. It was a placement scheme and I was put in a camp in Pennsylvania where I taught children aged four to sixteen with special educational needs. Even though this was nearly seven years ago I still speak to one of the mothers on Facebook to check how little Andrew is doing. It was so rewarding. However, as time went on I realised being a teacher was swamped with paperwork and bureaucracy, from planning and marking to going to safeguarding lectures. I have friends who are teachers and honestly they do such an amazing job. People just see it as a nine-to-three job with lots of holidays. It is so much more than that.

I actually went to the doctor at one point because my wrist felt like it was going to drop off I had done that many lesson plans, but it turns out it was just writer's cramp. Something kids these days don't understand. My lecturer would insist we all handwrite our plans and take notes during lectures but would give you 0.5 seconds to write them down. I'll be honest, a lot of the time I didn't have a clue what was going on and just filled my essays with big words like 'subsequently', 'nevertheless' and – my personal favourite – 'simultaneously', so that it looked like I knew what I was talking about. Still can't believe I thought I'd actually sprained my wrist. That is my second most embarrassing trip to the doctor; the first was the time I woke up after a night out and thought I was vomiting blood as my sick was red. Turns out I had forgotten about the five red Aftershocks I had downed.

Speaking of drinking, being a proper kid's belly has been a repeated pattern throughout my life and it is now the reason why I don't actually drink that much. I literally cannot handle my drink. How I managed to go out every single night of the week when I was a student (apart from Sundays, I mean don't judge me, even God needed a day to recover), I do not know. I think because I quit dancing to focus on my studies I had a void that needed filling. I got thinking about what I could fill it with. 'Vodka. That's going to be my new hobby.'

Me and my girls had it all planned out. Our week went like this:

Mondays were Gallery nights, normally a theme like 'Where's Wally?' or 'dress as an animal'.

Tuesdays were Revolution nights. We knew not to wear high heels on these nights; there were cheap paddle boards of shots and all the R&B music you needed to grind your ass off.

Wednesdays were sport society nights at Tokyo, so that's when we hung out with all of the hockey team.

Thursdays: those were Student Union and Salvation nights.

Fridays we'd order a takeaway and just have a little drink in the house.

Saturdays I would go home to see the family and then catch up with the girls from home or my boyfriend at the time for a little night out.

Sunday would be a family day and time to travel back to York. AND REPEAT.

I somehow fitted in studying and getting a 2:1 BA Honours, having part-time jobs throughout the whole of my time being a student and also being in the hockey society team. I now struggle in life to find time to fit in basic hygiene and keep up to date with social media, so I do not know how I managed.

Some of the best times of my life were made at university and a lot of the greatest moments were made with my uni girls, Sarah, Zoe, Jess and Siân.

Sarah is one of my oldest friends: I went to primary school, secondary school and college with her. We became really good friends at college and decided to pick the same university and live together there. I had the honour of being bridesmaid at her and her hubby Michael's beautiful wedding and am godmother to their first child, Jacob. She is my best friend, what I call my 'forever friend'. She is the most caring individual you will ever meet. She was like the sister of the group.

Zoe is the most similar to me in personality and the wild child of the group. She is my bad influence friend. We all have one. Everybody fancied Zoe; she is quirky, fun and always wore leopard print or tartan. (I will be attending her and Ricky's wedding this year – we have all grown up so much.)

Jess was the mother of the group. When you needed a shoulder to cry on Jess was our surrogate mam. If a lightbulb needed changing or we needed a spring clean we would all turn to Jess. She would make actual lasagnes from scratch and make wholesome meals for the house when all we had was noodles (pretty sure she's been baking since she was in the womb).

Siân was the straight talker of the group. She was brutally honest and told us to get our finger out of our arse when we were slacking with our studies, and she was also the one to tell us we needed bed and water instead of another 70p bottle of VK. Despite this, if you mentioned the words 'dance off' she would be twerking and doing the box splits in a flash.

I was the joker of the group, never refusing a night out and always up for a giggle. Apart from going out on the lash, some of the funniest moments at uni were when I was vegging in front of the TV with the girls. We would all just watch movies, gossip, slag everyone off and eat pizza.

We'd normally watch rom-coms because Zoe would pick the movie. Films I hate (despite being a Disney Classic lover), like *Dear John*. I hadn't even watched them and I could predict the ending. I'd be like, 'This is what's going to happen.'

And they'd say, 'Oh don't spoil it, you've already watched it.'

'No, it's just so predictable. They're going to die together or she's going to love the one that's poor because they always do, because love conquers all.'

I actually hate rom-coms. I'd rather watch *Saw* or *Scream*.

I feel like that's more real life. The shit that happens in *Saw* would be more likely to happen than *Dear John* or *Letters to Juliet*.

But Zoe chose them, so I would have to watch them. And everyone would be crying, and I'd be like, 'When is this going to be over?' I'd be crying through the sheer pain of watching it, and they'd be crying because they were so emotional.

Why are all rom-coms about two hours long? You can literally squeeze the whole plot into ten minutes: poor boy meets rich girl, girl then forced to get engaged with rich boy because his family and her family are friends, she realises she has to go with her heart and goes back to the original poor boy because love conquers all. That's the story done. Let's condense it and make it into a ten-minute YouTube video, acted by puppets. That would be easier.

And it's always the same actors and actresses. So then I'll start to get confused. 'So he dies?'

'No,' they reply. 'That's in the other movie.'

Another thing that annoys me is the girl will get dumped and she will accidentally bump into the love of her life a week later – hello, he's just a rebound! That's not real life. Why is no one on Tinder? Why are they not stalking their exes on Facebook? Because that's what happens in real life when you split up with someone – you start stalking the life out of them. They never do that. They never even get upset. They have a little cry on the night and then they're like, 'I've got to pick myself up and get out there again.'

I'm distressed for a whole month. I'm like, 'Oh, my life's not worth living, I'm going to be alone forever.' On a Sunday at around about eight o'clock at night, I start thinking of every bad choice that I've ever made. They never do that in movies. They need to make them more realistic.

The sole consolation was that during these movie binges I'd always be in the reclining chair. I think the others knew that if I didn't have the reclining chair, then I would be in my bedroom because I hated watching stuff like that. As I've said before, you can't decline a recline. So I'd just be lying right back, contemplating life.

Zoe, Jess and Sarah would be sat on the big couch and Siân would always be on the floor. Because she didn't live there, she didn't have her own chair space. She had to just sit on the floor. You have to get bumped up to that position of chair-sitting royalty. It's like if you visited the Royle Family, you'd have to sit on the floor as well. Where else are you going to sit? All the other chairs are taken. So Siân would sit on the floor all the time. God bless her.

Because I was never in charge of picking the movie I'd just end up downloading the films I wanted to watch on my Dell laptop upstairs after a night out. (Way before Netflix days, I'd have to wait an hour for it to complete and even then the film would buffer throughout.) Honestly, I'd be like an owl. I'd stay up till like four in the morning just watching horrors. I'd have a couple of hours' sleep and then go to my lecture.

I loved lectures at university, it's the complete opposite to school. At school you have to take what you're being taught as the gospel truth, but at uni it's all about questioning what you've been taught. I am not an argumentative person but I love a good debate. Especially when it was a 9a.m. lecture and I was still a bit tipsy (which was quite often).

I know the reason I'm quite a recluse now and why I don't

feel the need to go out all the time is because I was a social butterfly in York. For four whole years I partied non-stop so I've got all that out my system. I went to types of parties that I didn't even know existed: foam parties, school disco, UV parties, house parties, *Toy Story* parties, pyjama parties, everybody dress as something beginning with an F party, honestly any kind of party you can think of I've probably ticked it off my list.

'Where's Wally?' parties were the best. You'd always lose a friend because everyone was dressed the same. You'd be like, 'Have you seen my friend? She has blonde hair and is wearing a sort of slutty Wally outfit – low-cut stripy vest, blue tiny hotpants and those 3D glasses you get at the cinema but she's poked the lenses out of them.'

It was all harmless fun. That's what I said to my parents at home when I called them to tell them I had passed the 'initiation test' to become part of the hockey society. I didn't actually play hockey. I mean I did a couple of times but I had no interest in the sport aspect of it. I wanted into the hockey social club because they went out every Wednesday and most of my friends were in it.

'Hiya, Mam, you all right?'

'Yeah, we're all great, I've put you on that speaker thing so Dad can hear you too.'

'You alreet, kid?'

'Yeah, you sound concerned. Of course I'm fine.' I was very hungover, eating 99p noodles out of a plastic container but I wasn't going to let on.

'Just your mam seen you had all rips in your clothes last night on that book of faces.'

'Facebook, Dad. Mam, I've told you not to stalk me on that.'

'I can't help it. Anyway, I clicked onto a few people in the picture and I seen a picture and it looked like you had a bottle of wine Sellotaped to your hand.'

'I am fine, honestly. I'll explain, please don't freak out. So you have to be allowed into the hockey society by all the second and third years. They are in charge of the first years, us freshers, that's why we all had to dress as slaves and then we each do a challenge to prove ourselves worthy. That's why my clothes had rips in because I didn't want to actually spend any money on an outfit so I just ripped up a really baggy white top, wrote "slave" on the back and wore ripped tights with it.'

'Bloody hell, Scarlett, it sounds like a demonic cult.'

'No, Dad, it's just like when you get asked to down a pint at the football. Anyway coz they know me and Sarah are best friends, they set up a challenge for both of us. It was a pint glass filled with port, red wine, red VK and this red sambuca shizz. We had to drink it all, but not through a straw – through a tampon.'

Looking back, I suppose this was my first ever Bushtucker Trial in a way.

'And these are the people who are going to be future doctors, lawyers, politicians and teachers? They sound barbaric!'

'No honestly, it's a good laugh, trust me. One girl had to eat mealworms so I got off lightly.'

'But that doesn't explain why you had a bottle of wine stuck to your hand.'

'Right, well one of the rules they had is you are not allowed to go to the toilet while anyone is getting initiated. I told Sarah I wasn't peeing in a bucket in front of anyone so I was going to sneak out. Well, they noticed didn't they, so they Sellotaped a bottle of red wine to my hand as a punishment.'

What I didn't tell them is that I couldn't leave until I'd drunk the whole bottle. I mean, it should be made illegal really. How I was still standing, I just don't know. (At least I didn't have to do what David Cameron was allegedly made to do. If you don't know what I mean Google 'Pig-gate'.)

I mean, how bad is this? Jess, who I lived with, is lactose intolerant. So at the initiation ceremony, they gave her a bottle of milk and she had to drink it. I mean, really! They knew that – that's why they gave her it. It's evil, isn't it? In the second year, I didn't go to the initiations. I felt too bad putting the freshers through what we all went through. Some of those girls were really, really mean. But the thing is, regardless of that, the hockey society still organised really good Wednesday nights out. Swings and roundabouts, really.

So what would happen was, the social sec – my friend Chloe – would plan the Wednesday nights out. You would just get a text out of the blue:

'This Wednesday meet-up point: 7p.m. outside Salt & Pepper Takeaway. Theme: television. You have been given the character: a Banana in Pyjamas. C x'

Other people would turn up dressed as characters from *Baywatch* or *The Simpsons*. My friend had to dress up as Lisa, so she painted herself all in yellow and ended up not getting the deposit back from her landlord because half the walls in the house got stained. In hindsight, I wish *Gogglebox* was out at that time because I could have just walked around with a chair strapped to my back and sat down whenever I wanted. That would have been a perfect night for me.

People went all out on those fancy-dress nights. One night we had to go as something dressed as the letter F. One lass went as a full-on fence. She'd got a big long bit of cardboard and cut it out, so it was like a white picket fence. She had to walk sideways into all the bars.

You would get slagged off by the others if you hadn't made an effort. There was a lot of pressure. There was a girl called Fiona, and at the F party, she came as herself. The rest were like, 'That's shit. You need to go home, mate.'

The most memorable night out for me was the night I got burgled while I was dressed as a burglar. Oh my God, it was so ironic. One of the hockey club's nights out was a 'cops and robbers' theme. All the first years had to go as robbers. So I wore a black and white stripy jumper and a little mask, complete with a swag bag. We were in the club Tokyo, and Sarah and I were shattered. I just wanted to go home. Zoe and Jess said that they would follow, but we went to the kebab shop on the way home, so we thought that they would be back before us.

We were eating our chips with a tub of garlic sauce in the taxi, and then when we got back, all the lights were on. So we were like, 'Oh, Zoe and Jess are already in.' We knocked on the door and tried to open it, but the latch was on. We were like, 'Let us in, it's freezing!' but no one answered.

I rang Zoe and could still hear the music in the background. At that moment, my heart dropped. We peered through the window and Zoe's bedroom was upside down. All the drawers were pulled out. So I rang my friend Oliver, who was a rugby player and lived at the end of the road. I was like, 'You need to help us get in.'

He banged open the door, but what had happened was that the burglars had got a paving slab and thrown it through the back window. The neighbour was like, 'Oh yeah, I thought you just had your telly on loud.' What would we be watching that sounds like a paving slab going through a window?

The thieves had literally stolen everything. They'd even taken Jess's suitcase to put our things in. But obviously when the police turned up and we were all dressed as burglars, they thought we were taking the piss. They were like, 'Just so you know, this is wasting police time. You will be given a caution.'

'But we've really been burgled!' I cried, swag bag in hand. They genuinely thought we were taking the mick until they went in the house.

Sarah's mam Wendy came for us the next day. I just wanted to go home and burn my swag bag. When Wendy arrived she gave us all a huge hug. She made her way through the house. 'Oh God, look at the state of it,' she said. She was in my bedroom. 'I can't believe it, Scarlett, I am so sorry this has happened. They've trashed the place.'

'No, Wendy. They just took the laptop from my bed.' My room was a tip from getting ready. That's probably why they only took my laptop; they must have thought they had already done that room.

I was gutted they had took me laptop. Not because it was expensive because it wasn't, and it was like lobbing a sack of bricks around it was that heavy. But they'd also stolen the dongle that was in the laptop with all my work on. So then

I had to go to uni and give them the crime number because obviously I bet they heard that story all the time. 'Well, actually that work was stolen from me.' But it really was.

I had to just do the work again in two days. I think it was my worst mark ever. I got like 40 per cent, so I just passed. But it was too much to do in two days. I'd been doing it for like a month and a half. I sort of still remembered the books that I'd used so it wasn't as difficult. But still, trying to do six weeks' work in two days was almost impossible.

I thought that the lecturers would have given us a bit of leeway or given us a bit longer. But they didn't. They were like, 'It's still due in then.'

'But I've just been through the traumatic event of being burgled while dressed as a burglar and now you're telling me I've got to do all my work in two days!'

We can giggle about it now because we were dressed like that. I think if we'd just been in normal attire it would have been more of a traumatic event. They actually found some of our stuff – they were selling it in Leeds Market. One of the criminals was actually 'friends' with a couple of us on Facebook, and he'd seen that we were all on a night out. He was just a randomer that had seen our posts on Facebook. Firstly the picture that showed where we lived because we had stupidly put a photo of us outside the house, like, 'Yay, new house!' And the next post was us all dressed up, 'Yay, we're going for a big night out!'

I think what they had done is they'd just added loads of people who were friends on Facebook with the university. They knew freshers were going to have new laptops and stuff. It has taught me to be a lot more careful on social media.

So much that sometimes I even block my own mam off Facebook. Now this sounds harsh but she would call up and be like, 'You cannot go out dressed like that,' so I would just block her for a few nights so she couldn't stalk me, and then add her back again. Or she would say, 'I thought you had an essay to finish so why are you going on another night out?' To which I always replied, 'Mam, would I even be a student if I didn't do all-nighters and finish my essays at the last minute in the library?'

I decided to get a job to pay for my new laptop. I remember sitting in a little office in the Topshop in York about to have an interview for what would be the first in a long line of student jobs. It was quite easy to get part-time jobs in a busy student city. I had only been to uni for three weeks and I was already running out of new clothes. 'I'll apply for Topshop,' I thought. 'You get 60 per cent off; I'll have a new wardrobe before long.'

That job lasted three months. I take my hat off to Topshop girls; they make such an effort for work and that just isn't me. They would come in looking like they'd just walked off set from a Black Eyed Peas music video, wearing black lipstick matched with super-skinny jeans with some sort of avant-garde hairstyle. I would rock up looking like a hungover student in basic black leggings and an oversized jumper with my hair in a top-knot.

I didn't get as much make-up as I was hoping for Christmas so that was next on my job list. I managed to get a job at Clinique, with a whopping 70 per cent off make-up. I worked there for a few months – and loved it. However, after a couple of warnings I eventually got the sack for the most ridiculous reason. Apparently I was making all the customers 'too orange'. Yes, I am known to love a bit of bronzer yes, I did like to go a couple of shades darker tha people's skin tone; and yes, sometimes people's faces ended up a different colour to the rest of their limbs but I just like giving people that 'just come back from two weeks in Tobago' look.

My manager kept saying, 'You know, Clinique is all about looking *au naturel*.' But I'd reply, 'It's cold outside, let's make people smile. Everyone feels better with a tan, don't they?' I was gutted when I lost that job; no more £3 eyelashes that were so long I had to throw my head back to open my eyes.

My favourite job at uni was when I worked at a club called Salvation. It was the big club in town, but the queue was always massive. We didn't have to queue anywhere else in York because we were out so often we were friends with most the bar staff, door staff and DJs. But we didn't know anyone at Salvation. 'Well, I'll have to take one for the team and start working there then,' I told Sarah. I would sell shots or do promo for them. I was one of the arseholes in the street with a big bomber jacket on, giving leaflets out. You know, the ones that you cross the street to avoid. That was me.

I even remember the jargon I used to give to passers by. 'Excuse me, can I just stop you please? I've been looking all night for someone who looks like they know how to have a good time and wants to get mortal. I've only got a few of these flyers to give out – it's to make sure the club is filled with fun people to give the place an even better atmosphere.

So if you hand this leaflet in at the door you and your pals get free entry and a free shot. You know it makes sense.'

Even though we would be out in all weathers until stupid o'clock in the morning we had such a giggle. Plus there was a pasty shop that was open until about 2 a.m. so if morale was down we would all just go and get a big Cornish pasty.

I always had a job throughout uni. I was even a quantitative research analyst for three months. I always seemed to be skint though. I didn't even know where my money went. Recently I went for a catch-up with my friend Zoe. She had brought her friend Christie down with her. Zoe said to me: 'Tell Christie how many big shops you did when you were at uni.'

'What do you mean?'

'Tell her how many big shops you did.'

It is only when I was reminded of this that I started to cringe. 'Eeeh no, I can't!'

The truth is that I went to a supermarket once in the entire four years I lived in York, and even that was when my mam and dad came and they did a big shop for me. Other than that – and I'm going to sound so bad here – I ate all of my housemates' leftovers. Zoe would make noodles, and then whatever she left over, I'd eat. No wonder I was so slim at uni. I literally only ate leftovers. Or the other thing I'd do was just buy massive bags of pasta and have that with tomato sauce. I don't mean tomato pasta sauce; I mean ketchup. So I'd just have pasta and ketchup. Unfortunately, it was always rock hard. I didn't even know how to make pasta properly.

How scruffy is that? My mam would be like, 'Oh, you look like you're losing weight. Are you eating well?'

'Yeah, I had king prawn linguini last night.' I didn't tell her it was just scraps. But it wasn't lying, technically. I don't know what I would have done without Jess and her big portions. In fact I don't know what I would have done without any of my girls at university. I certainly wouldn't have ended up graduating. On my graduation day I didn't just leave York Minster with a 2:1 degree (and debt up to my eyeballs), I left with friends for life.

Best of all, they were friends for life who loved me for me. With the confidence I had learnt from dancing and with the encouragement from my family and what I'd learnt at secondary school, I walked into that university being nothing but Scarlett Sigourney Moffatt. I embraced my weird traits; I danced like a robot in clubs; I told the girls stories of aliens and conspiracy theories; I had the confidence to teach children and I changed my dance course even though it was completely changing the path I thought I wanted to take. Through it all, the girls helped me and I helped them. We built each other's confidence up every single day and we all wanted each other to succeed so badly. I have learnt that it's important when you find true friends to never let them go and to never betray them. As an Aesop fable once said:

'Betray a friend, and you'll often find
you have ruined yourself.'

Chapter Eleven

THOSE DARK
DOLE DAYS

★ The University of York lost a rubber duck they sent into space; there's a £200 reward for its safe return.

★ The average time spent by recruiters looking at a CV is five to seven seconds.

★ J. K. Rowling was on benefits three years before the first Harry Potter book was published. She couldn't afford a computer or even the cost of photocopying the 90,000-word novel, so she manually typed out each version to send to publishers. It was rejected dozens of times until, finally, Bloomsbury, a small London publisher, gave it a second chance after the CEO's eight-year-old daughter fell in love with it.

Getting a job in the 'real world' is a lot harder than getting a student part-time job at uni. It was really hard to find what I wanted: which was an actual career. Now in all honesty, I wasn't completely sure what career I wanted but I just knew I wanted to help children. I'd done placements working with children with autism and Asperger's and I found it really rewarding. I didn't want four hours here and a zero-hour contract there; I wanted a proper career. But there were just no jobs. Not even in the field I wanted, just in general. For every job that was coming up in the North East, there were 200 applicants, even for part-time jobs. It was just ridiculous. There was just nothing out there. I had so many friends at the time who were on zero-hour contracts. The recession had really changed everything.

When I graduated from York St John's I felt I had honestly been fed the dream: 'If you go to university, then you can have a career you love. The world is your oyster.' But it's not as easy as that. I remember thinking at the time, 'God, I wish I hadn't gone to uni.' I was up to my eyeballs in debt from my student loan and living off £40 a week. Now, looking back, I wouldn't change it for the world; I'm proud I accomplished what I did and it was a great experience. It just wasn't as easy getting a job afterwards as I had anticipated.

I just wanted to have a career, I wanted to work hard, be independent and make myself and my family proud. I ended up being on the dole for about five months before getting my job helping to assess medical information and helping disabled students at university.

I remember going to the dole office for the first time. I

arrived fifteen minutes early and was greeted by the security guard. It didn't fill me with confidence that they needed to have safety precautions. When I got there I tried to stay positive. I sat at the slate-grey desk and handed the lady my CV and we chatted about what jobs I would be suitable for.

'I have had a lot of experience working in customer service, I have worked in part-time retail jobs since I was sixteen as well as working as a checkout operator. I volunteered teaching drama and dance to children who lack confidence and I've done many placements with children with special educational needs.'

'Well, you know you haven't got enough experience in the workplace for teaching or caring for disabled children like you've specified on your curriculum vitae. I know you have done placements at university but it just isn't enough for the competition that's out there, I'm afraid. Everywhere is wanting people with experience so they can spend less time training, do you understand?'

I did feel slightly patronised but I stayed positive. 'Yes, I understand but someone needs to give me the opportunity to get some experience, otherwise I'm never going to get anywhere. It's a vicious circle.'

It just wasn't what I thought it was going to be. I knew I wouldn't be able to get the job of my dreams straight away but I just felt like they didn't listen to what I was saying. I know they're only trying to do their job of helping people get off Jobseekers' Allowance but some of the jobs I had to apply for I knew I was never going to get.

'So you live in County Durham, are willing to travel but can't drive. Hmmm, there's a job here just thirty miles from your home but it's a pizza delivery driver so that's no good for you.'

'No, I'm afraid not.'

'Here's a job that's just popped up on my screen today: a sandwich artist.'

'What's that?'

'It's someone who makes sandwiches. Right, because we are setting up this interview for you, you should be aware that your Jobseekers' Allowance will be stopped if you don't attend.'

'I never said I wouldn't attend.' I honestly didn't mind the idea of becoming a sandwich maker; to be honest I'd have taken a job eating the crusts from the sandwiches of kids who didn't want to eat them if it meant coming off the dole. I handed a CV in and waited for the call to tell me when the interview was happening. Well, days passed and I realised I clearly hadn't quite cut the mustard. Maybe I should have enclosed a picture of all the Billy Bear ham sandwiches I had made in the past.

The second time I went to the dole office, they said, 'Oh, you need to go on this three-day CV-writing course.'

'Are you joking? I know how to write a CV. I might have a lack of experience – even though I've had part-time jobs since I was sixteen – but I've been in education all my life. If there is one thing I can do and I have experience in, it's writing.'

So I had to go on this course, otherwise I wouldn't get my dole money. I went there, and they read my CV and went, 'Yes, really good.'

'Right ...'

'So if you could just help everybody else write theirs, that would be great.' For the next three days, I was a CV-writing teacher.

The next week when I went to the dole office, because I had had to go by bus to the CV-writing course, I had to give in my bus tickets to the dole officer so they could give me the £6 back. I could feel my face turn crimson but I genuinely couldn't even afford the bus fare because I was already in my overdraft.

I was given a new dole officer and she was very kind. She asked me, 'What was the course like?'

'In all honesty I would love to give you one good remark but it was a complete waste of time. They didn't amend anything on my CV. I didn't learn anything. I just felt like I was there helping everybody else.'

'Sorry to hear that. If you can fill this form in and bring it in next time I can pass these remarks on. Right then ... actually, I'm afraid it's flagging on my screen that there's another course you need to attend. It's only two days and it's on customer service skills. There's no way of getting around it.'

It was a dark period in my life and there were days I'd not get up out of bed and I'd just cry while scrolling through my computer on the Universal jobs page. I really feel for people who are trying hard but there's just nothing out there for them. At the dole office, I'd get talking to people while I was waiting. I remember there was one man who hadn't been able to get a job in eighteen months. He was only in his thirties. He'd literally worked every day since he was sixteen and he had been made redundant. Now he was applying for jobs, and he was just like, 'It's so frustrating. I want to work, but I come in here, and I feel like some people are looking at me like, "Oh God, you're so lazy."'

I think there's a stigma attached to job seekers, especially because of the programmes that are on telly now. Like in *Britain on Benefits*, they're literally zooming in on the one person that's in the town centre having a can at eleven in the morning. Not everyone is like that, but they pigeonhole everyone. They're like, 'Right, this is what everybody's like who's on the dole.'

It makes people hate the unemployed for no reason. Everyone thinks that 'those people' are all the same. But obviously they're not. I know you do get some people who fiddle the system and who can't be bothered to work. I also know people who admit they think it's more beneficial for them to be on the dole than to get up and go to work. But the majority of people are good people who do want to work, but the jobs are either just not out there for them or they're unable to work for medical reasons.

It is hard; I hardly stepped foot out of the house for those five months. The only time I'd get out was if I went for a walk or a wander round the shops with my friends.

'Oh, let's go to Costa Coffee,' they'd say. I'd be thinking, 'Shit, even if I get a small coffee, it's £1.40. God, I really want that hot chocolate with whipped cream and marshmallows and salted caramel sauce, but it's £3.60. I can't afford that.' I'd end up sitting there without a drink, pretending I wasn't thirsty. It was hard being twenty-two and not being able to go out with your friends. Me mam and dad offered to pay but I felt bad taking handouts.

They knew I was trying my best. But it was still just dreadful. I'd cry constantly. I'd be sat at the laptop, day in and day out. I couldn't go out anywhere because I had no money to do anything with. Then you're just seeing the same jobs over and over again that you've already applied for.

I had eight CVs. One for sales, one for customer care and so on. I just really wanted something. Anything. It was so demoralising.

I was like, 'God, Mam, why won't anyone give me an interview? I feel worthless.'

So then I'd rearrange my CV and she would say, 'Scarlett, I've read it, and it's fine.'

I even contemplated lying on my CV to get a job. 'Mam, I'm nearly over my overdraft limit, surely other people must be lying on their CV? We all tell little fibs.' But I knew they could check up, and then I'd be in trouble. See, the upside of having rough times is that it does teach you not to take anything for granted and to count your blessings when things do go well. Remember that when things aren't going completely the way you intended, you're allowed to scream, you're allowed to cry, but you are not allowed to give up.

In all honesty, like a lot of students when they first finish education in college or university, I didn't really know what exactly I wanted to do. I just knew I wanted to help people. I think sometimes when you have a certain qualification or a dream job in mind you can focus solely on that one pathway to get the job you want and dismiss anything else that comes your way. But sometimes you have to take a more circuitous route.

Eventually, I got a job at a mobile phone store selling

contracts (which I ended up loving). Which strangely took me to my next job sorting out students' finance. Which then led me nicely on to my dream job at the time of assessing medical evidence and helping disabled students. So I did get there in the end.

Sometimes, because we live in a world that moves very fast and we can get what we desire with a click of a button, or we stalk through people's lives (seeing what they want us to see) on social media, where they appear to have your dream job and dream life, we are harsh on ourselves. But we need to realise that life isn't always that straightforward and it doesn't matter if our own path takes a little longer to become apparent. Lewis Carroll sums it up nicely in *Alice in Wonderland*:

'One day Alice came to a fork in the road and
saw a Cheshire cat in a tree. "Which road do I take?"
she asked. "Where do you want to go?" was his response.
"I don't know," Alice answered. "Then," said the cat,
"it doesn't matter."'

Chapter Twelve

'YOU WANT ME TO WATCH THE TV FOR A LIVING?'

★ *Gogglebox* has now gone international: seventeen other countries have now got their very own *Gogglebox* including the USA (where it is called *The People's Couch*) and Slovenia (where it is called *God, Please Don't Let the TV Die!*).

★ In 2009, the United Nations proclaimed Mandela's birthday (18 July) to be Nelson Mandela International Day. The holiday asks people to spend sixty-seven minutes doing something good for others, which represents the sixty-seven years he spent working towards change.

★ Pease pudding is known as Geordie caviar. It's made from lots of squashed yellow split peas.

One of the big questions I always get stopped and asked in the street is 'How did you manage to get onto *Gogglebox*, Scarlett?' Actually that's a lie, it's: 'How do I get onto *Gogglebox*? Me and my family would be great on there.' The truth is I genuinely do not know, I'm sorry. I wish I had an email address I could just dish out to people. Me and my family didn't fill in application forms or go to lots of tedious auditions. In all honesty it was a favour gone wrong (or right, now that I look back).

My friend who I went to college with, Tommy Turnbull – great name, great bloke – was the one who made it all happen. He worked as a researcher for the TV production company Studio Lambert. One Thursday afternoon he called me up. I was sat on the couch in the living room watching *Time Team* with my dad (and moaning about how much I dislike *Time Team*).

'Scarlett, it's Tommy. I bet you know a lot of interesting people. Do you think you have any mates or relatives that are interesting enough to want to audition for a Channel 4 show? It would only take half an hour at most. Basically it's a show where people watch people watch TV,' Tommy explained down the phone.

'Pretty sure that's voyeurism, Tommy. I don't know, mate, they make programmes about anything these days. When would they need to be free?' I replied.

There was a long pause followed by, 'Anytime tomorrow. I know it's short notice but you would be really helping me out if you found someone.'

I called up all my contacts on my mobile straight away; I only have about thirty contacts so it didn't take long.

I mean twelve of them are immediate family, six are takeaways, three are hair salons and four of the names I don't even recognise. No one was up for doing the audition. I was gutted; I really wanted to help Tommy out. 'Oh well, fuck it,' I said to myself. 'If you want something doing properly do it yourself.'

'Hello, Tommy, it's Scarlett. I have bad news and good news. The bad news is I couldn't find anyone who wanted to take part, the good news is me and my family are up for doing it – well, I'm pretty sure they'll be fine about it, I haven't actually asked them yet. But give us a time and we will be ready, as long as it only does take half an hour.' Tommy was thrilled he had managed to get an audition in the North East. 'Mind, Tommy, we're not wanting to actually do the show for real. Remember, this is just a favour.'

Now I knew my mam had already watched the first two series of *Gogglebox*; this was back when they were on Channel 4 on a Wednesday night. So I gave her a call at work.

'Hello Burton's Bishop Auckland, Elisabeth speaking, how can I help you?' I knew if I called my mam at work she would be more likely to say yes in front of people.

'Right, Mam, tomorrow come home during your dinner hour – try and be back for half twelve because me, you and Dad are going to help my mate Tommy out by pretending to do an audition for *Gogglebox*.' I quickly hung up in order not to hear her response in case it was a no.

The next day a little crew of four people came to the house with a camera. We all sat on our couch, in our own little spots (everyone has their certain seat in the house).

'Right,' explained Tommy. 'We are going to show you some picture cards of celebrities and all you have to do is chat about them.'

First they showed us a picture of Piers Morgan, who I mistook for David Cameron. This resulted in us having a family argument about the bedroom tax, completely forgetting there were four other people in the room. Other pictures included Victoria Wood and Dawn French; we were told to stop chatting about them as we just couldn't shut up once we started recalling all our good memories of 'The Ballad of Barry and Freda' and *The Vicar of Dibley*.

Now before I explain the next picture card I feel like I have to defend myself. Although I have a good memory and will never ever forget a face, I will forget where I met you, how, in what circumstance and your name. So they show me the next picture card and I can't quite put my finger on who it is. Have I seen this man in a documentary? No, I think, he's from an advert!

'Oh, I love him!' I piped up cheerfully. 'I love savoury rice and this man was a life-saver at university. One microwave, one sachet and you had a meal in just two minutes!' My dad looked at me in such disgust you'd have thought I'd just smeared shit all over the living-room walls. 'Why are you all judging my love of Uncle Ben?' I asked.

'Because,' bellowed my dad, 'it isn't Uncle Ben the rice man, it's the great Nelson Mandela!'

I apologise profusely to the late, great Mr Mandela. I've

since watched at least fifty hours' worth of documentaries and YouTube videos on him and he is an amazing legend of a man.

Despite that slight slip-up, and much to my confusion, the next day I got a call from Studio Lambert telling me they want the Moffatts to be the new family on the third series of *Gogglebox*. Oh, and we would need to start filming on Monday, which was just two days away. Obviously we never actually planned to film and be on the television in real life and we were all baffled by the situation. It was actually my dad who was the most open to it. He just kept saying, 'Well, what's the worst that can happen?' Famous last words.

If you have flicked over to *Gogglebox* in your time and seen me and my family, you may already have some of your favourite moments. If not, you are probably reading this like, 'What the hell is *Gogglebox*?' So the following highlights will give you an understanding of some of the shit me and my family talk about in the comfort of our front room.

- The age-old argument for DC Comic fans: Batman or Superman, who is the best? I voted Batman. 'Superman looks exactly the same when he puts his glasses on and combs his hair … And everyone acts like it's someone else. I don't buy it. Batman has a proper disguise.'

- On that incident with Madonna nearly going arse over tit on stage at the Brits because one of the dancers stood on her cape: 'Have you been in an accident at work? Where there's a blame there's a claim!' (She should have got a good payout for that.)

- Me and my mam telling my dad to try these new nuts I'd just bought. We forgot to mention they were wasabi nuts and my dad, whose eyes are bigger than his belly, downed a fistful of hot nuts. (I've just realised how wrong that sounds when I say it out loud.) His eyes looked like someone had poured acid in them, his forehead started to sweat profusely and I am pretty sure at one point his nose nearly started bleeding.

- On Jeremy Corbyn being elected Labour leader. At the time, I hadn't actually heard his policies, I simply did what we all do and judged him on face value alone. 'He looks more like the next Doctor Who than the next prime minister, if I'm honest,' I said. But don't worry, I also have an opinion on Theresa May, that opinion being that it's a misfortune for her to have the same name as the hair product 'TRESemmé'. It must make hair appointments very confusing.

- As a family discussing the stress of results day for GCSE students: my advice was not to worry. After all, 'In the number one hit song "Give Me Everything", Pitbull rhymed "Kodak" with "Kodak" and look at him, he is a multi-millionaire.'

- The iconic scene in James Bond when 'M' dies. My logical thinking: 'Well, "N" can just take over.' I didn't understand what all the fuss was about – in alphabetical terms they had at least thirteen other agents left.

- On Martin Freeman doing a political video for the Labour Party ahead of the 2015 general election. My response? 'I'm not taking political advice from a fucking Hobbit.' (Now at the time of filming I never thought I would actually get to meet any of the people I was slagging off every Friday night. I had the safety net of my sofa, my parents and my own front room. I didn't have this safety net when I actually met Martin Freeman at Jonathan Ross's Halloween party. Not that I think Martin – who played one of my favourite characters from a TV show ever in *The Office* – actually watches *Gogglebox*, but you just never know. So I said hello and smiled very politely whilst power-walking past him.)

- And finally, everyone can agree with me here, when I watch *The Great British Bake Off* I get that into it I start really feeling like I know the contestants. 'I care more about some of these people than some of my own family by the end of it,' I said.

Now all of this was said whilst having a television crew in the house. Yes, I'm going to let you into a little secret, as another question I'm always asked is 'How does *Gogglebox* work?' Contrary to belief, we don't just switch a camera on and then start watching the TV. Unfortunately, it's a little bit more complex than that. For the past two years of us filming we would have two cameras, lights and a crew of normally five or six people in our dining room. Our favourite and a guy who has been there from the start is Matt, a sound technician from Oxford. Excuse the pun but he genuinely is a sound guy. He made us laugh with his quick wit, sarcasm and his love of northern chicken kebabs.

There was a time when me and my family had one of those rare moments in life where we were reduced to being speechless and that's thanks to one of the *Gogglebox* crew. We all just burst into a fit of laughter, staring at each other in disbelief. It was a moment off screen that I want to share with you all. We do laugh about it now but it is the most 'northernist' (definition: northernly racist) thing that's ever happened to us. As we don't have time to make tea or go and pop over to Asda or Sainsbury's halfway through an episode of *Downton Abbey* to get some nibbles, a kind member of the crew, in this case Karen, would pop out and get us something to eat.

I discussed the food situation with my mam. 'What should we get, Mam? I've had no tea. I mean Dad's saying he's not hungry, but he will be when he sees us eating so let's get a few bits.'

My mam agreed and turned to Karen. 'Karen, can we just get some bits to nibble on, like humous, crackers, even a bit of cheese if there is some, please? Thanks so much.'

The episode of *Downton Abbey* had finished (the one where Lord Grantham projectile vomits all over the place like a scene from *Saw*) and the door went. Yes, it was Karen, I could hear the rustling of the carrier bag. As we walked into the kitchen, stomachs rumbling all ready for our tea (northern for 'dinner'), we could not believe our eyes.

'I couldn't quite remember what you asked for so I just got some bits I assumed you would like,' announced Karen. There laid out on the table were four sausage rolls, a packet of

Scotch eggs, pease pudding and a massive pork pie. She may as well have thrown a few stotties and a crate of Newcastle Brown Ale in for luck. I mean if we were Irish would she have just assumed we wanted four jacket potatoes and a tin of Guinness each?

To be fair, if that happened to another family they probably wouldn't find it funny. But as a family with a warped sense of humour we often find that we are the only ones laughing. In fact, we often wouldn't make the cut of the show because of our inappropriate laughter. I remember when we all had to watch *Titanic* and the crew were like, 'You are not going to make the cut, stop giggling.' It is the scene where Rose is sprawled out, spread-eagled on the huge floating door and Jack is there, freezing his tits off with blue lips, God bless him. We couldn't stop laughing at the fact it was so obvious he could have fitted on the door with her. I get that he had to die as that was the plot but if the dude's got to sink at least make it believable and have her lying on a tiny door, maybe a wardrobe door.

Also if it's something that is meant to be serious like a documentary, me and my family just somehow completely miss the point and find something inappropriate about it. I remember we watched this programme about this man who loves watches and clocks. He has hundreds of clocks in his house. It was meant to be a really serious piece of television, and my dad was chatting about the timepieces and the mechanics of a watch and stuff, while my mam and I were just giggling the whole way through whilst trying to keep our eyes open. 'Jesus Christ, who has over a hundred clocks in one house?' my mam gasped.

'What happens when it strikes midnight in his house? It's going to be like *Mary Poppins*. His whole house is going to shake.'

Every time he would pick up a clock and touch it, I'd be like, 'Look at him stroking that clock!'

My mam would be crying with laughter. 'Behave!'

'Mam, the future, the present and the past walked into a bar. Things got a little tense.'

Meanwhile, the whole of mine and me mother's conversation would be going right over my dad's head.

Now it was always that way, me and my mam versus my dad, but then Ava decided she also wanted to film and it was then Mam, Dad and Ava versus me. 'What you watching for tonight's *Gogglebox*, Scar?' Ava asked one day with a cheeky grin. I knew straight away (it's the sisterly bond) just what she was thinking.

'Yay, you want to film with us, don't you?' I questioned. I was so excited. Ava is literally the funniest human being I know (despite still being at primary school); her wit and sarcasm is on point. She is like the lovechild of Stephen Fry and Ricky Gervais. I couldn't wait to film with her. As she was only eight when we started filming we gave her the option of whether she wanted to be involved each time. We didn't freeze her and defrost her when needed like they do with the children in soaps, she simply hung out with the film crew in the dining room or watched a movie, then an hour into filming it would be her bedtime.

'As long as you don't show me up by saying something stupid, Scar, I will do *Gogglebox*,' Ava replied. I agreed reluctantly that I wouldn't wind her up.

We started filming with a news item all about added sugar. Now I was honest and I openly admitted, 'I genuinely thought that "no added sugar" meant that there was like not a lot of sugar in the food at all.' I had the usual reaction of defeated sighs and an eye roll from my mam and dad before Ava kindly showed me up in front of the UK by delivering this perfect response: 'Scarlett, I'm a nine-year-old and even I know that, and you're twenty-five. Sort it out.'

Understandably, I didn't comment back or try and outdo her on her sassy comeback, I did the only thing I could do – accept defeat from a nine-year-old.

But it's stuff like nine-year-olds out-sassing sisters that makes the show so real. I feel the reason why *Gogglebox* got really popular was because it was reflecting the experiences of the people who were watching it. People were saying, 'They are just like us. They are watching telly on their sofas and commenting on it, just like we do.'

But what's lovely is because the show is so relatable, everyone who sees us in real life knows we are just normal approachable people. It's not like if you see someone like, say, Jeremy Clarkson on the street – that could be quite intimidating. We are just normal, average people. People feel like they know you because every Friday night we invite the audience into our home. Once *Gogglebox* started to get popular, the attention we got in the street really ramped up. I would have to set off fifteen minutes earlier to get places. I couldn't even go to Asda really. It's weird because essentially it is just a show where we are watching the TV but it's so flattering and lovely that people want to chat to me and other people on the show. Everybody knows a character in

Gogglebox. So a lot of people say, 'Leon is like my grandad' or 'He's like my grandad's friend.'

Leon and June are sweet, aren't they? I loved Steph and Dom too. I was lucky enough to get to meet them. They lived up to expectations! They haven't even been in the show for about four series, but they are so memorable because of their characters. They were super friendly, smelt how I thought they would (of rich mahogany and Creed cologne) and were about to go to the pub for a bottle of champers. But my favourites have to be the Siddiquis. They are by far my favourite family. They are so quick-witted. I think they are really underrated; they should be given their own show.

I still watch *Gogglebox* now even though we are not on as a family any more. People always ask, 'Do you miss *Gogglebox*?' The answer to that is, 'How can we miss something we still do?' We still all watch television together, we still laugh, joke and cry at the TV as a family, just the difference being nobody gets to watch us doing it any more. Basically, when I got asked to do *I'm a Celebrity*, the *Gogglebox* people gave me an ultimatum: 'It's either *Gogglebox* or the jungle.' To be honest it wasn't a tough decision to make; my family wanted me to go for the jungle and I just knew it was too much of an experience to miss. My family, the TV and our couch were always going to be there, the chance to go in the Outback with a bunch of celebrities wasn't.

Honestly, I loved having a job where I got to talk non-stop for several hours whilst watching the TV. Apart from the dry mouth. What I don't miss – it was the difficult part of *Gogglebox* – was when we had to watch a show we loved, because you didn't want to chat, you just wanted to watch and enjoy it.

We also had to watch a hell of a lot of shite, mind. But all those agonisingly boring documentaries were worth it when I would read my tweets and see that people had made comments about being cheered up after watching *Gogglebox*, or the fact that people would take the time out to send me letters. The greatest letter I ever received was from a lovely lady who was in hospital. She was having radiotherapy. She could only have one person in the room with her at a time, and they had to stand in the corner. So she couldn't watch telly with anyone. She was really close with her mam and dad, and she said to me that when she'd watch *Gogglebox*, she'd almost feel as if she was home and having that one bit of time where she was with her family. She'd put herself in my position and pretend that she was at home. I just think that's so lovely. The woman is all right now. She's in remission, which I'm so pleased to hear.

I think it's just amazing that people have the power to do that without even knowing it. You're just sat at home filming or in a studio filming and you're helping someone through bad times. I've had other letters where people have said, 'You helped me last Friday, I was so upset, I've just switched on *Gogglebox* and in that hour I just laughed and smiled.' It's not something I would have ever expected. When you start on TV, you don't even think that you're going to have that effect on people, but it's so rewarding. I always wanted a job where I could help make people smile.

I love all the letters and tweets and Insta posts I receive. I can't believe people take the time out to be so sweet. I also love a good natter with a randomer on the street. Sometimes when I meet people they are quite shocked by the fact I'm not this super loud, confident young girl. I often get 'Eeeh, aren't you quiet?' See it depends what day you catch me on. Sometimes I have days where I am the Scarlett Moffatt I love; other days I am Scarlett Moffatt struggling.

Now I don't quite know how to word this and I know that when you read it you're going to be like, where the hell did this pop up from? But that's the thing with mental health issues, they do just pop up when you least expect them. So now I'm going to discuss something I have never openly spoken about before because I feel ready to say it out loud. I suffer from anxiety and panic attacks.

Since filming *Gogglebox* I had been accidentally put into the limelight. And for the first time in a long time, well, since my Bell's palsy, I felt a feeling resurface. I felt out of control. I was always slightly worried when I filmed anything in case I was going to offend someone with what I said and it did have me on edge sometimes. Even though I don't purposefully ever mean to say anything bad, I'm only human and you can't please all of the people all of the time. So I guess I started noticing in myself that I was a lot more nervous around that time, a year into *Gogglebox*. I knew I had a problem when I started getting really agitated by silly things, like I could only have the music volume in the car on an even number otherwise I would worry that something bad was going to happen. I would imagine us crashing into a tree if the volume was at number thirteen.

Saying it out loud and writing this, I realise it does sound over the top but brains are very strange and unique things. I still now will write a tweet and if it doesn't get ten 'likes' in the space of five minutes I will have to delete it because I worry that I've written the wrong thing.

I worry that people are going to hate me if I don't give them 110 per cent. So if people do come up to me in the middle of the street and chat, even if I have somewhere to be I will be late for the meeting so I don't have to cut the conversation short. I've even missed a couple of trains because I get anxious thinking that if I say, 'Sorry I've got to go,' they will then tell everybody that I'm a dickhead.

I have days where I am feeling crappy and feeling like I'm having a bloated day or a bad hair day and I have to force myself to go outside. Sometimes I don't even step outside because I'm scared I'll get photographed and I worry that the papers are going to start slagging my weight off or the way I look. Most weeks during *Gogglebox* I would walk to my front door, cry, then walk back into the living room. I would give myself a pep talk, walk to the front door again, grab the handle, cry again and then walk back into the living room. Some days after nine or ten goes I would make it outside. But some days my head demons would get the better of me and I would stay indoors all day.

Now I knew that it wasn't right that I felt like this, but I felt like I was the only one in this situation and I was embarrassed; how could I speak about this to anybody? How could I tell someone that I worried that much over mundane things or that I sometimes felt like I was having an out-of-body experience? How could I say to my mam and dad, 'I have to walk up the stairs toe, heel or just walk up every other step otherwise I worry that one of my family members is going to die'? I would say to myself, 'Listen to yourself, Scarlett.' So I didn't tell anyone for over a year, I just kept these head demons to myself, listening to them and dealing with them by myself.

One night I decided to go out to the local with a few of the girls. Nights out – something that I loved at university – were now the bane of my life. I looked forward to people bailing on plans because I would just get so anxious about what to wear, who was going to be there, if there was going to be any trouble. But I knew I couldn't live my life like that. So we went out and some rough girl decided to start shouting '*Gogglebox*!' at me at the top of her lungs. She then proceeded to dance around me, being very intimidating. 'I am just going to the toilet,' I remember saying to my friend Billie. But I didn't, I just got a taxi home. I stayed all night at home, lying in bed crying, worrying if that girl knew where I lived, if that was just a warning of what was to come. I didn't even dare go to Asda the next day with my mam. I felt really dizzy and knew I could not live my life like this.

I didn't want to worry my family so I booked an appointment with the doctor. It was a female doctor, which for some reason calmed my nerves. 'So how can I help you today?' She smiled.

I started getting really sweaty and dizzy and thought I was going to faint. The words wouldn't come out of my mouth. I could almost see them scramble around in my brain. 'I think I'm mad,' I whispered.

'And why do you think that?' she said.

It all came pouring out. 'Well, I think stupid thoughts and I struggle to step out of my front door. Sometimes I feel like I'm having out-of-body experiences, sometimes I can sit and think about the same ten words that I've said to somebody over and over again and think because I've said that bad repercussions are going to occur. I have super good days where I'm normal

Scarlett, where I feel on top of the world and I'm happy and giggly. But I also have some dark days. Sometimes on those dark days I won't get out of bed, I'll literally lie in bed for the whole day, half of the day worrying because I genuinely don't feel good enough for what's happening to me. See, I've been given the opportunity to be on a TV show called *Gogglebox*,' I explained, 'and sometimes I feel like the opportunities I've been given I don't deserve. I'm scared I'll mess things up. I'm just a five-foot-and-a-fag-end Bishop Auckland girl, why am I being given this chance? I don't understand it. Then the other half of the day I spend crying in bed being angry with myself that I'm not just embracing what's happening to me and that I'm not enjoying the opportunities as much as I should be. I struggle to understand why people like me and get really anxious that I'm going mess it up.'

I sighed the longest sigh that has ever come out of my mouth. It was pure relief. I instantly felt better for saying it all out loud.

'Well, first of all you are not alone and you should not feel like you are a bad person for thinking these thoughts,' said the doctor. 'Trust me, there are other people who think things like this too. Can you tell me any other physical symptoms you have?' she asked.

'Well, sometimes I don't want to eat and I know that must mean these head demons are doing something to my brain because I love food. Sometimes I don't get to sleep until three or four in the morning because I feel like my brain is constantly thinking. When I get really bad I feel dizzy, I can almost feel the blood pumping around my body. It's as if I can hear my own heart skip a beat.'

'OK, Scarlett. So first of all I want to tell you that you are very brave for opening up like that. I know that it isn't easy. But I can't tell you enough that you are not alone; other people feel like this. You have an anxiety and panic attack disorder. Now I will talk through how we can help you. I would like to offer you the chance to chat to somebody, maybe do some cognitive behavioural therapy before we just prescribe medication, although there is medication for it.'

I was lucky that the doctor was so understanding. I came out with so many leaflets. Things I could do online, forums to chat to other people who were going through the same thing, exercises both physical and mental that I could do, meditation and mind space apps. I was just relieved that I wasn't alone, that I wasn't a bad person for thinking these things.

I went home and chatted about it with my mam and dad. No one's parents want their kids to feel this way, and they were constantly trying to reassure me, especially while we were filming. Now part of me thought should I be stopping *Gogglebox*, would that make me better? But I loved doing it. I couldn't let these head demons stop me from doing what I loved.

'I can manage this, can't I?' I said to my mam and dad.

'Of course you can, don't let anxiety stop you from enjoying life.'

Now, that is easier said than done, I know, and some days I still struggle with getting out of the front door. But speaking to family, friends and the doctor really helps. The first initial conversation is the hardest but I promise it gets easier.

Yes, I still have dark days; yes, I still have panic attacks, but as in life you have to take the rough with the smooth. I find exercise helps me and if I am worried about something, even the tiniest of things, I talk about it with my family straight away so that I'm not coping on my own.

See, I used to get so anxious watching the news for *Gogglebox*. (I once even physically fainted when we watched an item about Ebola – silly head demons.) I used to dread watching it on the television; actually I still sit in dread and fear when I turn on the news. I don't know what's happening to the world right now but there is so much hate. I would get myself really worked up about what sort of world we are creating for people like my little sister or even for my future children. But then my auntie Kirsty told me a quote by American TV personality Fred Rogers:

'When I was a child and I would see scary things
in the news, my mother would say to me, "Look for the
helpers. You will always find people who are helping."
To this day, especially in times of disaster, I remember
my mother's words, and I am always comforted by
realising that there are still so many helpers – so many
caring people in this world.'

This quote has changed my whole outlook on life and although I still sit in heartbreak watching the news, I now focus on the helpers.

Chapter Thirteen

SCARLETT MO'FAT TO SCARLETT NO'FAT

★ The *War of the Worlds* radio drama was first aired on Sunday 30 October 1938. It became famous for allegedly causing mass panic as people thought aliens were really attacking, although the scale of the panic is disputed as the programme had relatively few listeners.

★ Elvis Presley was rumoured to be a fan of the 'Sleeping Beauty Diet', a diet where a person is sedated for days at a time. The reasoning behind the diet was that a sleeping person wouldn't eat.

★ Worldwide obesity has nearly doubled since 1980.

As *Gogglebox* was just a hobby, and in all honesty television was never something I could imagine in my wildest dreams could be a full-time occupation, I always had a job whilst filming. One day I got a random email asking me to go in for an interview to cover a maternity position. It wasn't just any job, it was one of my dream jobs. I was about to become a breakfast radio presenter. The hours sucked arse; I walked to work as students were leaving clubs, owls were twit-twooing and McDonald's wasn't even serving breakfast yet, but I loved it. Getting to sit on one of those tall radio swivel chairs (every morning I had to get a bunk-up from my co-presenter as it was so high), feeling like the dog's bollocks with my headphones on, getting to chat and listen to music for a living. I mean I had to pinch myself every time I signed myself into work. However, I did think I would be able to rock up in a onesie with my hair in a scruffy bun every day, but now everything has gone digital we recorded a lot of the show so I still had to make an effort and actually brush my hair.

I was in a trio for Capital North East: 'Bodg, Matt and Scarlett'. I instantly clicked with Bodg when I found out his godfather was Len Goodman (the godfather of ballroom dancing). I loved Matt because I had never heard anyone be so enthusiastic about giving travel updates. And our producer, Thomas, was just the sweetest, most hard-working guy you could ever meet. He would get in even earlier than us, at like 4.30 a.m., to research what celeb gossip we could chat about.

We did hard-hitting items like 'What's in Craig David's fridge?' and got to interview amazing people (over the phone) like Tinie Tempah. My favourite part of the show was the throwback where people would tweet us to play songs like 'Breathe' by Sean Paul, or 'One More Time' by Daft Punk. I honestly would love to do radio again – it was one of the best years of my life. The only downfall was the fact there was a Gregg's next door and it's very easy to eat a whole packet of chocolate digestives with a cup of tea whilst listening to a four-minute rendition of Justin Bieber's 'Sorry'. I didn't feel bad eating them, I enjoyed them – although my waistline didn't and I did notice a lot of my clothes were having to be unbuttoned when I sat down to make sure I didn't implode on myself.

Now one of the things I especially love doing is eating. But I got to the stage where after I would eat a large meal I would feel really lethargic and I knew that although I was happy with my shape I was not happy with my health. Now I honestly believe you can be whatever shape you want to be. You can be pear-shaped, apple-shaped – hell, you can even be trapezium-shaped. But I think it is really important that you are happy and healthy in yourself.

Women are always made to feel bad about their shape. Look at any women's magazine, no matter whether it be for young girls or older women, you'll see examples of women putting themselves down. You'll see headlines like 'Fit Turned to Fat', 'How to Be Beach Body Ready', 'How to Drop Two Dress Sizes in Two Weeks', 'Hot and Not on the Red Carpet'. We focus on what women are wearing, how their hair looks, how fit they've got after giving birth. Why aren't we bigging women up? Yes, being healthy and feeling confident is an accomplishment but we aren't just aesthetically beautiful empty vessels. The women that are portrayed in these magazines are amazing and talented. Whether they are singers, comedians, actresses, authors, reality stars or simply great mothers, let's celebrate their accomplishments, not just how they look. If you look at any magazine made for men you can see how different their approach is. They have headlines like 'How to Get Rich Quick', 'Ten Tips on Being Successful', 'Why Your New Suit Should be Tailored', 'What Watch to Buy Guide' or 'Most Influential Men of the Year'.

What upsets me the most is half the time it's women writing the articles in women's mags. We are constantly bringing ourselves down and making ourselves feel shitty. If a guy is a little overweight he has a 'dad bod' or he is 'comfortable in his own skin'. Jesus, if my jeans mark my skin even slightly I'm branded 'fat', 'chubby', 'muffin top' … I've 'let myself go'.

I strongly believe every woman – no, every human being – should be a feminist. Now to be a feminist doesn't mean you have to go around burning your bra. Nor does it mean you have to go around wearing cardigans made from your own pet cat's hair (as I said on *I'm a Celebrity*, 'You can be a feminist and be a strong woman and still like fake tan'). It simply means that you want equality. If you don't want woman to be equal to men, then frankly what is wrong with you? Don't you want women to have the right to have equal pay, or do you think we all deserve less because we aren't walking around with meat and two veg in our pants? Don't you want women to be able to have the right to wear trousers to work instead of a skirt? The freedom to vote? To play sports? To marry who you want?

One of my favourite human beings, who is truly an inspiration to me, is Caitlin Moran. Her book *How to be a Woman* literally changed my outlook on life. My favourite quote from that, which I feel sums feminism up, is: 'What is feminism? Simply the belief that women should be as free as men, however nuts, dim, deluded, badly dressed, fat, receding, lazy and smug they might be. Are you a feminist? Hahaha. Of course you are.'

Because of this outlook, I don't believe women should be made to feel like they need to look a certain way, whether it be the clothes they wear, their hair, their make-up, or their size. I do, however, as a strong lover of Girl Power, want every girl to be fit and healthy so we can complete our mission to gain equality and die when we are very old and crinkly. This is why, as soon as I was starting to get some health scares and not feel myself, I decided to go to the doctor's.

When I arrived at the surgery for my appointment, I typed my date of birth and surname into the computer and sat on the custard-yellow seats in the reception area. Trying to inconspicuously cover my nose and mouth from the man next to me who had decided to cough openly and spread his germs all around the room, I was staring at the screen, waiting for my name to pop up.

Scarlett Moffatt Room Two Nurse Howarth
In I went. The nurse smiled at me.
'Hi Scarlett, what seems to be the problem?'
'I don't mean to sound like a drama queen but I just feel awful most of the time. I have been having terrible back and neck pain. I'm also having just constant, really bad headaches. And I am just permanently tired, even though I spend most of my time sleeping. I just have no motivation at all.'
'Have you had any weight gain recently?'
'Well, a bit ... I mean I have always been really slim up

until the age of twenty when I stopped competitive dancing. I mean really fit and full of energy.'

'And you are twenty-five now, is that right?'

'Yes, that's right.'

'OK, so I need to measure your height, weight and blood pressure and we will take it from there. Is that OK with you?'

'Yes, of course.'

'Hmm, five foot, your blood pressure is a little low ... and now if you can just pop on the scales?'

I'll be honest, I didn't want to. I was going to ask if I could take some layers off. I don't know why, it's not like I was going to be judged.

'Eleven stone and four pounds.'

'Does this mean I'm overweight?'

'No, it doesn't.'

'Thank God for that.'

'Your BMI is 30.09, so I am afraid you're actually obese. We will need to test you for diabetes type two.'

I burst into tears. 'How have I got myself to this state and how am I going to get out?'

Actually, I knew how, I just didn't want to say it out loud: I needed to move more and eat less. Every night was a takeaway and I had a job that involved sitting down with the only movement being clicking a mouse button.

Honestly, apart from feeling tired and the pains, I was super happy. I didn't feel like my weight stopped me enjoying myself. I wasn't bothered about not being able to wear crop tops and I was quite happy about wearing a kaftan by the pool on holiday. But what did bother me was that I was putting myself at risk of a serious condition. I wanted to live a long time, I wanted to dance around the house with Ava without getting beads of sweat on my brow. I was twenty-five; I shouldn't be getting tired from walking up a flight of stairs.

I honestly think if you are what the media calls 'a plus-size man or woman', that's great. Don't feel like you have to fit into what they tell us we should all look like. However, just make sure you are healthy. We all want to live as long as possible in order to spend as much time with our loved ones as we can. By just exercising thirty minutes a day we can do that. From that day at the doctor's I decided to lose weight. I didn't have an aesthetic image of what I wanted to look like, my goal was to be right in the middle of the healthy BMI scale.

I am not going to lie, it was bloody hard. I didn't completely change my diet but I just made wiser choices. Sweet potatoes instead of white potatoes, an apple instead of a slice of apple pie and, of course, I cut down my portion sizes. I had been eating for a family of four in one sitting, to be honest (no one needs a side of a full garlic baguette to themselves to accompany a plate of spag bol). I also stopped getting two Mr Whippy ninety-niners from the ice-cream van and instead kept a tub of sorbet in the freezer if I fancied something sweet.

I also really started getting into my fitness. I've always hated the gym; I feel intimidated whenever I go in. All those men making strange grunting noises at the weight machines and girls who don't sweat, they glisten. No thanks, I'll stick to exercising in the comfort of my own home in my pyjamas. That is the reason I brought out my DVD. I have been there; I know how difficult it is, I know what it's like to be busy and not want to have to walk to the gym in the rain and be the only one in there who isn't clutching a protein shake. I found some fun exercises and just wanted there to be something out there for women and men to be like, 'Well, if Scarlett can do it, I can.' Because I'm not superhuman; I'm just the average northern lass who likes a chip-shop dinner and doesn't particularly like yoga and cross training.

I also have my down days (sometimes weeks), when I have to motivate myself as I'm so tired from work I can barely even go in the bath and wash. Or days where I see an advert for a Burger King and go out and get myself a Whopper. That's fine! God, we are here for a good time not for a long time. Don't be so hard on yourself, people. It is OK to put on a few pounds, it is OK to not want to eat fennel salad and eat a Domino's instead. It's just everything in moderation so that we stay the healthiest we can be.

I was so happy when I got to my healthy BMI range and I must admit I actually enjoy doing the exercises. My family and friends said they got the old energetic five-foot pint-sized pocket rocket back. However, of course some people aren't happy. I had gone from getting trolled and slagged in the press for being overweight and a bad role model to now being 'too skinny' and being a bad role model. People were saying they liked the old Scarlett better (I mean I still have the same brain, thoughts and feelings, there's just less of me to squeeze into a jumpsuit).

I do not agree with body shaming. Whether it's for someone who's little or large, it is not OK. We need to get out of this mentality that we have the right to judge people. We do not. When we say awful things about the way someone else looks it says more about us than them. This is a very clichéd lesson I learnt but it's one I feel is really important in life, especially now because of social media and how easy it is to make a nasty comment about someone. It goes like this:

'If you can't say something nice,
don't say anything at all.'

Chapter Fourteen

LET'S GET READY TO JUNGLE

★ Myleene Klass's iconic white bikini from that infamous shower scene in *I'm a Celebrity ... Get Me Out of Here!* sold for £7,500 at auction in 2006 – the fashion designer gave the proceeds to charity.

★ Medic Bob is so popular on the German version of *I'm a Celeb* that he's had a hit single released based on the stuff he's said on screen.

★ The Australian coat of arms features two native animals, an emu and a kangaroo. Both of them can only move forward, which represents the notion that the country is never going backwards. (I mean they're also one of the only countries to eat both the animals on their coat of arms – but that is none of my business.)

'I'm a celebrity … *get me out of here*!' Ant and Dec boomed from the top of the camp. Perched on the corner of my couch at home, fire on full blast and unicorn slippers on, I said, 'Let's order a chicken kebab and have a glass of Baileys, eh?' I was always trying to entice my mam and dad into making a big thing of the first ever episode of the jungle every year. We all loved it, from trying to guess which celebrities were going to be in the opening title sequence to making our predictions of who was going to be crowned King (or Queen) of the Jungle that year. It has and always will be my favourite TV show. I love it more than *Red Dwarf, Bottom, The Young Ones* – even more than *The Royle Family*. It is my guilty pleasure and I look forward to it every year.

In the Moffatt household when the winner is announced and whisked off to that infamous jungle throne, it's a clear indication that we need to finish off the bulk of our Christmas shopping. The other human advent calendar in the Moffatt household is Michael Bublé. He randomly pops up shortly after *I'm a Celebrity* ends and you just know when Buble starts popping up singing swing hits, you should have all your Christmas presents wrapped and ready under the tree. Yep, November and December is definitely my favourite time of the year: Christmas decorations, selection boxes from the pound shop, you can wear as many layers of clothing as you like so you don't feel so guilty about having that extra roast potato or two … and, of course, *I'm a Celebrity … Get Me Out of Here!*

I had watched the show every year since it began in 2002. I remember going into dance class when we would be practising for the Christmas dance medal test and chatting about who we wanted to win and all the gruesome tasks they had been given. I was such a huge fan, a super fan. My absolute heroes were Ant and Dec. I loved hearing my accent on the television and just thought, imagine having Ant and Dec's job. They get to spend every day with their best friend and they always have such a good laugh. I knew *I'm a Celebrity* inside out.

I remember the first ever series I watched. I was twelve and a female comedian called Rhona Cameron went on a huge 'sometimes' rant and started slagging all of her camp mates off. 'Sometimes Uri Geller dramatises little things like farts like he's an alien who's never seen one before.' Me and my mam and dad burst into a fit of laughter. From that moment I knew I was going to be hooked on that show. My favourite ever camp mate was Peter Andre, especially in the shower scenes with his six-pack. I don't think I had Sky Plus then so I couldn't rewind or freeze-frame it, so I just used my photographic memory. (That reminds me, I haven't thought about Peter's six-pack in a while – I must have a long hard think about that later.)

But my favourite ever moment from the jungle was when Gillian McKeith pretended to faint and pulled her T-shirt down. She was a funny one, mind, always saying no to doing a simple trial like sticking your feet in mealworms – yet she smelt people's shite for a living! How can you say 'I'm a celebrity, get me out of here' when you sniff people's faeces as your job? You would think nothing would have fazed her. (To be honest, that show she did never made sense to me. It doesn't take Sherlock Holmes to work out that if you take a dump in a Tupperware box and get someone to sniff it, they're gonna say it stinks. Of course it bloody does, it's crap in a box!)

So imagine my delight when Daisy, Micky and Richard at ITV first approached me to ask me to go for a meeting about possibly being a camp mate on *I'm a Celebrity*. I could not believe it. But my initial reaction was: 'Well, first of all it's called *I'm a Celebrity*, and I'm not a celebrity. I know you've had what some people would class as D-listers on before, but I'm not even a Z-lister. Come to think of it, I am not even in the bloody alphabet. You can get someone better than me, honestly.' I was not selling myself at all.

But the producers were just chatting about what I would bring to the jungle. I was like, 'Well, I cannot really clean and I cannot cook. I hate camping. I probably would cry at every challenge. I don't really like adventurous food; the craziest, most alternative thing I've ever eaten is quinoa. The only thing I could bring and offer to the table is morale. I can try and keep morale up, I can always offer some daft jokes and I can talk about rubbish all day long, but other than that I don't really know what I can offer.'

They said they would be in touch and a couple of months later I got the call from Micky and Daisy. (It's that secretive that each celebrity gets given a code name. My code name was 'Little'.)

'Hi Little, how are you?'

'I'm really good, you two. How are you both?'

'Amazing, thanks. We are just calling to say we would love you to join the *I'm a Celebrity* gang and be one of the camp mates this year!'

'Oh my God, this is crazy. I'm actually going to be on the show? In real life? In actual real life?'

'That's right. What do you think?'

'Of course, it's a huge yes. I can't wait to be a camp mate. Ahh, I can't wait to get my hat and my red gilet with my name and number on the back!'

I was so excited and knew I had to take this amazing dream opportunity but I was equally as nervous. I had never been away from all my loved ones for that long before. I also knew what a wimp I am and in the back of my mind I was thinking, oh God, what happens if there's a challenge I can't do? I don't want to let all my friends and family down and embarrass them.

It was bizarre, I couldn't tell anybody even though I wanted to scream it from the rooftop. I wanted to parade through my home town of Bishop Auckland with a huge banner saying, 'I'm going in the jungle, I won't let the side down, town'. There was only the fantastic four of my mam, dad, Ava and my auntie Kirsty who knew I was going into the Outback of Australia.

When I told my mam, she was like, 'Please don't embarrass yourself.' It wasn't even like, 'Yeah, this is amazing.' It was, 'Oh please, for the love of God, don't embarrass yourself. I know you're scared of everything, but just try, just *try* not to be a Helen Flanagan. Don't be saying, "I'm not doing it", or "I'm a celebrity, get me out of here".' (Mothers, eh?)

I tried to spend as much time with my mother and my family and friends as I could, knowing I'd be away from them for a couple of months – which for someone who doesn't really leave her home town is a huge thing.

Because I knew I was flying out on Guy Fawkes' Night I decided to have a big get-together on my birthday, 17 October. 'Thank you all for coming, I'm really going to miss you all. Just know I love you all no matter what,' I announced to everyone after a few drinks.

'Why are you going to miss us, Dafty?'

'I don't know. I just feel like now we've got older we hardly see each other. I know with it being Christmas it's extra busy so I'm going to miss you.'

'Oh yeah, this hasn't got anything to do with your name being in the papers as one of the people who might be going into the jungle, has it?'

'That's stupid, isn't it? I bloody wish.'

And all the while I wanted to scream, 'Its true, I'm going into the jungle!'

Seven whole months I had to keep it to myself and the fantastic five. I agreed to do the jungle in April and honestly the time just flew by. I had my radio job and I was filming *Gogglebox* just a week before I flew out.

Imagine the excitement inside of my brain when 5th November crept up. I had had seven whole months of day-dreaming about what I'd get up to in the jungle and now it was about to happen. I knew I had to embrace every single minute of it; I didn't expect to stay in there long because, well, for one thing, I wasn't a proper celeb and two, I just watched TV for a living. I knew compared to who was going to be in there I was a nobody. I thought no one is going to vote for little me. So thinking I would be out within a week, I packed my suitcase full of casual stuff – packed to the brim it was, as I knew I'd have loads of time to chill by the pool.

When I finally got to Australia, I felt so weird. Even though I had known I was going for such a long time and I had tried to prepare myself, it did not feel real at all. The day I arrived I just wanted to get in there; I couldn't believe it was happening plus I didn't want ITV to change their minds. As far as I was concerned, the quicker I got in there the better, then they couldn't ditch me.

For the first week of being in Australia, though, you just chill in your hotel room. You are allowed out around the hotel, but you've got to have a chaperone so that you don't bump into anyone else on the show (I felt like I was in MI5, it was amazing). So you really honestly don't know who else is going to be in that camp with you as you aren't even allowed your phone or wi-fi to check. That's why when people are saying they miss their families and it's only been a week in the jungle, in actual fact they haven't spoken to their families for a fortnight.

Just two days before I went into the jungle, I found out on an Australian news channel that Donald Trump was now the US President. I remember thinking about this a lot in camp; I would just be sitting in my hammock so many times thinking, 'God, what world am I going to come out to? Will there even be a world there? I don't know if this show is even being televised any more. Has he stopped all the TV stations? Is he just broadcasting himself twenty-four hours a day?' It was really frustrating just not even knowing what was going on out there.

Eventually the day arrived, D-Day, and we had a quick last-minute meeting about the dos and don'ts of the jungle, which were all pretty much common sense. They asked if I had any questions. I only had one.

LET'S GET READY TO JUNGLE

'I really don't want to say the C-word on the show.'

'No, you cannot say the C-word.'

'So what do I say instead?'

'What do you mean?'

'Well, I would never say *that* C-word on TV, the one that rhymes with "runt". I mean "celebrity". If I can't do a trial, what do I say? Because, well, I can't say, "I'm a celebrity, get me out of here." I just can't. I'll have to say, "I'm sometimes on the telly, get me out of here," because the thought of saying the word "celebrity" absolutely makes me cringe.'

'Haha, don't worry, I am sure when you are covered in a hundred thousand bugs you will soon be able to say the C-word, believe me.'

I was ready for my dream to come true. I knew that in a few hours' time I was going to meet Ant and Dec. I was blindfolded and put some headphones on. 'OK, Scarlett, when we take the headphones and blindfold off, you are going to walk around the corner where you will be greeted by Ant and Dec.'

'Thank you. I hope I make it. My legs feel like jelly.'

I had so many thoughts going through my mind. There had been lots of speculation about who was going into the jungle that year. The papers back at home were saying it was going to be Nigel Farage. Oooh, I didn't know if I could stay if he was in there, I thought, because I'd want to push him in the camp fire. I was so nervous about who my camp mates might be. I don't know why but I was convinced the Chuckle Brothers were going to be in there. Imagine the trials ('to me, to you').

The blindfold was off. The headphones were off. It was

happening. I walked round and lived my fantasy. My two hundred bonds of hair extensions were blowing in the breeze, I could feel one of my eyelashes coming off, I had now realised my spray tan looked patchy in the sunlight, I had my £40 white and gold kimono dress on and gold heels that I couldn't walk properly in (Bambi on ice) but they looked good so it was all fine. Despite all this and having a sweaty tash, I could see my heroes in the flesh. It finally felt real, I was going on *I'm a Celebrity … Get Me Out of Here!*

'Oh my God, I'm going to meet the real Ant and Dec!' I was saying in my head. I held back the tears of excitement that threatened to come from being face to face with them. *Think of something cool to say*, I kept whispering to myself. 'Oh my God, it's really you, Wonkey Donkey was the highlight of my week as a kid!' I blurted out. (Smooth, real smooth, Scarlett.) I hugged both of them, getting a nice bronzer mark on Ant's crisp white shirt.

As I stood in the line-up, realising I was going to be living with legends like Carol Vorderman, Larry Lamb, Lisa Snowdon and Sam Quek (I mean a gold Olympian, not only that but a kick-ass Girl Power Olympian who, alongside her team mates, had put the words 'women's hockey' on everybody in the UK's lips), I could hardly contain myself. God, if my eleven-year-old self could see me now. All those nights I cried myself to sleep because of the bullying, wishing I could be anybody else but me, wishing I could fit in more. How silly of me.

If I could have a conversation now with my eleven-year-old self I would say, 'Scarlett, you think you're goofy, a little bit different to most other people; your brain constantly asks weird questions, you're a sensitive soul who feels like she doesn't quite fit in and struggles with accepting compliments. I am here to tell you all of those things are true. And sixteen years on, they're still true. But embrace it because those characteristics are what make you you! Great things are coming, kid, you've just got to believe in yourself. (Also heads up, don't admit to fancying Bart Simpson in a class discussion in Year 9; he is an animated character who looks like he has got severe jaundice – you will get unnecessary crap for it.)'

I guess what I've learnt is lots of us (me included) try to change the things that make us, well, us. But we shouldn't, we should just embrace it. It is crazy that I have only just realised that as I've got older, even though I read these words as a young child so many times:

'Today you are you, that is truer than true.
There is no one alive who is you'er than you.'

I have a lot to thank Dr Seuss for.

Chapter Fifteen

I'M NOT QUITE A CELEBRITY... GET ME OUT OF HERE!

★ All the camp-mates during their time in the jungle are allowed to choose one luxury item – which they may or may not receive at some point in camp. For my luxury item, I chose 'a bottle of fake tan and a tanning mitt'. (Funnily enough, I didn't need it.)

★ It had been claimed that Danny Baker was responsible for Bob Marley's death after treading on his foot during a charity football match in London in 1977. However, although Marley injured his foot in the game and cancer developed in his feet afterwards, Baker never played in the game. He believes the rumour started from a joke on his radio show.

★ Before Larry Lamb's acting career took off, his job was to sell encyclopaedias to American soldiers in Germany.

After I had been introduced on the show, I was feeling all sentimental and honoured to be stood there with my fellow camp mates and of course Ant and Dec. I was just so thankful that all of my camp mates looked friendly and happy. The year before they had had such a hard time with Lady C, and I didn't want to go through that sort of thing.

It was actually quite funny – when we were in the jungle, we didn't know that Larry Lamb used to date Lady C. One night when we were sat round the camp fire, perched uncomfortably on a wooden log, I was chatting away about her. I was saying, 'I'm pleased she isn't in the jungle with us. I'm glad that we haven't got any characters like her.'

Then Larry told me, 'Oh, I used to date her.'

'Oh my God, I'm so sorry, Larry. You should have spoken up sooner.' I was desperately trying to backtrack, saying, 'I'm sure she is lovely, she just didn't like any of the trials.' But we had literally all sat there and slagged his sweetheart off for about half an hour. He's still friends with her, so that was a very awkward moment.

Speaking of Larry, my bloody entrance into the camp. What was all that about? If you haven't seen it (please don't YouTube it), it was probably the most embarrassing moment of my life. In my head, I thought that I was going to enter the camp like some sort of Bond girl. I'd be really cool in some sort of jumpsuit, leaping from a helicopter. Instead I was sat in a canoe. Now I don't like any sort of water sports and canoeing is something I have never ever done properly and I don't want to do it again either. When I'm in a restaurant, along with the actual money tip I always give a life tip: 'Don't stand up in a canoe.'

Let me set the scene: I'm doing this challenge with Larry Lamb, who is like some sort of Bear Grylls–merman hybrid.

I am there in the torrential rain, my pretend silk (pilk) white dress is now see-through so it is revealing my Bridget Jones pants, my fake tan has now run all down my legs, my hair is stuck to my head and my eyelashes look like spiders' legs. I have got loads of soggy sachets of salt in my bra that I'd taken from a café and was trying to sneak in there. I have a leech on my right arse cheek and my canoeing skills are as much use as a one-legged man in an arse-kicking competition.

'This is not how I imagined my entrance to the jungle would be, Larry.'

He couldn't hear me at all. We had to find a little island with two flags, one for me and one for Larry and put our flag in the flagpole back on land on the other side of the lake.

'Have you found the flag, Larry?' I shouted.

'Yes, it's getting out lovely now the rain has stopped.'

After canoeing for about seventy minutes I finally found the flag. Now bearing in mind I couldn't even see the cameras at this point I genuinely thought something bad had happened to Larry. I could see a capsized canoe and my flag and that was about it. 'I can see the canoe, but I can't see you! Larry, are you OK?'

'Yes I'm fine. What you need to do is pull out the flag using the key in your canoe. But be careful, the water's freezing and the canoe will capsize when you take the key out.'

Now another little fact about me: I can't swim very well. I managed to get the very heavy flag but I couldn't swim with it at all. I just lay there floating like a rotten log in the lake. 'I'll come and get you,' Larry exclaimed. (Cue *Superman* music.) And save me he did. Honestly, you wouldn't believe Larry is seventy years old; the man is as fit as a fiddle. But as grateful as I was to Larry, it just wasn't the entrance I'd imagined I was going to have.

One of the first things my mam said to me when I got out of the jungle was, 'Honestly, the night before it aired, the papers' headlines were, "Scarlett Has to Be Rescued". I thought, "Jesus, how embarrassing, she hasn't even made it in yet, and she's already had to be saved!" I thought you were going to only last a few days in there.'

Once I finally got in, I quickly got chatting to my camp mates, trying to work out who I was the most compatible with. Now I always try to look for the good in people even if they're crappy personalities (life's easier that way) but I didn't have to try at all. It's a cliché I know but I honestly was so lucky to be put in a camp with such amazing people. I mean obviously me and Martin Roberts didn't hit it off straight away and we clashed quite quickly (I'll chat more about that later) but everyone else was lovely.

After being rescued (I'd still be in that canoe now to be honest if it wasn't for Larry), it was the start of a beautiful friendship for Larry and me. Larry (or Lazeruth as we all nicknamed him) is such a kind soul and would do anything he could to help us all. If I was missing home or it was all getting too much, it was Larry I would go and speak to. His wise words and his magic hugs seemed to make everything all right again. Everyone would agree with me that Larry was the boss; it didn't matter who got voted for by the public, Larry was our King of the Jungle. He is like a boy scouts leader; before Larry and I arrived no one knew how to light a fire so they were actually trying to burn Adam Thomas's trousers. I could be exaggerating here but Larry literally started a fire by just staring at a piece of wood and flint. He is at one with nature.

He didn't give a shit about any trials; when we had to do the Rancid Retreat which was a cold tub of water filled with fish guts in which they threw more fish and gloop onto us, he was just coolly diving underneath to collect the stars. At one point he put one of the dead fish in his pocket and said he would cook it later. Some of the boys got shown right up by him – all the boys would be doing press-ups with nothing but little tiny pants on (I mean seriously, I had such a hard life in there having to watch all them boys' six-packs glistening in the sun, I don't know how I got through it) and Larry would just strut into the middle of camp, take his top off and start pumping iron, out-squatting most of them. Sometimes he would even count in different languages just to spice things up a bit. He was definitely eye candy for those ladies with their free bus passes.

Yeah, Larry was the father of the camp and Carol Vorderman was the yummy mummy of the group. What a beautiful lady, inside and out. I loved listening to Carol's stories. She has grafted hard all of her life and made her mum, Jean, so proud. She has Jean (who sounded like a truly amazing woman) to thank for giving Carol the push to do *Countdown*. See, Jean saw an advert in a local newspaper about this new TV channel (Channel 4) and how they were doing a show that required a lady who was good at maths. That's an understatement: Carol is the mental arithmetic queen, Princess of Pythagoras. She can do mental arithmetic as quick as I can order a Domino's pizza (and that is quick), to the point where I'd take her answer over a calculator's. She sent a letter off to the channel without Carol knowing and encouraged her to go to the interview. I am so pleased she did because now the British public have got to know Carol Vorderman. Not many people can say they're a pilot, they're a graduate from Cambridge, they have an MBE and they've won Rear of the Year (*twice*).

One of the highlights of my experience in the jungle and one of the most surreal moments of my life is when Carol washed my hair for me. Because the shower and creek is so cold, your hair just stinks constantly; you end up with soap suds, dead bugs and all sorts in there. I think I managed to get a comb through my hair twice during the whole month I was in there. So this time I was lying on the creek and Carol had boiled some water for me and gave me a little head massage and everything. I mean *the* Carol Vorderman was washing my hair. Talk about surreal. When I was younger and my dad would finish work at two, he would pick me up from school and we would watch *Countdown* together. We would get a pen and paper out and play along. 'Two from the top and four from the bottom please, Carol.' I grew up with her in my house. I once even burnt down the kitchen in my mam and dad's house because of Carol and here she was playing Vidal Sassoon with me.

How that happened was I got that engrossed in a game of

Countdown I forgot I had put some potato wedges under the grill. The whole kitchen went up in flames and the firemen had to open every window in the house including the ones upstairs which brought black soot all up the new cream carpet. So we had to get a new kitchen and new carpets throughout. My mam and dad were not happy that day, mostly because of my response to one of the firemen.

'Are you OK?' he asked.

'Not really,' I replied. 'I'm absolutely starving, I was craving those wedges.'

Me and Carol had lots of in-depth chats about how there should be more regional accents on the the television. 'When you turn on your local news it should be someone with your local accent reading it out to you,' she would say.

'Exactly, surely everyone would be able to understand that person? They would have the same accent themselves or at least live in that place so they'd hear it all the time.'

We also had in-depth conversations about how women still haven't got equality. She told me about the time she went for an interview for a presenting role and they told her, and I quote, her 'tits weren't big enough'. (Bloody charming, eh!)

We bonded after our trial, 'The Big Bush Bake Off'. We kept getting the name wrong and calling it 'The Big Bush Off'. (But that's a whole totally different show, probably for Babestation not ITV.) Carol went first, gobbling down two turkey testicles presented as 'French knackeroons'.

'God, you ate them balls so fast, Carol.' It was as if she had done it before.

'They taste quite nice, like sweetbreads,' she said.

I went next. 'Look at the size of that!' I could not get to grips with how big the deer's penis was. I had to eat the tip of a 'sticky cocky pudding'. It tasted like really out-of-date corned beef. 'Oh, it's like meaty lard,' I said. I wouldn't advise having a nibble on it anytime soon. Carol ended up eating vomit fruit, which honestly is the worst thing I've ever smelt in my life. This was presented by Ant and Dec as 'sicktoria sponge'. She also devoured 'whole brain loaf' (sheep's brain) and a 'danus pastry', which was in fact an ostrich anus. One of the things I was pleased to get to eat was my 'bumoffee pie' (cow's anus). I mean I didn't understand how you could eat a hole, because technically an anus is a hole. I thought I'd be able to stick my tongue through it (I know that sounds gross) but honestly I was quite shocked at how little a cow's arse actually is.

One of the things I felt terrible about eating was the 'Cornish nasty'. It has genuinely put me off pasties for life. I had to eat a live beetle. I actually felt guilty about eating it, to be honest. I mean it had never done anything to me, and what an awful way to die. So apologies to the beetle but I did it. I asked Medic Bob what would be the quickest and most painless way I could kill it. 'Grab it between two fingers and bite its head off quickly,' he said. It tasted like a really hard Smarties shell.

I had completed three of my foods and only had two left. 'The next delight is "chocolate nip cookies". These are in fact camel nipples,' Dec announced with his cheeky little grin.

'One of my favourite foods is doner meat, I eat it sober sometimes and I don't even know what meat that is, so honestly I don't mind eating a nip or two,' I replied. They were just really chewy and later in camp I had to use the tweezers to get one of the camel hairs out from between my teeth.

One of the questions I often get asked is what was the worst thing you had to eat in the jungle and I'll tell you. A fermented duck egg. Jesus Christ on a bike, I can still taste it now. It was so huge. For those who don't know (as I didn't), a fermented egg is an egg that's basically a hundred years old. The yolk was a dark greeny-grey colour and it had the same texture as creamy Play-Doh with the taste of a sweaty rotten egg. I knew I had to eat it, I couldn't let the team down. Also before I went in there, one of the bits of advice my dad gave me (apart from leaving plastic spiders around the house and making me eat Scotch eggs as apparently that's what kangaroo balls taste like) was, 'I always say, what won't stick in your throat, won't stick in your arse.' But I swear I have never gagged so much in my life.

Poor Carol's final challenge was a live scorpion with the venom taken out. She just couldn't do it; I'm not surprised as it nipped her finger as she was holding it and her finger went bright red. Imagine if it had nipped her gum or tongue, ouch! I wasn't disappointed in her, though. I was sort of pleased because hooray, the scorpion lived.

Lisa Snowdon was my big sister in the camp. To everyone else she is known as one of the top models in the UK, or as a judge of Britain's Next Top Model, appearing in magazines like Vogue and Elle. To us in camp she was our go-to chef. Joel Dommett used to have her poster on his bedroom wall and here she was cooking him kangaroo loin and rice. I mean I was the cook for two days and it is hard work, cooking for twelve people who are absolutely ravenous from eating nothing but a portion of rice and beans for the day. Even when you have won loads of stars, the portion sizes are ridiculous.

One day, we won a crocodile arm.

'Woah, feel how heavy the basket is.'

'Oh my God, it's crocodile hands.'

I was a little confused. 'How many hands does a crocodile have, like, or is this from a couple of crocs?' They looked huge but it has actually got the tiniest bit of meat on it. It's all skin, and ooh, you can't eat that. You're chewing on what's essentially a cocktail sausage's worth of crocodile with some vegetables you've never heard of, most of which taste like celery. In fact, all of the vegetables in Australia taste like celery. I've never known anything like it in my life. Proper pissy celery vegetables – even if it looked like a potato it tasted like a celery stick. That's why me, Sam, Ola Jordan and Carol would sit on our hammock and cry with laughter watching Lisa cook. She would try every single vegetable and fruit to decipher what it was.

'That looks like an apple that, Lisa,' I'd say.

'Let me just take a little chunk out of it. Yeah, you're right, it's an apple.'

She had the right idea being the cook; you would be full from sampling before your food even hit your tin canister.

I loved our chats by the camp fire. 'Lisa, apart from your family and loved ones, what do you miss the most?'

'Hot showers and a nice bubbly bath, what about you?'

'I miss condiments; I would bathe in a bath of offal if it meant I could have a pinch of salt with this meal.' To be honest I smelt like offal for most of my time in Australia. Noddy changed his bloody clothes more than me.

While I literally looked like I had been born and raised in the jungle Outback with my ferrel hair, bug-bitten skin and the fact Adam and Joel washed my bra in cooking oil so I had a constant whiff of a greasy café, Ola Jordan was glowing. We were all already used to seeing Ola with all of her fake tan, make-up and beautiful gowns on *Strictly* but she looked even better without it all on. Ola had a beautiful tan and she was strutting around in a bikini with no wobbly bits at all. It was remarkable, sometimes I would watch her walk and literally nothing would wobble. She would use the mosquito repellent as a shimmer oil for her legs and made little bandanas. Meanwhile I had to use a belt on my actual knickers because I'd lost so much weight my arse was always hanging out of my shorts.

As a massive ballroom and Latin lover obviously I wanted to become best friends with Ola; she is the princess of dance. To get as far as she has in the dance world is incredible and I have such admiration for her. It takes dedication, drive, hard work, skill and patience to get to where she has. I would love listening to her stories about *Strictly*. She used that competitiveness and drive in all of her tasks – she was a little pocket rocket. The time me and her had to go head to head and down fish guts was gross. Although Ola won, technically we both lost. Even with half a tube of the *au naturel* green tea toothpaste, our breath still stank of carp.

From one dancer to another, I loved spending time with Jordan Banjo. He is a prime example of how you shouldn't judge a book by its cover. Now I try to never ever judge but first impressions count and because I'd met hunky men like Jordan before I must admit I thought he was going to be a little bit cocky and arrogant. Knowing that he is part of the huge dance troupe Diversity, once dated Little Mix's Jesy Nelson and is about eight foot tall with a ten-pack, I thought he was going to ooze with confidence. I couldn't have been further from the truth. What a gentle giant. He is actually quite shy and isn't the massive party animal I thought he would be; in fact I found out that he actually doesn't drink alcohol at all and he is as close to his family as I am.

Me and Jordan also had a shared passion. I'm not talking about dancing, I'm talking about naps. Actually naps sounds too childish, let's call them 'horizontal life pauses'. We both had at least an hour's worth of horizontal life pauses a day. With me being just five foot I was as snug as a bug in my hammock; I looked like a little parcel of ravioli all neatly tucked away. Jordan, on the other hand, being six foot five, looked like a sausage roll in his hammock, with his head and feet poking out. I'll be honest, that is half the reason I was so shocked I even made the final three, never mind won, because I thought the show would just be cut-aways of me drooling in my hammock.

Another camp mate who completely shocked me was Wayne Bridge. I had heard so many stories about footballers and how they're bigheads. Well Bridgey is not one of those. He is one of the most humble and sweetest guys ever. He loves his wife and children so much, when he would chat about them you could see his eyes bursting with pride. I really wanted him to get to the final because I know he would have loved the Cyclone so much (the huge slip and slide which is super fun but results in you being bruised). He looked out for everybody and without realising it entertained most of the girls with his campfire routine doing one-armed press-ups whilst making sure the fire was roaring. Obviously being a footballer he was super competitive and when me and him went up against each other in a challenge where we were covered in this honey stuff and bugs were dropped on us, he genuinely felt guilty about winning. 'I should have let you win, Scarlett.'

'Of course you shouldn't have, Wayne, you won fair and square. Go and enjoy the bloody banquet and stop being daft.' He is the sort of guy I want my little sister to marry when she is older.

Me and my dad met up with him and his wife Frankie recently actually, as we share a love of *The Walking Dead*. We went to this *Walking Dead* screening of an unseen episode. To be honest that's the only premiére sort of thing I've ever been to. I am so pleased I did because – and I'm writing this with a huge smile on my face – I met Jesus. (Not the actual Jesus as in God's son, but Paul 'Jesus' Monroe, the character from *The Walking Dead*.)

I have always been a massive fan of zombies, thanks to my dad – well, 'fan' is the wrong word. I've been 'made aware' of zombies since a young age. My dad is convinced that movies are there to prepare us for what's about to happen. So there is an increase of alien movies at the moment as aliens have already made contact and the government is going to have to introduce us all to them soon. Same as the increase in zombie shows. My dad is prepared for what could be a zombie apocalypse.

I told this story on Channel 4's *Sunday Brunch*. 'So my dad is ready for the zombie takeover to happen in our lifetime. He has stored tins of food, a hot stove, bottles of water, a first-aid kit, a radio and old welding masks in our attic. I haven't got a clue why we need the masks, like, and how much use they will be, like – but we are prepared. We have also had a chat – me, Dad, Mam and Ava – about our exits and where we would flee to. We are pretty sure we would lose my mam along the way as she has said she probably will give up within the first twenty-four hours.'

When I got home from filming *Sunday Brunch*, my dad was really quiet.

'Do you fancy a brew, Dad?'

'Nah, you're all right.'

'You OK with me, Dad? You seem quieter than usual.'

'Not really, kid. What did you say that on *Sunday Brunch* for, man?'

'Sorry, Dad, I didn't mean to embarrass you.'

'Embarrass me?'

'Well, yeah, is that why you're upset?'

'No, I'm annoyed. I mean now when the zombie apocalypse happens everyone knows to come to our house. Come on, Scarlett, think about things before you speak. We haven't got enough supplies for everybody.'

And it's conversations like that with my dad that made me miss him so much in the jungle. He is one of a kind. I was so happy I had been given such an amazing bunch of people to share my *I'm a Celebrity ... Get Me Out of Here!* experience with, because I knew my mam and dad didn't have to have any moments where they felt upset watching me. If I'm happy, they're happy.

So like I said, we were all having such a great time in camp, being a tight little team, having a giggle, winning loads of stars in the trials. That was until Martin Roberts (from *Homes Under the Hammer*) and Danny Baker came in to camp to stir things up. And yep, shit hit the fan.

Now Danny Baker was who I wanted to win and he is a man I have a lot of respect for. He is pure genius and I had watched his work in action on *TFI Friday* with that lovely tangerine-haired man Chris Evans when I was little. Martin, on the other hand, well, me and him got off on the wrong foot. I don't know if it's because I asked if *Homes Under the Hammer* was like *Changing Rooms* and did they go into every house and stencil the kitchen and laminate throughout, or whether it was just because our personalities clashed. I now think he is just really misunderstood and he is completely harmless. I think at first I just found it a shock at how negative and snappy he was. He didn't get my sarcastic humour. But honestly towards the end of our experience he was one of the people I enjoyed spending time with the most.

I remember one night Lisa Snowdon made him some beans and rice on the little hotplate we had been given. Mind, dry beans and rice with no condiments and nothing but lukewarm river water to wash it down with is utterly vile. The beans are completely tasteless and have the texture of dry rabbit droppings. The rice is like eating tiny shards of flavourless glass. And the lukewarm water tastes like plastic as it has been melting in the canisters all day. But hey, it's better than nothing.

The reason we were cooking on a hotplate and not the camp fire was because our team had been banished to the top of the hill. Our groups had been separated, and the other team were eating ostrich steak. You could smell it from our camp, and I was like, 'Oh God, what I'd do to that ostrich steak right now.'

Lisa appeared with our beans and rice. 'Here you go, Martin.'

'It's fine, Lisa, I don't want any.'

'What do you mean? You'll be hungry.'

'No, I'll just wait for the food to come.'

'This is the food.'

'No, when they switch the cameras off.'

'Martin, people don't lose a stone in here for nothing. Plainly this is all we eat. There are no Mars bars being dropped in.' I was crying with laughter; he had me in stitches. It made me completely forget about being hungry because I couldn't focus on anything else but wetting myself from laughing.

I felt for Martin, I really did. Plus he was a latecomer and was a big tea drinker like me. The headaches you get from caffeine and sugar withdrawal, eugh. Larry, bless him, would boil hot water and just give it to you in a cup, so you felt like you were drinking tea. So you were just drinking hot water, but it was nice just sitting on your bed holding your cup. Me, Martin and Wayne Bridge would often pretend to be eating biscuits with our cup of hot water – imitating dunking a digestive biscuit smothered with chocolate. I would have eaten a bucket full of kangaroo testicles if it meant I could have been given a packet of chocolate Hobnobs. It was during this role-play that me and Martin had the most political conversation the camp had ever witnessed.

'What's your favourite biscuit to dunk?'

'I love a custard cream.' Jordan peeped out from his hammock.

'Nah, it's all about the chocolate digestive, plain and simple,' Bridgey chipped in.

'Do you know, it depends what time of year it is,' I said.

'What?' Martin snapped.

'So at Christmas time it's all about the hearty biscuits that make you feel warm inside. I'm talking chocolate digestives, chocolate Hobnobs and ginger snaps. Summer time it's all about the light biscuits. Your Rich Teas and custard creams. Any other time of year you can have a bourbon with a cup of Yorkshire tea.'

'What about Jammie Dodgers?' Martin exclaimed.

'Woah pal, you can't dunk a Jammie Dodger. Same as you can't dunk a Jaffa cake.'

'Of course you can.'

'Right guys, back me up on this, you can't dunk a Jammie Dodger. It spoils it. You've got to keep the jam intact to get the best out of it. If you dunk it the jam will go in your brew. This is ludicrous, Martin, you're making your brew undrinkable by dipping that in.'

And so #biscuitgate began. Never did I think people would be having a debate over Twitter about dunking Jammie Dodgers. But yeah, hallucinating about food was one of our greatest pleasures while sitting round that camp fire. It helped with the sugar withdrawal symptoms. It especially helped us on day three, which is famously known as constipation day. I knew that, so that was the one day that I said I would clean the dunny (up there for thinking, down there for dancing!).

The only argument I had in camp was with Martin. I

had been voted president by the lovely public of the United Kingdom, which meant I wasn't allowed to do any jobs myself, I had to just delegate. (Plus I got to sit on the only comfy seat in camp.) We split all the chores fairly and it was working really well. I put Adam Thomas with Martin so he could motivate him but to be honest Martin didn't listen to me, Adam or the rest of the camp. We were running low on water and Adam was busy getting firewood.

'Could you please go and collect some water, Martin? We are running low.'

'No, not yet. I am busy.'

Now I realise you lovely lot watching only got to see me ask him once. I had in fact asked him several times over the course of about five hours. I couldn't take it any more.

'I can only ask you so many times to get some water politely, Martin. Come on, you don't speak to any of the men the way you speak to me. If I was Larry or Wayne, would you have said no?'

Then Danny (my hero) Baker stepped in. 'Mate, she's president, if she says do something you've got to do it. But you don't, you always answer her back like she's some silly kid and she isn't.'

Now look, I am an adult and I don't need anyone to fight my battles for me but I was feeling really alone that day so I was grateful for Danny's intervention. I just felt like I was banging my head against the Bushtucker Telegraph as Martin was just not listening.

But like I say, I really like Martin, we chatted for hours and after that argument it actually made us come closer together. He apologised and that was enough for me; he didn't mean to make me feel like that and I know he would genuinely never want to make anyone feel upset. I have a lot of time for Martin. I also have a lot of time for Danny and when he went I was devastated. He was my winner. I just couldn't understand why he had been voted out so soon. But I knew he wanted to be in that Versace Hotel with his wife Wendy and he had done trials and experienced camp life so he got all he went in there for.

The camp just seemed too quiet without Danny's stories and his singing. I couldn't believe he had just got over throat cancer; his attitude to life is one I'll take with me always. He embraces every day and what a life he has led. From playing football to meeting Bob Marley, to selling records to Elton John and being besties with Chris Evans. When I got home from Australia, I was kindly invited round to Danny and Wendy's home. They found out I had no heating (you'll hear more on that later but basically when I first moved into my flat in London it had no heating at all and it was like living in an igloo) and so they warmed me up and made me an absolute spread of lamb chops and about ten different kinds of potatoes. As I pulled up to Danny's house I was in shock. I thought their house was absolute house goals, it was beautiful.

I found out that me and Danny actually had some things in common. Both of our mums were amazing human beings and called Betty. He has a love of Noddy like me (I mean I'd had my toy Noddy for twenty-four years and I didn't think anybody could love him as much as me but Danny had original illustrations in his home). His first-born daughter is called Bonnie and my first-born chihuahua is called Bonnie –

I have had her since 13th September 2015 (she was only ten weeks old) and I treat her like my child. And also we have both done radio, although obviously he has done it for years and actually knows how to work the buttons on the screen.

I loved that day round Danny's, it was one of the best days in London I've ever had. We – that is, me, Danny, Wendy, their kids Bonnie, Mancie, Sonny and his girlfriend – drank wine, wore Christmas paper hats and watched some of the trials of the jungle back.

Of course, that's the most notorious part of *I'm a Celeb*: the Bushtucker Trials. And I can assure you, they are quite as bad as they look! One that stood out for me as particularly appalling was 'Croke-e-mon Go'. I used to be claustrophobic, and I've never been scuba diving or anything – Jesus, I didn't even dare to put my head under the water in the bath for a long time. I'd get properly freaked out. I couldn't even go in some lifts as I'd feel anxious. Sometimes I could go in them if they were mirrored or you could see through them, but not being able to see an exit for me is terrifying.

So you can imagine how I felt as I stepped into a tank full of eels. I sat myself down and could feel them against my skin. Trying to stay calm, I then had to put my head in another tank. The trial hadn't even begun and I could feel myself hyperventilating. Medic Bob fitted me with a snorkel and I knew I had to endure hell for the next four minutes. 'It's just four minutes of my life, that's all,' I told myself. 'If you can do this, Scarlett, you can do anything.'

Medic Bob outlined what I needed to do. We called him Dr Gloom, because even though he's got a smiley face, it's always bad news. He may as well have said, 'Basically, you could die, but we're on hand so try not to panic and try not to die on live telly. It wouldn't be good viewing.'

'Bob, what happens if I swallow some water?'

'I am going to show you some techniques because you will be swallowing water all throughout the trial. You need to breathe in through your nose then out through your mouth, spitting the water out as you go.'

I was like, 'What happens if I swallow too much water and drown?'

'Just calm down, you'll do fine. If you want to get out at any time, signal with your hands or pull hard on the rope to the left-hand side of the tank.'

I closed my eyes and focused on my breathing. I couldn't hear anything Ant and Dec were saying. OK, what song can I sing, I thought, what will take my mind off things? So in my head I kept replaying 'Tragedy' by Steps (fitting, I know). They dropped toads in the tank with me; they came down hard onto my head. I bit down into my snorkel so hard my gums bled a little. I did not want to lose the snorkel; that was my breathing apparatus. Six yabbies came next, followed by more slithering eels. I had eels by my feet and eels by my ears. A hundred soldier crabs were lobbed in next, then spiders. Then all of a sudden the water drained and I could see Ant and Dec's smiling faces through my misty goggles. 'Yes, I've done it.'

I was sat there smiling; it was my worst day and best day in that jungle. My worst because that was a huge fear of mine, my best because I'd just faced it and kicked its arse. The jungle was so good for my confidence. It is bizarre but on the walk back from trials you think about the oddest things.

On this day I remembered the piece of paper my little sister Ava had given to me just a week before I went to Australia. She had scribbled a Winnie the Pooh quote on it. It read:

'There is something you must always remember.
You are braver than you believe, stronger than you
seem, and smarter than you think.'

Chapter Sixteen

AND THE NEW QUEEN OF THE JUNGLE

★ Celebrity camp-mates are given red socks to wear so that blood from insect bites doesn't show up on camera. (Reassuring.)

★ Ridiculous amounts of creepy crawlies are used during jungle trials. In 2004's 'House of Pies' trial, 1.5 million flies were used. (Lucky for Brian Harvey, the flies couldn't actually fly, due to the conditions they'd been bred in).

★ *I'm a Celebrity ... Get Me Out of Here!* has been going for sixteen series starting back in 2002. Over this time it has seen ten kings sit on the throne and six queens.

'We are in the final three guys, we have made it to the very end.'

'Bro, this is crazy.'

Adam was jumping around, we were like three big kids hugging and jumping around in a circle, we could not believe it.

'I feel so lucky that we all came in on the first day and we are all leaving on the last day. We've experienced it all.'

See, a lot of the camp mates wanted to get back to reality and to see Australia and live it up in luxury at the Versace Hotel. But I know for a fact that me, Adam and Joel, well, we weren't arsed about that. How many people get this opportunity to experience something as bizarre as *I'm a Celebrity ... Get Me Out of Here!*? I didn't think it would happen but I really wanted to make the final three. I had imagined what it would be like for so long and it wasn't even what I thought it would feel like. I knew how amazing all the camp mates were, so for people to actually pick up their phones, tablets, iPads, laptops and actually take time out to vote for me, well, that meant I felt accepted.

'Guys, this means we get to have the final feast together.'

We weren't all hugging for too long when we realised what was coming.

'I know the feast sounds good but to earn it, ha, it means we have to do our final trial, doesn't it?'

Adam went first and came back looking shell-shocked. He had tackled the jungle classic, 'Fill Your Face'. He had to put his head into a clear fish bowl-style helmet where 3,000 crickets, 300 cockroaches, 10 giant burrowing cockroaches, 10 scorpions, 10 millipedes and 20 spiders were dropped in to keep him company. He had aced the trial through gritted teeth and won us all a starter plus a drink each. Joel and I both knew he would ace it; after all, you don't get given the nickname Mr Bushtucker Trial for nothing.

Joel came back from his trial holding his stomach. 'Oh no, you've done the eating challenge, haven't you?' I said. I started to get a lump in my throat and a sickly feeling in my stomach.

'That was the most disgusting thing I've ever done,' he said. 'I had to eat a furry moth, a pig's snout, fish eyeballs, goat penis and blended scorpion.'

He aced it, I was so proud. I must admit, as selfish as this sounds, I was also gutted. I wanted to do the final eating challenge. Not because I enjoy the taste of liquidated scorpions but because I had already managed to get through one eating trial so I knew I could get through another one. My mind began to run wild with the possibilities of what my final trial would be. 'I hope mine isn't anything to do with being underground, or in a coffin or a cave.'

'It won't be, it'll be fine. You can do whatever is thrown at you, Scarlett,' Adam said. Adam was good at motivation. His camaraderie and laughter kept us all going through camp.

'Thanks, Adam, and thank you, Joel. Bloody hell, we all have a main course now.' My mouth was watering already at the thought of real food, on a real plate.

'Good luck, Scarlett,' the boys shouted. I went and sat in the Bushtucker Telegraph to talk about how I felt. This was going to be my final ever trial. I couldn't believe it. Where had the time gone? I didn't want to leave. Yes, I was missing everybody back home but I genuinely was having the time of my life. I was living my dream.

My final ever trial was to win all three of us a dessert and a treat. Oh what I'd do for a bit of apple crumble and custard. Or a cup of tea with a Tim Tam (which are basically the Australian version of a Penguin biscuit, but it's like a really sexy Penguin biscuit – I ended up bulk buying them at the airport and bought 240 Tim Tams at duty free).

As I walked up the hill to see what final horrors awaited me, I noticed something peculiar. I couldn't smell anything. Most of us had learnt to identify insects by their smell alone (not a skill that I thought I'd have to acquire or a skill that I hope has to come into use again). We would walk into a trial, and I'd be like, 'Right, so I know there's mealworms and crickets involved.'

Medic Bob would be so confused. 'How do you know?'

'I can smell them.'

You just get to know the smell of different insects. Here's a little insect chart for you:

- Crickets: similar to old pumpkin guts like a sweet but deathly sort of smell

- Cockroaches: smell musty, like damp clothes

- Mealworms: basically smell like an alley with loads of dog shite in it (you know, the type where the poo is that old it's gone white like chalk)

I suppose no matter how much you watch the show you would never know that, I mean it's television not smellevision. I've watched the show religiously though the years. In fact,

I've watched it all, judging everyone throughout. I wish I hadn't now because you don't actually realise how difficult it is until you're in there. I remember watching some trials and screaming at the TV, 'Jesus, do these people not know what they've signed up for? They do know surely that they're free to leave whenever they want – they've chosen to partake. No one's forced them! Big wimps, the trials can't be *that* bad.' But believe me, they're even worse than you imagine.

Back at my final trial, I was ten seconds away from finding out my fate. I was greeted by Ant and Dec; it was so encouraging to see their smiling faces and to encounter people who didn't smell of sweat. That's why I couldn't smell the insects, all I could smell was soap, deodorant and cologne from the boys.

Dec asked the questions. 'What would it mean to you if you won, Scarlett?'

I knew exactly what it would mean to me and trying to put it into words was proving a difficulty for my brain. As a kid, now this will come as a surprise to you, but I've always been a bit weird and I wasn't accepted in a lot of social groups. I always felt a bit of an outsider looking in. So I feel that if I won I would be showing my little sister that it doesn't matter, you can just be you and people will accept you for that.

It meant more than just a crown and a title for me. I was doing it for all the little outsiders out there, to prove they can do anything they set their minds on, that they're stronger than they think.

'Good luck, Scarlett, you are – if you choose – about to do the final trial of the series. The Cavern of Claws.'

My brain was like, right, what has claws? Erm, cats, no, that makes no fucking sense, Scarlett, why would they put you in a cave full of pussies? Erm, tigers? Right, head, you're just being ridiculous now. Oh God, it's going to be rats, isn't it?

'You have five minutes to dig into the cave above and to the side of you where some surprises lurk along with the stars.'

I was put in a cave where I had to lie flat on my back. I felt like I was in a coffin, I could barely stretch my arms in front of me. As they closed the cave door I felt trapped and for a moment I didn't think I was going to be able to do it. But then I remembered what I had just said to Ant and Dec. I whispered to myself, giving myself a little pep talk and doing something I detest – referring to myself in the third person. 'Come on, Scarlett, you can do it, it's just five minutes out of your life. You've overcome worse things than this,' I whispered.

It was so dark, that kind of darkness where you can't even see the shadow of your hands in front of your face. I could barely hear Ant and Dec. I lay there with my mouth tightly closed, grabbing onto my goggles, ready for anything that was about to happen. The cave started to fill with cold water and – joy of joys – rats. Obviously, because the rats wanted to get out of the water, they all started to burrow under my neck, as that was the warmest area. One was trying to nibble at my collarbone. I had scratches on me afterwards for about three weeks. I was clawing at the walls, scraping them with my little nimble fingers. All sorts of creepy crawlies were falling on me, but I didn't care; I just knew I wanted to get out of that confined space. I was like a woman possessed. I was screaming and pulling bits off the wall, pulling anything off! I was literally pulling the prop apart. I had bits of plasticine in my hand from pulling it away. I did it: I got all the stars in a minute and a half because I just wanted to get out.

Even then, I apologised to the rats. When I got out, they wouldn't get off me, so I was like, 'Please, I'm sorry. I know you've just been scratching me, but you need to get down now.'

One strange aspect of the show is that you can't see the cameras – they're hidden. So you essentially feel like you're all alone. It was a great experience for me though. The only downside was missing my family. Even though I knew they were watching, I often forgot. Many a time I would say, 'Oh, I can't wait to tell my mam and dad.'

And Ant and Dec would remind me: 'Scarlett, they're watching. They're going to see this.'

But every time I did a trial or something funny happened, I'd just want to pick up the phone and be like, 'Guess what's happened here?', even though they would already know.

I just wanted to discuss it with them and talk to my friends – 'Carol Vorderman washed my hair today!' I wanted to tell someone so badly, but you can't. It was just unreal.

The really good thing is that nothing has altered between my friends and me. They just see what I do as an extra job. I don't ever feel that anyone I'm close to has changed the way they are with me or treated me any differently. They just see it as extra-curricular.

'What are you doing today?'

'Oh, I'm filming.'

'Oh, right, have fun.'

It's actually people who I don't really know, people who were horrible to us at school, who all of a sudden want to be my best friend. It's really bizarre – the number of people who bullied me at school who are now saying, 'Remember when we did this?'

'No.'

I think they want fame by association. But I don't want them to think that what they did at school was all right. It's not that I'm holding grudges – I think you become a bitter person if you do that – but I just don't want to associate myself with those people or think that I ought to be nice to them. I don't have to be any more.

It's so funny because as a family we never missed an episode of *I'm a Celebrity*, so I know the programme back to front. When I was in the jungle, my knowledge of the show was a standing joke. All my camp-mates called me 'the encyclopaedia'.

I'd be saying to the others, 'We haven't done the second eating trial yet. One is normally at the beginning, and then we do another one later.' So I'd be waiting for it. I would also tell them, 'Eight more days till Cyclone. Seven more days. Six more days.' I'd have a countdown.

I knew, too, that I was going to be doing a trial underground because there hadn't been one yet. So I went into the Bushtucker Hut and told the producers, 'You do know that I hate being underground.'

'Don't worry, your trial is not underground.'

'Yes, it is.'

'No, it isn't.'

'Yes, it is. I know it is. We may as well start to talk about it now because I know that I am doing one underground. I've watched this show since I was twelve. Do not try and make out that I don't know what I'm talking about!'

When it came to the final day, I was ridiculously nervous. The three of us – Joel Dommett, Adam Thomas and I – were sitting down in the camp waiting to hear who was going to be the King or Queen of the Jungle.

My mam and dad have brought us up with a lot of manners. So every time that I was saved, I would say thank you. I was the only person that said thank you. But I remembered Sam Quek had said, 'You need to stop saying thank you. It comes across desperate.'

'It is not. I'm just genuinely thankful that people have voted.' I cannot help it. I also say sorry when I shouldn't. I am just very English.

So every time I was saved, I was like, 'This is so bizarre. Why have I stayed and Carol Vorderman, Larry Lamb and all these amazing people have gone?'

When it was down to the last three, and Ant and Dec said Adam had come third, I was just looking at Joel as if to say, 'What?!' We were both bemused. Joel and I had spent the whole time in the jungle sleeping. I thought, 'How can we be as entertaining as Adam? He's so funny all the time.' Adam has the most contagious laugh and honestly he is so cheeky. His character from *Emmerdale*, well, that's basically him, he played himself – a cheeky loveable guy.

Then it was just Joel and me. I was pleased that Joel was technically, no matter what the outcome, the new King of the Jungle because he is a decent bloke. The one question all my friends asked me when I got out of the jungle was, 'Did you fancy Joel?' Joel is kind, funny, he has the sweetest mum, Penny, and he's just as awkward as me (I've never known anyone else like that in my life). But even if we were both single, he dates models and unless I'm modelling watches you won't be seeing me walking down any catwalks soon.

Getting back to the final, statistically it is men who normally win – I think because it's mainly young girls who vote. In fifteen years, only five women had won: Kerry Katona, Carol Thatcher, Stacey Solomon, Charlie Brooks and Vicky Pattison. I thought, 'I know that I haven't won, but this is still amazing. I got to go in at the beginning and then I have lasted until the end.'

As Joel and I left the camp, I remember walking across the bridge and actually hearing other people. That was weird because for ages it had just been a small group of us. So to hear other people was like, 'Oh God, I feel I am going back to reality.'

I almost did not want to leave because it was lovely in the camp; it was like a little bubble and there was no TV or phones. I thought, 'Oh no, it's over.' That's all I could think of as I was walking across the bridge. My mind wasn't even thinking about who had won. I just kept thinking, 'Oh, it's over.'

What was it like the moment I found out I'd won? Amazing! It all went so quickly. We stood and we watched our best bits, and I stood next to Joel and held his hand. I was all ready to say, 'Yes, mate, you've won!'

Then, when Ant and Dec announced the outcome, I was just in hysterics because I was really shocked and I didn't think that I would ever win. I just burst into tears. I couldn't help it.

I was sitting on a throne in the middle of the Australian jungle. I had just been crowned Queen of the Jungle on *I'm a Celebrity ... Get Me Out of Here!* The shock and awe of it all completely overwhelmed me.

Why was I crying on the throne? I honestly do think it was because I went from just sitting on the couch watching *I'm a Celeb* to sitting on the couch watching it and being on TV watching it, to knowing that I was sitting on that throne while people were sitting on their couches watching it. It was really weird. It was not like anything I'd ever experienced.

Another reason for the tears was because it all happened to me so quickly. I was sort of catapulted onto TV. It is not like I'd been doing adverts since I was a child, where people gradually learn what it's like to appear on TV. I was never that person really. I was in a complete daze.

I still find it hard to believe. I was thinking, 'Oh my God, I'm sitting on the throne, and it's just bizarre.' Even Ant and Dec said, 'I just feel like I need to give you a hug,' because I was just in shock.

I was like, 'What on earth is happening?' Then when I walked across the bridge, I jumped because the fireworks were louder than I was expecting. Thank God I didn't fall off.

I could see my mam, but I couldn't get to her because the people had to take photographs of me first. So you can see me on the bridge trying to get to her with everyone shouting, 'Stay there!' I started crying again because I just wanted to give her a big hug.

Even today, I look back on that moment and go, 'Wow,

© ITV/REX/Shutterstock

© ITV/REX/Shutterstock

Little Miss Moffatt,
sat on a tuffet, eating
her rice and beans.

Along came a spider...
on top of a frog!

Reliving our jungle days with my favourite
camp-mate, Danny Baker.

Us posing with tear-filled eyes and genuinely shocked faces, after finding out I
was the new Queen of the Jungle just five minutes before.

First breakfast out of the jungle – I've never been so excited to eat toast with the family in my life.

My forever friends looking all grown up: Zoe, me, Sarah and Jess.

Above left: That's neat, I really love your tiger feet. Sarah-Jane, me and everyone's favourite granny, Mary Berry.

Above right: Northerners taking over the NTA's!

When everyone orders fancy desserts but Stephen only eats beige... so gets two scoops of vanilla ice cream.

Right: *Now I gotta cut loose*!
Me and Kevin Bacon being
footloose on set.

Below: Yes, that's me and my boyfriend.
Jokes. That's me and the legend that is
Tom Hardy.

Come on now, we could
swap heads. Just call me
Scarlett Carr.

By Guv'nor, it's Mary
Bleedin' Poppins.

My favourite photo of all time. Living the Disney dream.

Fun in my twin Alan Carr's dressing room at the LGBT Awards.

Mother-daughter selfie before the BAFTAs.

The hardcore party animals of nanny's house parties. Josh, Ava, me and Noah.

Coming full circle… presenting *I'm a Celebrity: Extra Camp* with the amazing 2008 King of the Jungle, Joe Swash, and 2016 runner-up, Joel Dommett. Love them both!

how did that happen?' It is bizarre, but my dad always claims it stems from him. He has always said to me – and I'm sure every dad says this to their kids – 'You are destined for better things. That is why we couldn't give you little first names. We had to have you up there, on another level.' That's why I was called Scarlett Sigourney.

But it's very nice that my parents always had great faith in me – and they were right to as well, you know. My success means that some people's dreams are a little bit closer because when I was growing up there were literally no women with northern accents on the telly.

You never think it's possible, but now that it's happened, it's a good thing. I feel that because I'm from such a small town that nobody has heard of, it is nice if kids watch me and think, 'Oh well, I've got an accent like that. So I could maybe do that if I wanted to.'

It was so sweet. All my friends and family back home were so supportive. I couldn't wait to see everybody and thank them after my mum told me what they had been doing.

'Oh, Scarlett, wait till you get home, you are going to be so overwhelmed. Everyone has been so supportive, it has been unbelievable. There's a banner with your face on in Bishop Auckland pound shop, the Mitre pub has loads of pictures of you up, every shop has posters, people had T-shirts with "Vote Scarlett" on, Jackie Taylor [my mam's mate] even got a van printed with your name and face on. And have you seen the video of the party yet?'

All my family had had a huge party for me on the night of the final. They got big cut-outs of Ant and Dec and a throne. They had crowns and a big cake decorated with spiders. They all got T-shirts they'd walk around town in. Honestly, it was incredible.

They recorded everybody in the Mitre pub from the moment Dec announced, 'And the new … Queen of the Jungle is Scarlett Moffatt!' Everybody got up and cheered; my family were crying. Watching all the happy faces of the people I cherished the most made all of the awful trials and challenges worthwhile. My auntie Janine and uncle Richie started dancing on the chairs, our Demi and Ben were buzzing, the Potters – Adele, Kerstie and Tammie – were bursting with pride. When my mam and dad showed me that video back at the hotel that's when it hit me. I had just won. It wasn't a dream, it wasn't just a fantasy, I hadn't made it up in my mind – it was really my life.

All of my best friends (the girls, I call them) had a party in the local BR (this is the old British Railway Working Men's Club). They were there with their vodka and cokes and had recorded the final too. I couldn't believe their reaction, I mean you know your friends love you but when things like this happen you realise how much. Even my friend Bam who doesn't get emotional about anything was in tears. My bestie Sarah and Nicola Morris were hugging, Kelly was jumping up and Sam and Billie summed it up: 'Fucking get in,' they screamed.

It felt amazing to win. Weirdly, winning the jungle helped massively with my anxiety and panic attacks. I realised that I could fight my head demons and I was in control. I was way stronger than I thought. I also realised that I needed to stop being so anxious about being accepted. After all, people had gone out of their way to vote for me, for SCARLETT

MOFFATT – that's little me. I felt like I had finally been accepted, not just by other people but by myself. I realised there and then I had to stop being so harsh on myself.

As Bruce Lee said:

'Defeat is not defeat unless accepted as a
reality in your own mind.'

Chapter Seventeen

CHRISTMAS TIME, COLD MASHED POTATO AND WINE

★ According to tradition, you should eat one mince pie on each of the twelve days of Christmas to bring good luck. (Yule be pleased I told you this fact).

★ Six million – that's the number of rolls of Sellotape that will be sold in the UK in the run-up to Christmas. (5.95 million – that's the number of rolls where you can't find where the tape ends).

★ The chances of a white Christmas are just one in ten for England and Wales, and one in four for Scotland and Northern Ireland.

Hopping off my seat slightly dazed and jet-lagged (after twenty-seven hours of travelling), I clambered down the aeroplane steps. Arriving into Newcastle Airport was an amazing feeling. It felt so good to be home. Smelling those Gregg's sausage rolls and seeing people without coats on even though it was December just warmed my heart. I couldn't believe how many people had turned up to the airport to greet me – I don't mean family, I mean people who I'd never met who had supported me throughout the jungle. I grasped my little sister's hand and tried not to cry. I will remember that feeling for the rest of my life, I was just on a high. A Christmas high.

Apart from telly, one of my great loves is Christmas. I believed in Santa until I was eleven. I found out he didn't exist from my teacher in Citizenship class. She said something about different beliefs and about how no grown-up believed in Santa. I was like, 'What?' All the kids were laughing. So I went home and asked me mam and dad, 'Why did you not tell us when I went to secondary school that Santa wasn't real?!'

'Sorry, we just wanted you to believe,' my mam replied.

'I'm at big school now. You should have told us that Santa wasn't real, man.'

But I think my parents just wanted me to believe in kiddie stuff for as long as possible. That shattering disillusionment when I was eleven hasn't put me off Christmas, though. I still absolutely adore it. I'm the biggest Christmas fan ever. You know the super-enthusiastic main character in the movie *Elf*? That is me! I'm like, 'It's Santa. Woo hoo!'

I just buy stuff that I don't even need – anything that's red and green or looks festive. I'm all into it. I don't ever buy coffee from coffee shops, but if the cup has got a Santa face on it, I'm like, 'Oh my God, I need it in my life.'

I start buying mince pies in November and eat pigs in blankets as a snack (it's festive, it's allowed, the calories don't count). One of the highlights of the year for me is when Gregg's do their Christmas specials. They do chicken bakes with stuffing or cranberry sauce in them. Sometimes they really mix things up and have turkey pasties. They also do special hot chocolate where you get cream and marshmallows and gingerbread men with candy canes so they are more Christmassy. I literally put about 40kg on at Christmas. You can't help it. Every night you've an excuse for a Snowball. I quickly put on the weight I had lost in the jungle.

Me and my dad have a little tradition, the Moffatts' 'Twelve Days Before Christmas'. We drink a pint of Baileys each night on the build-up to the big day. My dad and I drink Baileys like it's water. I can't work out how many units of alcohol that is but to be frank, I don't care. Like I said, it doesn't count because it's Christmas.

As for my Christmas shopping, it's like a military operation. It takes some planning. I make a list of everything and then just have a whole day where I shop. And I like proper wrapping. Sometimes I spend more on the wrapping than the actual present for the person.

I have a theme to my wrapping every year. So last year it was brown paper with ribbon. I also made a little stamp saying 'Scarlett', so I could stamp every present. Yes, I get carried away.

I've normally got it all done by the first of December, and I always go really overboard with my little sister. In the past,

I've got her things like a trip to Disneyland Paris, iPads, dressing tables. So she gets a big present off me and a big present off my mam and dad. I do treat her like she's my child. Obviously it had to be an online shopping trip the year of the jungle win as I had like five days to get presents bought and to try and get over the jet-lag.

We have a ritual on Christmas Eve. Ever since I was little, my mam has given us all new pyjamas. We're allowed to open one present every Christmas Eve, but obviously it's the pyjamas. Every year my mam will say, 'Oh no, not that one, not that one. What about the present wrapped in Disney princess paper?' And every year me and Ava just say, 'Mam just give us the present that you want us to open.' And it's always the new pyjamas.

For the last three years, these have been matching onesies. Last year Ava and I got matching Pokémon onesies. We were both Pikachu. As well as the matching onesies, we got new slippers and dressing gowns. Our mam gets new ones as well. That way, we're all ready for Santa.

Then we always have a Christmas Eve buffet. It always has to be the same: pickled onions, sandwiches, garlic bread, chips and dips, mince pies and pizza (that's been stood there for about three hours, so it's freezing). Then we all sit down together to watch *The Grinch* in our new pyjamas.

I like Christmas to be very traditional. One year, my mam wanted a trendy black Christmas tree. But my dad, my sister and I like a tacky Christmas. You know the sort of thing – loads of lights, stickers on the window, tinsel that doesn't have to match, baubles of every colour, and those plastic little Santas that look like they're coming down the chimney.

Stuff like that everywhere. Even in the bathroom, just stuck everywhere.

Whereas my mam wants everything to be coordinated. When we had done our living room out in that haphazard way, she said, 'I'm going to get a black Christmas tree.'

'What?'

'Well, it will match with other things.'

'But things don't have to match at Christmas, Mam. What will Santa think?'

'Don't be stupid.'

'No, what will Santa think if he comes down that chimney and he sees a black Christmas tree?'

'But he's not real!'

'La, la, la. I don't want to hear that in our house. He is real.'

Then there's the ritual on Christmas Day. At least fifteen of us always go to my nanny Christine's house. My nanny's house is quite small, and she only has a table with four chairs. So the kids are sat eating their Christmas dinner on the stairs and on the floor.

But I wouldn't have it any other way, even though it is organised chaos and by the time the mashed potato comes out, everything else is cold.

Grandad, my nanny and my uncle Mark do the cooking. They all chip in. But our family doesn't get involved in that at all. Definitely not. We just sit back and get drunk.

Sometimes we bring condiments. So we'll do the cranberry sauce and mint sauce, but that literally is it. We also bring the booze, which is the most important bit, I think. We always buy a lot of booze. Baileys, obviously, loads of wine, Prosecco, Bucks Fizz.

After the lunch, we always put the telly on, have a sit around and just chat. By this time, my nanny's a bit tipsy, and she'll put Jive Bunny on. The 'Jive Bunny Megamix'. It's always the same. It begins, 'Come on everybody, come on everybody.'

'Now the party starts!' we shout, and so we drink some more.

Then we just play loads of games. We'll play bingo for money. We have an actual spinning bingo machine, and my nanny brings out the tickets. It's twenty pence for one and a pound for a strip. The prize for a full house is normally at least a fiver. So you have to be prepared to flash the cash.

After that, we play a quiz which my nanny sets every year. We normally get a lot of questions on *Carry On* movies. That is her favourite subject. So a couple of days before, you catch up on all the lines in the *Carry On* films.

But the ridiculous thing is, even though she sets all the questions, my nanny still joins in the quizzes. We split into teams, and every year we're like, 'You can't join in, Nanny, because you know all the answers!'

Nanny replies, 'Oh, I can't remember the bloody answers.'

'But you've just written them all!' And somehow her team always wins.

She divides the quiz up into actual sections, so she'll have a *Carry On* section and the next section will be pop music of the sixties. Every section is about her era, basically, so we're all just looking at each other, as if to say, 'What?'

After the quiz, we play this accent game. One person is given a movie quote. They have got to say it in a certain accent, and then the others have to guess the accent. My uncle Mark's the funniest. He's just so bad. Everything sounds Welsh.

He's like, 'No, it's Jamaican.'

'Then why do you sound Welsh?'

Loads of funny things always happen at my nanny's house on Christmas Day. One year my mam was sat on the edge of the couch and when she moved, the whole arm of the chair came off. She was like, 'Oh my God.'

'Prop it up, prop it up,' I said.

So she got loads of Argos catalogues and propped it up. Then when everyone came and sat down, my mam said to my dad, 'Sit there if you want.' So he sat down, leaned on the arm and it fell off.

He got the blame. My nanny went mental at him. She was like, 'Mark, what have you done?'

'I don't know my own strength, Christine.'

My mam and I were just looking at each other, thinking, 'We can never discuss this.' Except when I put it in this book.

Then at about eight o'clock on Christmas evening, we go back home and just chill on the couch. We end the day with a kebab or a Chinese. They deliver kebabs and Chinese on Christmas Day. That's why Bishop Auckland, our town, is known as 'Bish Vegas'. Maybe because it's so glamorous, or maybe because it's got a lot of slot machines!

Boxing Day is just as much fun. Normally everyone comes round our house, and my mam does a buffet with lots of drink. We have pies, sausage rolls, vol-au-vents. We have a sort of open house policy where people just turn up. It's really nice.

Of course, a lot of the food is frozen, but my mam will say that it isn't. She'll tell me, 'Oh, I just took these sausage rolls out of the oven.'

And I'll say, 'Yes, but you've just put them in the oven from the bag.'

'Well, no one needs to know that.'

'I think they're going to know that you haven't been up this morning at 4 a.m. making your own pastry. Mam, we know you!'

I have lots of favourite memories from Christmases past. One of the best ones was when my grandad was pretty drunk. He was like bouncing up and down on a wired fireguard and he was singing 'Yellow Submarine'. But instead of 'We all live in a yellow submarine', he was singing, 'We all live in a green tambourine.'

He got everything right – except the colour and the object! He really didn't realise, but we all started joining in anyway: 'We all live in a green tambourine.' I always remember that because we were all crying with laughter.

I also have very fond memories of lots of family games at Christmas. Sometimes we play on SingStar, and that always causes arguments. When people lose, they go, 'Well, I should have got better marks than that!'

And I say to them, 'It's just a game. It's for fun and it's for kids.' These people are all forty plus, so they should just calm down.

However, drink and games do not always mix very well, especially when you're playing Trivial Pursuit. That always causes rows. Oh my God, I remember once we were playing and my uncle Daniel literally threatened to leave. He was like, 'Well, if people aren't going to start playing fair, I'm getting up and I'm walking out.'

After that, it was a bit awkward. We were like, 'We should

probably just stop playing.' It wasn't really in the spirit of Christmas.

Another funny aspect is because we all take a load of presents round to my nanny's, we all end up going home with the wrong presents. We sometimes even end up with our own presents that we'd given to someone else.

We just put all the presents in different bags. At the end, you're like, 'I'm sure I had a £50 gift card from Next.' But you never see that again. You wind up with a toast rack instead.

On a more positive note, you can also end up with fifty selection boxes of chocolates. That's one of the things I love about Christmas. Normally chocolate bars are 70p each, but at Christmas time selection boxes are a quid from the pound shop and so you get five bars at 20p each. Woo hoo!

Christmas is also an excuse to eat your own bodyweight in Ferrero Rochers. If it was happening in April, everyone would ask, 'Why are you eating a whole box of Ferrero Rochers on your own?' But if you do it at Christmas, no one bats an eyelid. They're like, 'What's that? Ferrero Rocher? Can I have one? Can I have a whole packet?'

At any other time of the year, everyone's like, 'Oh, that is just pure greed.' But at Christmas, no one cares. You can eat five selection boxes on the trot and half a litre of Baileys, and no one judges you. It's the only time of the year that that's appropriate. In fact, it's encouraged. It's almost the law. If you're not doing that, you're doing Christmas wrong, in my eyes.

Looking back, my all-time favourite Christmas present was a Cabbage Patch Kid because I had just wanted one for so long. When we lived in Shildon, Santa used to come round the streets and ask all the kids what they wanted for Christmas. It was honestly amazing.

So you'd hear a bell and there'd be Christmas music, and Santa would suddenly come into the street on a float. All the kids would be stood outside waiting. Once you could hear the bell, you'd be like, 'Oh my God, he's coming, he's coming!'

One year, I met Santa in the street, and he asked me, 'What do you want for Christmas?'

'A Cabbage Patch Kid, please.' And obviously, the next day I got one. I remember thinking, 'Oh thank you, Santa. You listened!'

A few weeks before the big day, I'd always write a wish list for my parents, or I would get the Argos catalogue and just circle everything. My mam would be like, 'Pick ten presents that you really want, put a star next to them, and just circle another ten in case Santa can't get the ones with the stars next to them.'

But I'd just be like flicking through and saying, 'Want that, and that and that.' In the end, I circled everything in the toy section.

One year I remember getting a toy kitchen. It had a little microwave and little pretend pans and pretend slices of pizza. I was always playing on that. I think that is the only time that I've ever enjoyed spending time in the kitchen. It's certainly the only time that my mam has ever heard me say, 'Do you want some food?' All she hears now is: 'Can I order you something?'

I bet she's like, 'Where's that little girl gone, the girl who just loved to cook my pretend pizza in a pretend oven?'

The other Christmas present I loved was Mr Frosty. That was

a snowman which made slushies. You'd put in ice and water and freeze it. Then you'd move Mr Frosty's arm up and down, and it would make a slushy. Oh my God, that was amazing.

I loved things like that. I was such a geek as a kid, and now my little sister's exactly the same, which I'm really pleased about. It means that now at Christmas I can give her those things as well. One year, for instance, I gave her a microscope.

I remember getting a microscope when I was younger. It had slides containing half-insects and stuff. Then I'd write down all my observations. Things like, 'Fly, definitely dead. Chopped in half.'

I'd also get those chemistry kits where you could add bicarbonate of soda to water and observe the reaction. I'm delighted that my little sister likes things like that now.

In addition, every Christmas I got an art kit from Argos. You'd open it up and exclaim, 'Oh my God, I'm like the real Neil Buchanan. I am from *Art Attack*.' That's how I felt when I got it.

At first, my parents would give me a big pad of A4 drawing paper, all wrapped up. I'd be over moon. 'Yes, I know what's coming next! I've got the paper, but I've got no art stuff.'

And then I'd open the next present, and it would have all the felt tips and the wax crayons and the stencils and the paint – which you were never allowed to use. Everything was circular. Oh my God, I used to love stuff like that.

I feel like actually now that's what kids miss out on. Now it's all about technology. It's all about watching stuff on YouTube or iPads or laptops, whereas as a kid, I loved just drawing. I could spend hours doing that. I think that has been lost a bit.

Also, I feel we've lost our passion for actual board games. I remember getting really excited about Frustration and Mouse Trap. I'd always play those games and then give up halfway through. No one ever won, because you'd just get bored of it or have an argument.

I'd be thinking, 'I've being playing Monopoly for three hours now – or is it three weeks?' Or I'd be playing Cluedo and saying to myself, 'I'm actually going to kill someone soon. Just pass me the lead pipe now. I'm going to be the one with the candlestick in this living room in a minute if we don't stop playing this game. They solve real-life crimes quicker than we play this.'

I much prefer Christmas songs. My favourite is 'All I Want for Christmas'. It's one of those songs that when it comes on and you're drunk and with all the girls, you're all like, 'Yeah!' You think you can hit the high notes. You're holding it and waving your fingers around. We're all looking at each other, like, acknowledging each other and thinking, 'We're hitting the high notes, and we're amazing.'

Every year, when I have a drunken sing-song with my friends like that, we all shout in unison, 'We should form a band!'

Then the person who doesn't think they are a good singer says, 'I can be the manager!'

Someone else says, 'I'll be the roadie!'

'And I can drive the van!'

And we're all like, 'Why have we never thought of it before? Why have we been ignoring this talent all these years?'

So we spend every Christmas thinking of a really shit girl band name. We always used to say that we would be called

Girls Are Allowed. I'd say, 'That's amazing. The name is similar but not quite the same. Will people think we are a tribute band, Nicola?'

'No, they'll know that it's not. It's a totally original thing.'

'I know. When we write "Girls Are Allowed", we won't actually use the word "are", but the letter R, backwards. That's really quirky: Girls R (backwards) Allowed.'

I always feel really blessed because I know that a lot of people don't have that wonderful family and friend bonding time at Christmas. Sadly, these days that's not always the case, is it? A lot of families split up and move away and lose touch sometimes as well.

Our Christmas is very informal. It's not like we have to get dressed up or anything. We all just chill out in our comfies and slippers. But it's still such a special time of year.

Even though our family meet all the time – it's not like we haven't seen each other all year – it still feels different at Christmas. My mam sees my auntie and my nanny every day, and whenever I'm home I always go and see them. But Christmas is something else. It's also the time when it really brings it home that it's just lovely to have really close family. We are like the Brady Bunch and I wouldn't have it any other way.

It was bizarre after the jungle because everyone got swept up in the show, and as a result no one was very organised with Christmas. So we decided to eat out for Christmas dinner, something we had never done before (and will never be doing again). Although it was nice not doing any washing up, there's something lovely about chaos at Christmas. I know the dream that is sold to you on the TV is being knee-deep in presents and expensive crackers, having a civilised turkey dinner with all the trimmings, then sitting by an open fire roasting chestnuts with a lavish tree sparkling with antique baubles in the background. But it's just not Christmas for me and my family if everything goes to plan. Dare I say it, I missed eating cold mashed potato last Christmas. I missed not having enough elbow room to cut my meat up and banging into the person sat next to me, I missed being able to sit in my slippers and not be judged for it. In the words of my good friend (well, I feel like he is) Dr Seuss:

'What if Christmas, he thought, doesn't come from a store.
What if Christmas, perhaps, means a little bit more?'

Chapter Eighteen

LONDON AND ITS SMASHED AVOCADO

✷ To pass the Knowledge, the insanely difficult London geography test required of black-cab drivers in the city, you must master 320 basic routes, all of the 25,000 streets that are scattered within those routes, and about 20,000 landmarks and places of interest within a six-mile radius of Charing Cross.

✷ The word 'avocado' in Nahuatl Indian (Aztec) means 'testicle' because of its shape, so the word 'guacamole' literally translates as 'testicle sauce'.

✷ Cock Lane, near Holborn Viaduct, didn't get its name due to any association with poultry, but because it was the only street to be licensed for prostitution in medieval times.

T ears streamed down my face.
'Scarlett, what's wrong?' My mam, dad and Ava looked so concerned.

'I don't even know how to say it because it doesn't feel real but I have been offered a place to present the Best Seats in the House competition for *Saturday Night Takeaway*!'

'Ahhhhhh!' my dad screamed and picked me up.

'This is amazing! Wow, dreams do come true, Scarlett, you're right,' my little sister yelled.

Now was the time to tell them what I'd been thinking about all over Christmas. 'You know, I have always wanted to see what it's like living in London and now seems a perfect time. If I rent somewhere for a year then I can see if it's the place for me. I've got to take a chance.'

'I agree completely, kid. We will help you look for a flat.'

Just three weeks later, I was at Darlington station listening to an announcement.

'The next train arriving onto platform one will be the 12.29 Virgin service from Edinburgh Waverley to London King's Cross, calling at York and London King's Cross,' the tannoy announced. Holding back the tears with a lump in my throat, standing next to everything I owned – two suitcases and a backpack – it was really happening, just three weeks after the discussion of moving to London. I waved my mam goodbye. Yes, I had lived away from my family before but never this far away. I was off to live in the capital city, London. I was like a real-life Dick Whittington. I should have been super excited but I just felt distraught at the fact I couldn't pop round my mam and dad's for a cup of tea, or to give my little sister a cuddle or to go and have a natter and a kebab with my best friend Sarah.

It was a huge step for me, suddenly moving hundreds of miles away, especially after everything had been such a whirlwind recently. I had only been down to London a handful of times in my whole life so I bought a map of London and the Underground (such a tourist) just so I could get my head around it all. I could walk from one end of my town to the other in half an hour, whereas London seemed like this giant country. As soon as I arrived into King's Cross station, well, let's put it this way, 'I knew I wasn't in Kansas any more.'

I knew straight away things were going to be different living down south to up north when I got into the taxi to take me to my new flat. After I got over the fact there was a card machine in the taxi (which I'd never seen before), I realised the taxi driver hadn't done the normal three things all northern taxi drivers do.

1. **Tell me what time he had been working since.**
2. **Tell me what time he is working till.**
3. **Moan about Ubers.**

Normally you couldn't get taxi drivers to stop talking but no, not a mutter of a word. I mean the driver was pleasant enough and he got us there safely but it just wasn't the same. I have so many stories that involve taxis back at home. Like the time I had no money on me so I gave the driver some garlic and chips as payment. Or the time I thought I had money in my room at uni so I ran up to get the £4 and realised I had spent it on four VKs the other afternoon. I had a brainwave and remembered I once read somewhere that stamps were legal tender. Knowing I had three packs of first-class stamps (as

I'm a traditionalist and still like to send letters to my family), I ran down the stairs clenching the Queen's lovely face.

'Here you go, mate, it's legal tender,' I explained.

'You've got to be taking the piss.'

'You've got to accept it, pal, it's the law.' He reluctantly took them off me, not wanting to argue with a nineteen-year-old girl who was by some standards 'slightly pissed'. I knew I was never ever going to get away with this sort of stuff with southern taxi drivers.

Down in London, anything that could go tits up with a flat in the first week of moving in happened. There was no heating, the water didn't work properly, I had no duvet as it hadn't been delivered yet, nor had the TV arrived – oh, and the fridge didn't work. So to sum it up, I was sat the day after New Year's Day with ten layers on, wrapped in an itchy blanket, watching Netflix on an iPhone screen and drinking tepid tap water. I couldn't even have a cup of

tea because I couldn't keep the milk fresh.

Treating myself to breakfast the next day (as I didn't want to sit and catch hypothermia in the flat) I made my way into Camden. I could not believe the choice that you guys down here get. I love the north and I'm not meaning to make it sound like we only have the simple things in life but in all my twenty-six years of living up north I was never asked the following questions.

'What kind of tea would you like?' the waiter asked.

Thinking they meant Yorkshire Tea, PG Tips, etc, I shrugged. I didn't want to sound too fussy. 'Oh anything, honestly,' I said.

To which the response was: 'Breakfast tea, decaf, green tea, peppermint tea, chamomile?' The list was endless.

'Just normal tea please,' I replied.

'Great, would you like milk with that? We have soya, almond and unsweetened,' he added.

'Just like cow udder milk please,' I requested. Other people eating in the café were in hysterics, as they could see how anxious I was getting with all the choice.

'Would you like any sugar lumps, brown sugar, sweeteners?' This was slowly turning into a breakfast interrogation. In my mind I was screaming, 'I just want a fucking cup of tea, mate, with milk that comes from a cow's tit and a teaspoon of sugar – the kind that looks like white sand please.'

Even the choice of toast was borderline ridiculous. Not just the usual white or brown, oh no. 'We have rye, wholemeal, gluten-free or sourdough, madam,' the waiter listed. I don't get why anyone would want to eat toast with sourdough in it. I knew I needed to embrace living down south so I decided to try something I had never heard of that is on every menu in London.

Avocado. The vegetable that is actually a fruit that is the 'good' kind of fat (again something that I'd only just realised was a thing). I don't know what it has got in it but it is addictive. I have it nearly every day now, smashed, sliced, mushed. For my breakfast, dinner and tea, it goes with everything. I tried to introduce it to one of my best friends, Billie, when she came down to watch me do an episode of

Saturday Night Takeaway. I took her for breakfast down here and she giggled.

'What you laughing at?'

'Mate, why are you eating nacho sauce with toast?'

'Nacho sauce? It's not guacamole, Billie, it's avocado.' I don't think I've quite managed to convert her to the avacoolo gang just yet.

I really love London, it is so diverse and vibrant; it has so much culture. It is virtually impossible to be bored here. Also, despite the rumours and what people say, everyone is just as friendly down south as they are up north. Everyone I have met has been so helpful and kind – but there is less chat. I think the difference is it's so fast-paced in London and everyone has somewhere to be, people literally just do not have the time to stop and chat in the middle of the street. Also because everyone is busy and career-orientated, when I'm not filming it's very rare I have anyone to do any fun stuff with. There's no one I can just ask to come round my flat to have a cup of tea and a chocolate biscuit. It is so hard to make friends as an adult, especially when you're in a new city.

Regardless, it is an amazing place but I'll be honest I just cannot see myself settling down here. Not just because it's not socially acceptable down here to walk along Oxford Street eating a sausage roll at 10 a.m. (which it is walking down Newcastle Northumbria Street) but the house prices are actually ridiculous. My dream – and I know that it's years away yet and it probably will never happen but aim for the stars and all of that – is to have a house with an annex, so my mam, dad and little sister can live with me. I would love it, because I think it would be a bit much if they lived in the same house with me 24/7, but if they lived just a stone's throw away, ahhh, I would be in my element.

Anyway because of that dream I will definitely have to move back up north as unless I want to rent all my life I could only afford a garage or a shed in London.

I'll be honest with you, before I came down to London I thought everything was more expensive, not just the houses. I thought I was going to have to take a bank loan out when I came down to London because my dad was like, 'Oooh, cans of pop cost £8 there.'

But they don't! They're literally exactly the same price as at Asda back home. He's like, 'Aww, a big shop will cost you a bloody fortune, pheeeew!'

'Dad, it won't!'

'Have you seen the price of a loaf of bread down there?'

'It's exactly the same, Dad!'

When I went home last, he'd bought me loads of PG Tips and Yorkshire tea. He was like, 'Put this in your case.'

'Why?'

'Save your money.'

'But it's exactly the same price in London. I'm not abroad, do you know what I mean?' If I go to my local Sainsbury's in London and I buy PG Tips it's exactly the same cost as if I go to the local Sainsbury's at home. But he just can't get his head round it, he really can't.

He will call me and ask what I'm doing. 'Just eating a peanut butter sandwich, Dad,' I'll say.

'Bloody hell, how much did that cost ya once you bought everything to make it with? Bet it was twenty bar or at least fifteen quid.'

God bless him, he doesn't have a clue. It's all because one time I took him to Camden Market to get an ice cream and he asked for a Mr Whippy ninety-niner with monkey blood sauce and a flake and it cost £2.10.

'How much? I'll have my eyeballs back ta, pal, I mean how can it be a ninety-niner if it's £2.10, mate?'

'Dad, stop it now, you're embarrassing me.' Although to be fair he had a point.

When my dad isn't phoning me up asking the prices of London stock he is normally asking how my weekend's been and that involves me talking about either whatever I have been filming, bigging up the London sites or sometimes involving Ant and Dec (and Lisa and Ali). Whoever said you should never meet your heroes is talking crap. They're genuinely the kindest and funniest people I have ever met, they even invited me over their house a few times for Sunday dinner – Stephen Mulhern comes too and we have such a giggle. Even if he does manage to baffle my mind with his magic tricks (I'm telling you now, Stephen is like Jesus, I bet if you asked him he could turn water into wine). I also go to their local pub and it is just so lovely because I feel like I'm at home again. Obviously the boys and Stephen are super busy filming lots of exciting things like *Britain's Got More Talent*. So when I'm not stalking them lot I spend most of my days being a tourist. I have done ghost-hunting trips, Madame Tussauds, the dungeons, Shrek world. I even bought a Union Jack umbrella to walk round Covent Garden with.

I do seem to spend most of my days alone. I'll be honest, though, if there's one thing I've done in London which I never used to do up north, it's spend time by myself. Now obviously we are all by ourselves sometimes, but I mean I am purposefully not spending time with another human being other than myself. I'll text people and say I'm busy with work when really I just want a day all by myself. It is great, I love it.

This sounds proper big-headed but I have now realised I love my own company. I used to hate being left with only my own thoughts, I would get so anxious and overthink everything. But since I gained more confidence from the jungle I go for meals out by myself. It is one of my favourite things to do (as sad as that sounds) as I spend most of my time surrounded by lots of people constantly chatting so it's nice to not have to interact with anyone and to be able to just appreciate what I'm eating (plus I don't have to share any of my food or wait forever and a day for the other person to decide where and what they want to eat). I take long walks with my dog Bonnie and we sit on Primrose Hill and I read my books. I walk around Camden Market with a tray full of halloumi fries and I people-watch. In fact I make up scenarios about the people I'm watching. I make up a name for them, a job, how they met their partner, if they're having an affair. Sometimes my brain makes up such a funny story about the person I actually laugh out loud.

Having a day by myself in my flat in London is the best. One of my favourite things to do in the house is pretend I'm on *Strictly Come Dancing*. I even do the voices of the judges: 'seven'. I put my Adele *21* album on full blast, put loads and loads of mascara on and then go in the bath and stare at myself in the mirror as the mascara runs down my face while I sing along, pretending I am in fact in one of Adele's sad music videos. 'Never mind I'll find someone like you, I wish nothing but the best for you too.'

I sometimes order loads of food from Domino's (I mean a

large pizza, seven franks hot sauce chicken wings, four cookies, one big garlic dip and a 1.5 litre bottle of Coke Zero) and when the food comes I pretend to shout through to some make-believe person in the house so the delivery driver doesn't think I'm greedy. 'I think that's our food that's arrived. I'll go and collect it, you get the plates out ready, thank you, sweetheart.' Then I take great satisfaction in eating it all by myself while watching shit-your-pants scary movies on my Mac. Not caring how I'm eating with garlic sauce all down my chin (after all, calories don't count when no one sees you eat them).

I will stalk fit girls on Instagram to the point where I know their life story. I talk to Bonnie (my dog) in strange accents and at least once a day I say the following, 'Come on, Bonnie, you can talk to me, I swear if you speak in human language so that I can understand you, I will not, I repeat will not tell a single soul.' All of the above in my home is normally done in nothing but my Bridget Jones big white pants and my hair in a top-knot with toothpaste all over my face while I'm trying to dry my spots out. I just have completely fallen in love, well, with myself since moving to London.

I think it's important that we really enjoy spending time with ourselves. To realise that being alone doesn't mean we are lonely, it just means we get to forget about everything for a little while and just enjoy being our weird and wonderful selves. As the American politician Ann Richards once said:

'Learn to enjoy your own company. You are the one person you can count on living with for the rest of your life.'

Chapter Nineteen

SATURDAY NIGHT TAKEAWAY
(MINE'S A CHICKEN KEBAB)

★ Turkey has thirty different variations of the kebab (get me on a plane right now!).

★ The idea behind helicopters has existed since as far back as 400BC, when vertical flight was invented in China in the form of a flying toy made from bamboo which created lift when spun.

★ In 2007, the mayor of Chicago decided to award the singer Jennifer Hudson with her own special day, calling 6 March Jennifer Hudson Day.

I will set the scene. It is Thursday 23rd February 2017 and I am about to have my first ever script meeting. Now, I don't actually know what a script meeting is at this point and I'm hoping it can be something that I can just wing. I walk into the cosy little room in the ITV studios holding a cup of tea. The tea is actually burning through the paper cup but I am pretending I'm not getting third-degree burns on my hands as I want to play it cool. Ant, Dec and all the lovely ITV bosses are sitting around the table.

'Hello, how are you?' Dec asks. I nod.

'Looking forward to your first script meeting?' Ant adds. I nod. For some reason, words will not come out of my mouth, and then I realise it's because my brain's concentrating on the heat from the tea. Put the bloody tea down, Scarlett!

This sounds silly on reflection but I was so shocked that everyone at the meeting was so nice. When I thought of big

Smiles with the big boys, Ant and Dec.

TV bosses I thought they would be like Mr Burns from *The Simpsons*. I thought you had to be mean to get to the top of your game, like in *The Devil Wears Prada*. But they're just genuinely lovely, passionate people who are good at their job. We started the meeting with a little introduction and a chat about what we had been up to. I couldn't believe I had got myself so nervous, but it shows how much the whole show meant to me that I wanted to make a good impression. (I'd relaxed so much by the end of the first meeting I was even dipping biscuits into my tea; I felt right at home.)

'So for the first episode we were thinking you could hop on a motorbike, get over to Battersea, jump on a helicopter, and bring someone who's watching the show on the television to come back with you in the helicopter to sit on the best seats in the house to watch the show in the studio,' said one of the producers. 'Little Ant and Dec can serve you food prepared by Jamie Oliver and there will be a little glass of champers waiting for you all.'

I started laughing. I mean, no way was that really going to happen. 'Imagine, sounds like a scene from *Batman*!'

'So you up for it?'

'What, in real life you want me to do that?'

'Yeah, what do you think?'

'Oh my God, this is actually going to happen. Of course I'm up for it!'

I wanted to kiss and cuddle everyone in the room but I knew that would be unprofessional. I couldn't believe that Ant and Dec and ITV were trusting me, little me, on my first ever episode of live TV presenting in a studio. And I was getting to be a bloody Bond girl.

'I have never actually been on a motorbike before,' I admitted. 'In fact, I've not been on a push bike in over fourteen years.'

'That's OK, you can have a little practice so you feel comfortable with it and if you don't, do not panic – we will think of another plan.'

Now if this had happened before the jungle I probably would have said no to even trying to go on a motorbike; the fear and anxiety would have been too much. But because I had gotten through things that I never thought I'd be able to manage, I thought to myself, well, you've been through worse, Scarlett, it'll be fine.

So when the day came I was ready to swerve in and out of cars on the busy roads of London whilst riding on the back of a motorbike. It was 27 February 2017. Now this date might ring a bell as it is just my luck that the day I decide to face my fear of bikes is the day that Storm Doris hits the UK. Yep, that's right – 90mph winds was my first ever motorbike experience. The only way I can describe what it was like being on that bike is something that you may have witnessed yourself. Have you ever seen a fly or spider on the window pane in your house and you've blown it and it has just skidded out of control, not knowing what the hell's going on? Yep, that was what we were like, skidding through the roads of London. I mean, if I can get through 90mph winds I can get through a bit of rain and late-night London traffic on a Saturday night. So I agreed to the adventure of a motorbike and a helicopter.

Fast-forward to Saturday. My alarm went off at 7.02a.m. and I was literally skipping around the house in my unicorn slippers. 'I just can't wait for Saturday, ooooh it *is* Saturday.' I couldn't even drink my brew I was that excited. All my friends were texting me 'Good luck, we will be watching' messages. My mam, dad and Ava were on their way down from Bishop Auckland to London to watch the first episode live. I arrived at the ITV studios at 9.30 a.m. for the script meeting and rehearsals. Now obviously you can't really rehearse going in a helicopter and bringing people back into the studio so I just learnt my timings and felt confident; I had forty minutes to do my thing and the rest, well, I would just have to wing it.

I didn't have time to be nervous as I was far too excited by the fact I was about to be sharing a stage with Ant and Dec. I felt like I was being pushed to new heights – and then actual heights by spending the first episode flying around in 'a real-life helicopter'. My task was to tell people watching the show to get my attention if I was in their street. So I had people flashing their lights on and off but they were at the very top of a block of flats and I only had five minutes to do my thing. There were six people waving out of a window but I knew I was only allowed to fit three people in the helicopter and I didn't know how I would say, 'Sorry, you three can't come.' Then I spotted a house with its living room and bedroom light on. There was a random cat next to the house which was taking a dump – I mean, it is live TV. I knocked on the door and the couple had their TV on delay because they don't like watching the adverts.

'Would you like to come and watch *Ant and Dec's Saturday Night Takeaway* with me?' I said to the guy who opened the door. 'I'll take you to the studio now in a helicopter!'

The guy was gobsmacked. 'Oh my God, yes, let me get my wife.' Then he closed the door on me and went back in the house. Now it's not entertaining for anyone to watch me just stood outside a door, so I did what every northerner does in that situation: invite myself in, sit on ya couch and tell you to hurry up and get ready as I've got the helicopter parked up without a ticket and there's traffic wardens hanging around.

Flying back after I'd accomplished the mission that ITV and Ant and Dec had set me felt amazing. I did it; I had done my first ever live presenting on *Saturday Night Takeaway*. But I couldn't get too excited: I had to stay composed in the helicopter and act professional. I did forget to tell the couple they would be scooting off on motorbikes as well but I think adrenaline had kicked in for them by that point and I could have said we were going by elephant and they'd have agreed.

We made it back to the studio in the nick of time and we sat down on the best seats in the house. So I was watching the show from a sofa. I mean it was just like my old *Gogglebox* job.

The End of the Show Show was just an ad break away. Now due to all the travelling, my eyelashes were hanging off and I had helmet hair but I didn't care. I whipped off my clothes while the amazing hair and make-up team made me look show-ready and I slipped on a little dress and heels. I was about to go on stage and sing 'Spotlight' with Ant, Dec, Stephen Mulhern and Oscar-winning legend Jennifer Hudson. 'Well I don't like living under your spotlight.' The light came on me for my bit and I could see my family in the audience – my smile was cheesy because I had to bite the insides of my cheeks so that I didn't cry with happiness. I mean what a first episode, I will remember that for the rest of my life.

My first ever Green Room was an experience too. Everyone after the show chills in this room and there's a little buffet. I was going to get a bottle of Prosecco for myself and drink it with a long straw but my mam said I had to give a good first impression. So I drank the full bottle but out of a champagne flute. Ava got a tour of the studio by Ant, bless him; she said her life was made now. We stayed till about half eleven and then made our way back to my house and ordered a pizza.

'I know I keep saying it, but I cannit believe this is my job.'

'I know, to be honest we are going to come down every week and watch it live,' said my mam.

'Oh really, I'd love that, Mam. It was nice standing on stage and being able to see your faces. At least I knew three people would be laughing at my jokes. God knows what's in store for me on next week's show, I just want it to be Saturday every day of the week.'

Every Friday at the script meeting it felt like Christmas Eve. I would get that excited nervous tummy knowing that I was just one sleep away from something magical. I felt like I was ten again when I was filming *Takeaway*. Honestly, I would just constantly be in shock – it says something when you're twenty-seven but you have to wear a Tena Lady pad because you're scared that one week you might get a little over-excited.

I mean I got to do a live sing-a-long with Steps. I was obsessed with them; when I was a kid me and my mam went to see them five times. I still have their board game in me attic. I would get me hair in braids like Faye and as it wasn't as easy as Googling and printing the lyrics off back then I would listen to their songs on repeat whilst writing the lyrics down. I remember having the rehearsal to practise the 'Tragedy' dance on the Saturday afternoon. I said to Mike, who was my fabulous producer, 'Seriously, I was born ready for this. I do not need any help with the Steps dance moves.' Mike just giggled away as I started throwing my hands in the air to 'Tragedy', shaking everything my mamma gave me.

I got to clap along in the studio alongside Little Ant and Dec while Ant and Dec joined Take That in a medley. And I played a new game called Game of Phones where I relived my call-centre days. My auntie Kirsty and uncle Mark came along to that show. Now that was a good night in the Green Room; we just plonked ourselves in a corner with a bottle of Prosecco each and people-watched.

Another week I got to watch the Kaiser Chiefs in the End-of-the-Show Show. That reminds me, I had actually met Ricky a month before this as I'm friends with Grace, his fiancée, who is a stylist. Now she kindly invited me to come along to one of the Kaiser Chiefs shows at the O2 arena, which was amazing. I got a little bit tiddly and ended up with a few others including my friend Showbiz Liz (legend) having a house party at Grace and Ricky's, leaving at about five in the morning. Now that is late for me, I like to be tucked up in bed by maximum 1 a.m. I am an absolute party pooper. Anyway the following day as I was hungover I ordered breakfast (Domino's) and I got papped. I knew at that point when my pictures were making the actual paper just from ordering a pizza that it was a slow news day; I mean who gives a flying fuck that a then-twenty-six-year-old girl is hungover and ordering a large pepperoni with seven chicken wings, wedges and four cookies (I was very hungover – I needed carbs)? They'll be papping me taking my bins out next (oh wait!).

My favourite ever episode was when I got to take part in *Ant and Dec: the Musical*. I loved the singing and dancing, and I got to play Ant and Dec's mother (they were twins in this production) and myself alongside Peter Andre in the jungle scene. Never in a million years would I have thought my dreams would come true of sharing a stage with Ant and Dec and meeting the most amazing talented people who I had watched on television my whole life. I mean I even got to play Sling a Sausage with Peter Andre, a man whose poster I had on my wall as a teenager (it was an online game involving hot dogs and a wall with cut-outs, you dirty-minded people).

I am so bloody grateful that Ant and Dec and ITV believed in me so much to give me that opportunity. It was a life-changing experience and one I'll treasure forever. Especially the grand finale in Walt Disney World Florida that was just magical and a real dream come true. See, I have always been a big supporter of the idea that you're never too old to believe in magic:

'You are never too old to dream a new dream.'

Chapter Twenty

BY GUV'NOR IT'S MARY BLEEDING POPPINS

★ In Disney's 1991 animated film *Beauty and the Beast*, the beast is a multitude of animals. He is a composition of a lion's mane, a gorilla's brow, a buffalo's beard and head, human's eyes, a bear's body, a wild boar's tusks, and a wolf's tail and legs.

★ Dwarf names that didn't make the cut in Disney's *Snow White* were: Jumpy, Deafy, Dizzy, Wheezy, Hickey, Baldy, Gabby, Nifty, Sniffy, Swift, Lazy, Puffy, Stuffy, Tubby, Shorty and Burpy.

★ Devices called Smellitizers can be found all over Disney parks. They emit scents in certain areas to match the surroundings, so the smell of baking cookies and vanilla is around Main Street, salty sea air surrounds the queue for the Pirates of the Caribbean ride and there's fresh citrus on Soarin'.

Disney has always been such a huge part of my life. My friends all say I live life through the eyes of a Disney princess. I always have and hopefully always will. I am constantly singing (in my best high-pitched, birds-tweeting-around-me, old-woman-knocking-on-my-door-offering-me-apples sort of singing voice), I waltz around the house and I always try to see the positive in every aspect of my life.

As a kid I would endlessly sit on the edge of my bed, eating Parma Violets and watching *Beauty and the Beast*. It was my favourite thing to do – I watched it that much it got to the point where I could honestly recite the whole script to you. I felt like I truly knew Belle when I watched her, sitting in my bed with my Groovy Chick duvet wrapped round me. That brunette lass from a small village, the one who felt like she just didn't quite fit in, the one who people thought was slightly strange as she would constantly have her head in a book ... I honestly felt like I could relate to Belle. We even had the same scraggly hair. (Up until Belle came along, Disney gave me unrealistic expectations of hair. I mean, whose hair looks like Ariel's when you get out of a pool? And don't even get me started on Princess Jasmine – come on, all that dry heat and humidity and not one bit of frizz? That's not real life!)

I love everything about *Beauty and the Beast*. Especially its morals. It taught us girls that just because Gaston is fancied by all the town, that he is a proper lad, that he has rippling muscles, that his arse looks like two eggs in a hanky, that you could grate Parmesan cheese on his abs and he has the glossiest hair ever seen on an animated man, it does not mean he isn't the bad guy. You can be the most handsome guy in town but can still be a chauvinistic fuck boy. I mean I'm not saying I agree with bestiality either. Or marrying someone that's locked you up against your own free will (Stockholm Syndrome?). But beauty is only skin deep and that message is important.

My flat in London is covered in *Beauty and the Beast* memorabilia. I have Cogsworth the clock, Lumière the candle, a Chip cup, and a Mrs Potts and Chip salt-and-pepper shaker. I have endless Disney quotes in frames. In the spare bedroom I have: 'Dear Peter Pan, I've left my window open. Please come rescue me.' In my bedroom I have the famous Belle quote: 'I want adventure in the great wide somewhere, I want it more than I can tell.' In my living room I have a famous Walt Disney quote: 'It's kind of fun to do the impossible.' I even have one in my toilet, obviously a Winnie the Pooh quote: 'Life is a journey to be experienced, not a problem to be solved.' I know at twenty-seven it's probably a little extreme but I believe you are never too old for Disney.

When the *Takeaway* team first told me, 'We are doing the live final show in Disney World Florida,' I could not control my emotions. When they continued, 'And you will be performing in front of the castle on Main Street, during a parade, dressed as Mary Poppins,' I knew then that all those years of believing in dreams wasn't silly: they do come true.

Waking up on the morning of travelling I experienced an emotion I wish I could bottle up and give to every single person. I literally felt like I was floating on air all the way to the airport. Meeting up with all of the two hundred fans of the show who had won tickets to come and watch the final was unreal. Everyone was on such a high.

As a treat for myself, I bought some magazines from WHSmith. Now although I love all the normal mags (you know the ones with cool, sexy names that entice you to buy them like *Cosmopolitan*, *Heat*, *OK!*, *Look*, *Closer*, *Reveal*, etc., where you find out all the celeb gossip whilst learning what you should be wearing and how to do your highlighter properly), when I'm on a plane I read things like *Take a Break*, *That's Life!*, *Chat* and *Real People*. Magazines that are basically *Jeremy Kyle* in print, with a few crosswords, and which tell you where the best place to buy your sausages for a casserole and how you can turn eight empty litre bottles of Coke, a piece of plywood and an old blanket into a new lounge chair for your living room. I absolutely love them and they got me through the long flight.

We arrived at an early hour of the morning at the Floridian Hotel in Orlando. I was with my good friend and producer Mike Spencer (he is one of the geniuses behind *Love Island* – you can thank him later). I knew I was going to get no sleep. I sat in my Belle pyjamas eating a full marzipan-shaped Mickey Mouse in the dark, knowing that in four hours I had to be up again to start rehearsals at the park. It was intense practising the next morning but I didn't care because I wanted to make sure I got everything perfect – this was a once-in-a-lifetime opportunity and I wanted to remember and feel every single second of it.

The day of the show arrived – four days of having fun at rehearsals had flown by, and I couldn't believe the day had finally come. Virgin Atlantic were kind enough to fly my mam, dad and Ava out to watch me. I felt like a movie star. They came to meet me in my very own RV which had my name on the door; it had a little movie director's seat with a light-up mirror and a fridge which was full of Fiji water (which obviously I had never drank before as it's about four quid a bottle so I made sure to drink my own bodyweight of it) and lots of chocolates and goodies.

'What do you think, Moffatts?' I said to my family. Ava hugged me so tight I could hardly breathe.

'This is just unbelievable,' my dad replied.

'Just think, Scarlett, if you could go back in time and say to those bullies that this is what would happen, or to the time you were nearly over your overdraft. It just feels surreal,' said my mam.

'It is bloody barmy. I still don't understand why it's happening to me but I suppose there's no point in over-analysing it. Best to just bloody enjoy it.'

The lovely Josh who was our Disney tour guide showed the family off to their seats, along with my old dance teacher Joan Martin (she was over in Florida by chance and I was delighted at the thought she could come and watch some of my moves).

'Enjoy the show!' I shouted. After getting my hair and make-up done I was escorted to the back of the stage. The crowd was huge. We were not expecting this; it was like the whole of Disney World had stopped to watch our show. We had Christina Ricci (I know, another childhood memory of *The Addams Family* and *Casper the Friendly Ghost*) as our guest announcer, CeeLo Green singing 'Forget You' and Cat Deeley (another one of my childhood legends – remember *SM:tv Live* with *Chums* and Wonkey Donkey?) as the thief who stole the missing crown jewels.

Now I have to admit I also wasn't prepared for the Floridian heat of 38 degrees Celsius. At one point in the show I had to run to the other side of the park to get everyone in the audience popcorn. I literally ran a mile, in the heat, in heels, with seven minutes on the clock live! But I absolutely love the thrill of live TV. Knowing that at any point it could all go tits up keeps the adrenaline going.

It got to the part in the show I'd been waiting for (well, for my whole life really), doing what I loved: singing and dancing. It was the 'Supercalifragilisticexpialidocious' scene. Ant, Dec, Stephen, me and Little Ant and Dec went down Main Street on a horse-drawn carriage with every single Disney character surrounding us, singing to the rooftops.

'You know you can say it backwards which is "docious-ali-expi-istic-fragil-cali-repus," I sang to Ant. I was led to the stage by two dancers and with tear-filled eyes I performed my little heart out. It was a thirty-second solo dance break to some, but to me in my head I was the real Mary Poppins on that stage. I could see my family and my old dance teacher Joan Martin in the crowd. The whole audience stood on their feet as Ant and Dec and Stephen made their way to the stage. The fireworks went off and the applause was like an army of drums banging.

The show was unreal and honestly watching Ant and Dec performing in their suits, in the heat, in Florida, LIVE, I just felt so privileged to even be on the same stage as them. I know that I'm the luckiest girl alive to be given these opportunities and to be learning from the best British TV presenters of our generation. We all sat and had a glass of champers afterwards to celebrate; even Holly Willoughby and her husband Dan

Baldwin came along as they were on holiday in Florida with their little ones.

Along with my little sister being born, my dad beating cancer, my graduation day and winning the jungle, that finale show in Disney is and always will be one of my favourite memories so far in my life.

Me and the family decided to stay on in Florida for another week. We literally went on every single ride, ate in every single restaurant, saw every single show and sang every Disney song possible. Ava even wore a Belle dress one day when we went to the Be our Guest restaurant. One of the waiters said to Ava, 'Oh Belle, I do apologise, the Beast did not tell us his wife was joining us for dinner this evening. One moment and I shall bring the master.'

With that, the lights dimmed and 'A Tale as Old as Time' came on. The waiter took Ava over to the Beast where she got to dance with him. It was just magical and a moment she will cherish forever.

Then, just when we thought the week couldn't get any better, I got a text from Warwick Davis (by the way, a little sidenote: he and his family are the nicest and kindest people you will ever meet).

It said: 'We watched the show. Are you still out here?'

'Yes, I'm with the family xx'

'Great, I'm here too at the *Star Wars* convention. Would you like to come along?'

'OMG!! Really?? That would be amazing xx'

So we met up with Warwick and his family, Sam, Annabelle and Harrison. Sometimes I just pinch myself and say, 'I can't believe this.' It doesn't even feel real. Honestly, the majority of times when things happen, I guess especially this last year, it feels like I'm watching it on the sofa with my parents. And then I get home and lie in bed and it'll hit us.

Sometimes things don't sink in for a long time. It's like it's not really happening. Then all of a sudden some time later, I'll just be sat watching the telly or on the bus going home and then I'm like, 'Oh my God, that really happened!' It is very overwhelming.

At the *Star Wars* convention we watched a show with Warwick and Anthony Daniels, who plays C-3PO. He was amazing, so funny. He actually wore a gold suit, and he had a cannon that he just randomly let off. It fired little golden sparkles. He's got his act very well honed.

Obviously, we were the only people there who weren't dressed up. So we stood out out like a sore thumb. Everyone really went for it. People had literally stuck fur to their skin to look like Chewbacca. How painful is that?

People had made their own costumes, and it must have taken them months. It was just unbelievable. People were embracing the characters and walking around as if they were them.

If someone from the Dark Side passed by, everyone else would move out of the way, as if it was real. There were lots of Darth Vaders and people in the actual Storm Trooper outfits. They must have cost a fortune – at least £3,000 each. And so hot as well in the Florida sun. Ava, me and my dad were saying, 'This is amazing!'

But I'm afraid my mam did not enjoy the convention so much. In fact, it was the worst day of her life. She hates *Star Wars*. She just says she doesn't get it. But she didn't just go off to the theme park. Oh no. She stayed with us all day and just moaned the whole way through.

She kept looking around at the people in costume and going, 'Oh my God, what a set of tits!'

And I was like, 'Be quiet! This is a once-in-a-lifetime opportunity. There are loads of people who would have loved to have come here.'

'I don't care. I think it's shite. There's something missing in all these people's lives. There's no need to dress up like that as if you're not yourself.'

'It's the same as us loving Disney, Mam. It's exactly the same.'

'It's not. It's not the same.'

'It's just escapism. If I could walk around like Belle or Tinker Bell, I would – if they did a costume big enough.'

Then the announcer said, 'And now a special preview.' It was a little advert for the new *Star Wars Rebels* cartoon. They showed that, and then he asked, 'Does anyone want to see more?'

And everyone was whooping and cheering, 'Yeah!'

'OK, you're going to watch an exclusive episode.'

It was a half-hour episode. And my Mam started crying. We were there about eight hours. She was sobbing, 'I can't take it any more, I need to get out.' But she couldn't just sneak out then because there was high security in the theatre. So she had to watch it through tear-filled eyes.

The minute we got out, she asked, 'Can we go now?'

We got an Uber, and the driver was saying, 'Oh my God, you're so lucky. I love *Star Wars*.' He actually had a *Star Wars* air freshener hanging from his rear-view mirror.

I was thinking, 'Oh my God, of all the Uber drivers we could have had!'

Warwick had given us these gold weekend passes that allowed you to get into everything but we were leaving the following day.

'Do you want the passes?' I asked the driver.

'What?'

'Do you want the passes?'

'What do you mean?'

'Well, you can have them. We're not going to use them again, we leave tomorrow.'

'Are you joking? I'm going to take the whole day off tomorrow. I'm going to ring my wife now and tell her the good news. Thank you so much!' He loved it.

I just thought, it is pure fate that our Uber driver was such a massive *Star Wars* fan – it was meant to be. After all, it takes no effort to be kind and if you can't be kind in Disneyland then it basically means you have no soul. As Cinderella once said:

'Where there is kindness there is goodness; where there is goodness there is magic.'

Chapter Twenty-one

THE TIME I WATCHED *JEREMY KYLE* WITH KEVIN BACON

★ The nineties UK classic TV show *Gladiators* had a total of thirty-four gladiators. Eunice ended up being a stunt double for Angelina Jolie and Rhino appeared in films such as *Pirates of the Caribbean: On Stranger Tides*, *Batman Begins*, and *Argo*.

★ In *Footloose*, the actors who played the parents are barely older than the kids. Dianne Wiest (mother) was only nine years older than Ariel (Lori Singer) at the time and John Lithgow (father) was twelve years older.

★ The BAFTA Awards' famous mask was designed by US sculptor Mitzi Cunliffe and it weighs 3.7 kg.

This year has just been proper mental and I know I'm never going to get a year in my life that's greater and that's why I've loved and cherished every single minute of (what some would call) work. I honestly have been like a pig in shit, I've been lapping it up. I've been blessed enough to be part of two of my favourite television shows of all time with my heroes: *I'm a Celebrity ... Get Me Out of Here!* and *Saturday Night Takeaway*. I used to have no luck at all, couldn't even win a bloody raffle me, but this year I've been lucky enough to be able to present backstage and give out an award at the National Television Awards (NTAs), which was actually my first ever invite to an awards ceremony. In fact it was the first time I'd ever set foot on a red carpet (well, apart from a Blackpool B&B that me and my mam once stayed at where the carpets were red and the walls were green).

I took my dad as my date and we were given a blacked-out car to take us (no joke) thirty seconds across the car park. We giggled as we made the long trip from my dressing room to the carpet, but we felt dead posh and that. Once we had taken selfies with people, signed autographs and had our picture taken by the press, I went backstage and sat in my dressing room while the family went up into a box to watch.

I was so nervous. I had actually bought my outfit for the event four hours earlier in Topshop. Not ideal: I had had an outfit made for me but when I got it I looked like I worked for a really shit airline in a blood-red ill-fitted suit complete with shoulder pads an American footballer would be jealous of. So I ended up wearing an £80 suit with a black vest from River Island underneath. But it was fuchsia pink, I had my hair in a high pony and my skin was highlighted to the gods so I didn't care.

It was funny though when interviewers asked, 'Who are you wearing, Scarlett?'

'Well, I'm wearing myself, mate, but my outfit is from Toppers – £80 it is and the vest's £6 from River Island.'

When I first walked on stage to hand out the first NTA of the night with Dermot O'Leary (the king of live TV), my throat started going that dry it was as if water had never touched my lips in a year. I was so nervous but managed to somehow read the autocue whilst having someone tell me how long I had left to chat for in my ear. My first ever interview of my life was with none other than Danny Dyer. Now I absolutely love Danny Dyer – I have a bit of a crush on him to be honest – so needless to say I was shitting a brick and my heart was skipping beats. 'Please don't swear, Danny, I'm not saying you would but it's my first interview and I love you.'

'I won't, darling. You got nothing to worry about, sweetheart.'

And I knew he wouldn't, he's a good egg is Danny. After finding out on *Who Do You Think You Are?* that he was in fact royalty and was related to William the Conqueror and Edward III, I wanted to know more about how it had changed things around his house.

'So, have things changed now you're royalty?' I asked him.

'No, and the Queen still hasn't welcomed me into the Windsor fold. Give me a bell, babes.'

I didn't even know what to reply so I just said, 'You are the most Cockniest person I have ever met.'

I soon eased into the interviewing after being able to

chat to Ant and Dec, the lovely
Holly Willoughby and Phillip
Schofield (who by the
way are literally the nicest
people in showbusiness).
Before I knew it, the
night had nearly ended,
so I slipped on my tiger
slippers and was about to
head out when I heard,
'Mary Berry is coming
backstage, *Bake Off* has just won!'
'Ahhh, shit, it's so dark back here, I don't
know where my shoes are.' I couldn't find
them in time to chat to Mary Berry and have a photo with
her, so I now have a framed picture in my living room of me
and the person everyone wants to adopt as their gran, Mary
Berry, with huge lovely tiger slippers on my feet.

The day after the NTAs I was on a high, I had so many
amazing tweets and Instagram posts about my presenting
job, I felt like a professional. That was until I read the
papers. Now in some articles I was in the 'hot' section with
what I was wearing but in one particular newspaper I was
in the 'not' section. Why, I thought, I liked my outfit, did

they think it was too pink, did it clash with my orange tan? No, apparently 'I didn't show my figure off and it wasn't a gown.' I mean the person who wrote the article was clearly an Einstein for pointing out the obvious that I wasn't wearing a dress. Also I had short shorts on, my legs were out, but did they have to be? Erm, no! I could have worn a turtleneck jumpsuit if I'd wanted to. It's so sexist how I was told I basically wasn't revealing enough. Come on, guys, it's 2017! Women can wear what the hell we want and we don't need some journalist to tell us if we are hot or not!

Next came the BAFTAs, which I was super shocked at being asked to present an award at (as in all honesty I wasn't even expecting an invite to attend in the audience). I know how much of a prestigious event it is and I was completely honoured. Not many people get invited and the people who do are absolute stars. I always love watching the BAFTAs and seeing all the amazing frocks but being there in person was breathtaking.

I took my mam along as my date and when we arrived we were escorted to a lift, a lift that David Haye was casually standing in. I clenched my mam's hand and whispered, 'O. M. G. It's David Haye, Mam, look.'

'I know,' she whispered. 'I can see, it's only a little lift, he might hear us.'

We giggled and went to our seats. We then spent the next half an hour before the show being fan girls and admiring the room.

'Joanna Lumley is five rows in front of us, Mam.'

'Sweetie darling.'

'Look to your left, Benedict Cumberbatch is there. Look to

your right, there's Jennifer Saunders. And look down there, it's Dame Joan Collins.'

'Now seriously, Scarlett, how does she look that good? She looks younger than us.'

The awards ceremony began and me and my mam were just in awe. Halfway through I was taken backstage with Aisling Bea who I was presenting the 'Reality & Constructed Factual' award with. I bumped into Charlie Brooker, Charlotte Riley and was sat next to none other than Chuck Bass (Ed Westwick) from *Gossip Girl*. Louis Theroux was backstage too and we ended up having a conversation about feminism (one to tick off my bucket list). Me and Aisling had created an *Anchorman*-style sketch to present the award where we would read out full stops, pauses and mistakes on the autocue. Luckily people laughed and I could now relax.

Me and my mam were so hungry after the show. Obviously we didn't dare eat anything before the BAFTAs as I only have to look at a chip and I bloat to the point where people mistake me for being 'with child'. The food was divine and my mam told me to 'stop being a tit' because everything that came out I would say, 'Oh so for the main we are having BAFTA glazed carrots, with BAFTA mash, with BAFTA beef with beautiful BAFTA gravy lavished all over it for a bit of BAFTA moistness.'

'Right, stop saying BAFTA or I will be BAFTAing out of the door, into the BAFTA taxi, all the way to your BAFTA house, got it?'

It is a night me and my mam will both remember forever and I wish I could do it all a-BAFTA-gain.

I have also got to take part in absolute nineties nostalgia

by bringing back the cult classic *Streetmate* (which I will chat loads about in the next chapter) and of course by participating in *The Crystal Maze*. All I need now is to have Jet from *Gladiators*' legs wrapped round me, a cameo on *Absolutely Fabulous* and to present the weather on *Big Breakfast*, and my childhood is officially complete.

The set for *The Crystal Maze* was massive compared to what I thought it was going to be, like I was actually out of breath when I made my way from the futuristic zone to the medieval zone. I felt like I was actually travelling back through time. I knew I would be the first and only person to get locked in on one of the challenges because my mam had already predicted it. I was put on a team with Steve Jones, David Coulthard, Jodie Kidd and Joey Essex. Now I have always loved Joey, this was only the second time I had ever met him but he is a genuinely lovely chap. Yes, he only wears a watch for decorative purposes as he can't tell the time but that doesn't make him a bad person, does it? He is someone that, if I ever got the chance, I'd like to have a tour of Essex with; he could show me the sights.

We managed to get most of the crystals (they kindly got rid of one of them to get me out of the room I was locked in). We really did all put our hearts and soul into it as we did it for Stand up to Cancer, a charity close to all our hearts. We managed to get 112 gold tickets in total. Now as an avid fan of *The Crystal Maze* I knew we had to make sure we got rid of all the silver tickets out of the dome as they cancelled the gold tickets out. So me and my nimble fingers picked out every silver I could see. We managed to get 112 gold and only seven silver tickets: £20,000 won for cancer research. We were over the moon. We even got our very own 'We Cracked the Crystal Maze' commemorative crystals for keeps.

People on the television are super lucky, I mean getting the chance to do *The Crystal Maze*, it was so bloody fun, I'd have paid to do it. Another 'job' which I can't believe is a job is *Celebrity Juice* with Keith Lemon. When I went on there I was on Fern's team with Jonathan Ross (Wossy). Opposite me was none other than Holly Willoughby, Baby Spice Emma Bunton and Gino D'Acampo. We were carrying furniture whilst getting hit with plywood by a little person. I watched Wossy lick a man's arsehole (obviously he wasn't to know), Gino entered a sex party and I nearly died (at least three times) in a mechanical chair while shouting out answers to questions like:

'Name three things you find in a cage?'

'A hamster, a rat, a person!'

'Three places you can't take your clothes off?'

'In public, the zoo, a nursery!'

One of the many highlights this year was filming adverts. I did some online adverts for Suzuki where I had to stick as many Post-it notes on a car as possible, play the *Generation Game* and pop balloons inside a car with my nails. Another one was for Virgin Atlantic which I absolutely loved; I had to be interviewed by three children on my knowledge of Disney and Virgin (obviously I aced it).

And then there was my advert with Kevin Bacon for EE. Now my advert was straight after the one he did with Britney Spears (no pressure) so I was honoured to be chosen. In my head, as the other adverts were filmed in studios I had assumed we'd be doing the same, but little did I know it would be filmed on a cold beach in the middle of nowhere in Hastings. Beautiful place but I have never felt cold like it. I was wearing a sack, a little pair of shorts and some thermals. I had to pretend to eat a witchetty grub, which brought back all sorts of traumatic flashbacks from the jungle. I did joke with Kevin Bacon, 'Do you want me to save you a bit in case you're hungry later?' but I don't think he heard me. I would love to experience that day again – it was just bizarre, but also I never knew you could have that much fun whilst not being able to feel your whole body from freezation (I understand this isn't a real word but you can keep it, same as the word me and my mam use for someone who is really nasty, we say they are full of evility).

At one point me and Kevin Bacon (I had to restrain myself from singing *Footloose* every two seconds) were sat having a cup of tea watching *Jeremy Kyle* on set. I mean there's something I never thought I would be able to write down. I think the tagline was: 'Who stole my grandad's dole money?'

Now I was trying to act cool around Bacon (that's my nickname for him as I've met him for ten hours so obviously that means we are now soul sisters) but at one point I was strutting up the hill when a gust of wind came and I heard Jadeen (my agent) and Nicola (who sorts my hair and make-up out) shout, 'Scarlett, your pants!' To my horror I was standing there with my shorts wrapped round my ankles; luckily I had big granny-pant thermals on underneath otherwise Kevin would have got a shock. 'I'm not intentionally mooning you, Kevin,' I apologised. I was so mortified I could feel my face turn beetroot. Luckily he just giggled and saw the funny side

To my horror I was standing there with my shorts wrapped round my ankles.

of it, but I will never live it down and I can never watch *Footloose* in the same way again.

Life is very surreal at the moment. Sometimes I just sit and think, *oh my actual God*. It is so overwhelming how my whole life has changed in such a short space of time. To be honest I never want it to end. I mean if it did, I'd be happy to go back to my life being a disability advisor but I just feel so lucky to be having these experiences.

Now even though the positives outweigh the negatives, there are a few bad points, like getting papped even when you're just taking your dog for a walk or taking the bins out – and because of that the pressure of feeling like you should make an effort to look good all the time. But the worst part is the social media trolls or the people who comment beneath the *Daily Mail* articles (I've learnt not to read them now). But I don't hate the trolls; like I've said before, I pity them. They're lacking something in their lives, God bless them.

The positives, though, I mean where do I begin? It was only a year ago I was watching people like Tom Hardy, Ant and Dec, Alan Carr and Rylan on the television, and now they're in my phone book. I was watching shows with my family ordering a chicken kebab and having a glass of Lambrini and now I'm *in* the bloody shows. I pop to the shops for a pint of milk and people want to stop and have a chat and a selfie with me. The magazines I would read lying in bed hungover on a Sunday (contemplating what is my life), I'm now in. This has all happened in the space of a year. The strange thing is that even as I write this book I still don't feel like a celebrity. I don't think my family and friends would ever let me, to be fair. I'm treated no different and rightly so. They do, however, often tell me to stop for a second and take it all in.

My mam always says, 'You don't know how long this journey is going to last so enjoy it while it does.' And that is what I do: that's why you will very rarely see me without a smile on my face and that's why whenever I get a chance to involve my family and friends, I do. I have a really small group of close friends and family and to be honest they're the only people I really bother with. I used to think when I was younger it was about having loads of friends but as the story 'The Vixen and the Lioness' in my *Aesop's Fables* taught me:

'Quality is more important that quantity.'

Chapter Twenty-two

THAT'S A STREETMATE

★ Davina McCall appeared as a dancer in the music video 'Word Is Out' for pop princess Kylie Minogue, wearing a striped sweater and beret.

★ Statistics show that women who use online dating are most afraid to meet up with someone who ends up being a serial killer; meanwhile, men said they are most afraid of meeting up with someone who won't allow them free time or let them meet with their friends whenever they want.

★ Scientists believe it takes humans just one-fifth of a second to determine whether we fancy another person.

My phone vibrated as I was alerted that my car had arrived and was waiting outside the restaurant Pescatori, where I had just had a meeting with Channel 4. We had been discussing bringing back the nineties cult classic, *Streetmate*. A very fancy Onyx Mercedes had arrived and the driver got out of the car to open the door for me.

'Thanks very much but you didn't have to get out of your car to do that,' I said. He giggled away and confirmed the address of where I was going. 'Yes, that's right, just near Chalk Farm tube station, cheers.' I sat on the ivory leather seat in the back of this very fancy car, staring out of the blacked-out windows.

'There is wi-fi service in the car, Madam, bottled water on the side and some Polos inside the arm rest,' the driver told me.

'Wow, I've never been in a car with free Polos before, thanks,' I said. I quickly pocketed the Polos (I love a freebie).

The meeting had been amazing and there was one person I needed to call to let her know I had got the gig.

'Mam, I'm going to be hosting *Streetmate*!'

'Wow, you're going to be a little mini Davina! I'm so proud.'

'Oh, I hope I do Davina proud. If I can be a tenth of the presenter she is I'll be super happy.'

'Ah, I'm sure you will be, love.'

'Mam, I'm buzzing that it's been brought back. I mean it might actually encourage people to meet face to face, to start to date the old-fashioned way again, like walking up to someone in a bar or a supermarket and asking for their number.'

'You never know, Scarlett.'

'I mean, let's be honest, Mam, what with all these dating apps and people sliding into everybody's inbox and having sneaky DMs on social media, there's no ambience to dating any more. You just swipe left or right at a photo that's been filtered to the hills and hope you're not being catfished. I mean, no one walks around in real life with a constant Valencia or X-Pro filter, with the saturation turned down and a slight bit of Facetune. It's just not real any more. Also I feel like no good love story started out with some bloke sending a picture of his penis to his potential future wife and mother to his children.'

'Scarlett, that's dirty.'

'Why Mam, that's what happens these days, like some of the girls have these apps and have even been sent messages the day after a night out asking if they were in Vodka Revs last night, rather than the guy just going up and asking them for their number when they were actually out. People are too scared of rejection. No one likes the thought of somebody saying no to their face. But they don't mind doing it to other people via a screen. I just think shy bairns get nothing, you've got to ask. What's the worst someone can say: "No, you can't have my number"? Well then, they were never the one anyway.'

'I do think you watch too many Disney movies and you have grand ideas of what love should be like, Scarlett.'

'No, I think apps and dating sites are great, especially if you have a busy profession or you don't have a lot of time, or you don't enjoy going out or you're shy. It's a great way for people to meet. Plus, then when you meet up with that person you feel that instant spark and it's not that awkward small talk as you already know a little about them. I just hope that with *Streetmate* I can build people's confidence up when it comes to actually going out and talking to people you don't know.' That was what I really wanted to achieve with the show.

I was about to film my first ever episode of *Streetmate*, just two months after the initial chat about presenting the show. I was given the task of presenting fifteen episodes; that's thirty dates, that's sixty potential people who could have found true love by the end of the series (or just a lot of shit, awkward dates). Love makes me giddy, and my heart just melts when I see an elderly couple walking hand in hand down the street; however, I must add I also love seeing the single independent characters. Being single is just as great as being in a relationship sometimes. No awkward meetings with the in-laws and having to pretend you like them. And you don't have to endure watching a whole season of a show you have no interest in at all. Although on a negative note, you are always put on the shit table at a wedding, sat with the odd uncles and black sheep of the family. But whether you're single, coupled up with bae, engaged, married, divorced or asexual, I say embrace it!

I had arrived into Bristol to film the lovely George. He wanted a girl aged between eighteen and twenty-four who, and I quote, 'wore earrings and had skinny blue jeans with a white T-shirt on'. This was going to be harder than I first anticipated. People are so bloody fussy. I was just looking at people who were smiling and looked like they had brushed their hair that morning, but some people have a very specific type. We had one girl who kept turning everyone down because she specifically wanted someone who was wearing chestnut-brown brogues and a tweed jacket. I mean, come on, people can change their bloody shoes! Also they might be a builder and have to wear steel toecap boots to work, I mean a tweed jacket just doesn't look right teamed with a high-vis. I had to tell some of them, 'Look, this is why you're single, stop being so fussy' (I know it's harsh but I just wanted them to find love).

I'm not saying go for somebody who you don't fancy at all but if there's one thing I've learnt doing this show and which I've passed on to my friends, it's this: if you have more than four things on your list of your 'ideal partner' then you need to knock some off. Because sometimes this 'ideal partner' just doesn't exist.

Bristol was great, I'd even been given security. Now this wasn't because I think I'm big time like Beyoncé and need protecting, it's more because sometimes people get a bit carried away when they see a camera and, well, turn into knobheads, to put it frankly. If one more man dabs in front of me or shouts the infamous phrase 'F**k her right in the p*ssy', I'll scream.

However, the first security man wasn't actually sure what his job entailed and was just comical. He kept disappearing and turning up with things like pulled pork sandwiches, a bag of homemade fudge for his wife from a market and selfies with local landmarks. He also told us we needed to get a taxi to get to the Bristol Canal dock. The taxi ended up costing £1.80 and the destination was literally round the corner, I mean it took us longer to get in the taxi, fasten our seatbelts, tell the driver where we were going and pay him than it would have done to walk all of twenty steps. We quickly got rid of Frankie and ended up with the lovely Justin and Michael. Michael actually ended up fancying one of the ladies who I was trying to find a date for (she was a doppelganger for Janet Jackson – nineties Janet Jackson not 2017 Janet Jackson). After a lot of flirty banter (flanter) I decided to set them two up on a date with each other and they ended up leaving hand in hand (cutiepies).

One of my favourite dates was with seventy-six-year-old Geraldine Firequeen. What a hoot! She rocked up looking like a glamorous gran with flowers in her hair and a spring in her step. She had been married four times and wrote erotic novels to pass the time and classed herself as a white witch. After telling me she was psychic, I decided to put her powers to the test.

'Can you guess what star sign I am, Geraldine?'

'Ooh yes, definitely Pisces.'

'No, not quite, I'll give you another guess.'

'Cancer?'

'No. And again.'

'Taurus?'

This went on for another couple of minutes until she finally guessed correctly, 'Libra.'

'By George, you've got it, Geraldine, you have the gift.'

We proceeded around the picturesque town of Didsbury (I'll openly admit at first glance I thought it was somewhere where posh northerners went to die, but I take it all back, it's very trendy and the people there are very welcoming and friendly). After Geraldine had eyed up a fishmonger, a guy in Tesco and a twenty-three-year-old estate agent, I finally found her dream man sitting in a quiet country pub: Jeff. Let me paint a picture of wor Jeff. He was a tanned seventy-one-year-old Sean Connery lookalike with a turtleneck jumper casually set off by a suit jacket. He collected classic cars, sailed and played the trumpet. I knew Geraldine was going to be thrilled.

She came into the pub and met Jeff for the first time. 'Wow, you've sparked something in me which I haven't felt since 2005,' she proclaimed.

'Well, I'm speechless, it's so lovely to meet you, Geraldine,' he said.

I started to cry as I watched the two meet. I think it's lovely that even if they didn't find romance they found a new companion; they swapped email addresses (which is cute) to stay in touch. You are never too old to make new friends or to find love.

That reminds me – I often film bits called 'vox pops'. It's where I run up to random people on the street and ask them questions. So I asked one husband and wife, 'Can you remember your first ever date with each other?'

'Yes, even though we've been married forty-five years.'

'And what was the date like?'

'Bloody dreadful.'

It's so funny some of the answers people would give me. I even got proposed to by a man with two tear tattoos on his face at one point. But the funniest vox pop I did was with two eighty-year-olds. They both had blue cardigans on as if they'd purposefully matched for the date, they were holding hands and he kept giving her little kisses on the forehead. It was beautiful to watch that they were so in love.

'Excuse me, sir, could you please tell me what was the first thing that attracted you to this beautiful lady?'

'Of course. We first met at a bus stop, she was waiting for the 181 and she had a lilac cardigan on. I was drawn to her brown eyes; they were glowing with adventure and made me feel young again.'

'Wow,' I gasped. I was quite taken back by such a poetic response. 'Feel young again?' I continued. 'So how long have you been together?'

'Oooh, about three years now, lovey.'

'Ahhh, this is such a great story. Do you mind if I ask you a couple more questions but we film it for this new show *Streetmate*?'

'What, to be on TV? Oh no, lovey, we can't be doing that. You see my wife doesn't know I'm out with this one. We meet up once a week and head into Cheltenham. I've been married to my actual wife for over fifty years and she's been with her husband for over forty.'

I paused, waiting for the laugh or the punchline, but no, there wasn't one. I mean I didn't think that people cheated on each other after a certain age – shows how naive I am. Needless to say, we didn't use that part for the show.

That night I was ready for my bed; some of the days were 7.30a.m. starts and we would finish at 9.30p.m. I didn't mind as this was my dream job, but this running around was doing nothing for my bunions (sexy, I know). I ordered room service (a tuna sandwich, as normal) and started flicking through my phone. I noticed I had a new message on Twitter.

@scarlettmoffatt from @thisisdavina

'I just wanted to say good luck with *Streetmate*, you are going to smash it xxxxx'

Oh my giddy aunt. The fact that Davina firstly knows I exist, and secondly has wished me luck. It meant so much, I felt like that was her seal of approval. I hope I haven't let her down. I tried my hardest to hook everyone up and get as close to their 'type on paper' as possible.

The next day, me and all the crew travelled back to London to film in Covent Garden. Now I'm going to be totally honest with you as there's no point in lying, I thought London was going to be really difficult. Even though everyone's friendly, the thought of running up to people when they're clearly in a rush got me anxious. 'What happens if everyone just says they're too busy?' I said to Suzy the producer. 'I mean everyone's got somewhere to be in London, they might think if I run over to them that I'm trying to sell them something or that I'm one of those annoying people that ask if you've ever been in an accident and if you want to sue the person responsible?'

But I had nothing to worry about; it turns out people do want love in London. However, filming took longer than expected what with me having to stop every five minutes with anxiety from all the bloody pigeons. I mean they're everywhere, watching us with their beady eyes. They don't care about flapping their wings inches away from you looking like they're going to kamikaze into you. And where's all their babies? I mean seriously, have you ever seen a baby pigeon?

The most bizarre thing happened in Covent Garden. I was trying to find a date for this fifty-year-old man. He kept picking out twenty-year-old blondes so I told him, 'Remember, they've got to fancy you back, this is a two-way thing!' I didn't mean it rudely but seriously some people think because a TV camera is there, people are automatically gonna say yes. Anyway I was starting to give up hope when I spotted a beautiful-looking woman in her forties in the window of Carluccio's. 'Are you single?' I mouthed. She nodded and I ran in there faster than eight-year-old me when I heard the ice-cream van. To my disbelief she was on FaceTime to her dating coach (you can't make this stuff up). Not only that but she was flying back to Melbourne that night so was super keen. 'Yes, let's just do the date now,' she demanded confidently. Turns out she is a socialite in Australia and is famous in her own right. She was even bridesmaid for the princess of Denmark. Eeeh, the people you meet and the stories you hear when you take time to stop and chat.

I'll be honest, their date didn't go amazingly well, neither did anyone's really. I mean they all had nice, fun times but out of thirty couples only one of them actually became an item. But I guess that's love, you've got to kiss a lot of frogs before you find your Prince Charming. Or in my case a lot of mammy boys and egotistical, cheating, lazy boys with 'little man' syndrome.

I mean seriously, they say love hides behind every corner, but I must have been walking around in circles half my life. But love works in mysterious ways. Everything happens for a reason and fingers crossed in fifty years I will be sat with the love of my life, in a garden with a donkey called Aurora, being proper pensioners, drinking cups of tea, dunking digestives, moaning about the weather and saying phrases like, 'We only had one dishwasher back in my time, bloody kids these days, they don't know they're born.' Some people (me included) had an image of what the man of my dreams should look like, but I didn't realise that by having a specific type in my head I was turning everyone down who didn't quite reach up to that image. I was letting so many incredible people pass me by.

So whatever makes you happy – dating, not dating, relationship status: taken or relationship status: single – just be you! As some genius once said:

'Be weird, be random, be who you are.
Because you never know who would love
the person you hide.'

Chapter Twenty-three

CROSS MY PALM
WITH SILVER

★ The pyramids were originally covered with casing stones made of highly polished white limestone. Because of this, it is said that the pyramids could have been seen from the mountains in Israel and maybe even from the moon.

★ When Stephen Hawking was nine, he was ranked the worst student of the class (bet he doesn't lose sleep over that school report).

★ Mystic Meg the astrologist's real name is actually Margaret Anne Lake.

Now call me Mystic Meg and cross my palm with silver, but I kinda predicted the future. You may want to book me for some tarot card reading and crystal chakra realness once you've read this, so hold on to your horoscopes. In April 2016, I released my last book *Scarlett Says* (where I basically just chatted about my thoughts on everything from Jeremy Clarkson to the moon landings). In it I did a little section on 'Dream jobs: five jobs I would love to do'.

Obviously being Ant and Dec's sidekick was up there. I quote: 'Imagine hanging out with those boys all day and having a laugh. I would love it.' Well, in response to Scarlett from the past here's Scarlett from the future: 'You will love it, it is a great laugh and how the fuck did you manage to make this happen?'

Another job I said I would have loved was a radio presenter. I wrote that I would 'chat shit all day and finish work by lunchtime, it would be mint'. Now in response to that I can now say: 'It's a lot harder than it seems. It is an amazing job, but only once you've managed to prise your eyes open – as they're stuck together with sleep from waking up when the moon's shining – and you've had your first three cups of tea and half a packet of chocolate digestives.'

Now one that didn't quite come true but I'm putting it on this list as I feel that I am one step closer to getting an interview for this job is 'Stephen Hawking's assistant'. I have so many questions and I feel like he could answer them for me, plus if I was his assistant people would take my outlook on some theories seriously instead of looking at me with a blank expression.

So when I was doing *I'm a Celebrity … Get Me Out of*

Here!, me, Adam and Lisa were chatting about Egypt so I thought I'd pass on my views about how I think the pyramids were made.

'I proper believe that the fact the pyramids are there is proof of time travel. I watched this documentary and then read up about it loads after, and Stephen Hawking has said it would be possible to travel back in time; we would just need to go faster than the speed of light.'

Lisa and Adam seemed genuinely interested so I continued.

'Now the speed of light is exactly the same number as the coordinates of the Great Pyramid of Giza – which is 299,792 [the speed of light is actually 299, 792, 458 metres per second, and the coordinates of the pyramid are 29.9792458°N]. Now this cannot be a coincidence. Also the pyramid lines up exactly to the star consolation Orion's Belt. How would the Egyptians know that so many years ago?'

Now at this point Adam is proper interested.

'Yeah, I actually sent my idea of what all this means to Stephen Hawking but I never got a response,' I continued. 'Coz I think the pyramids are from the future, I think someone from the future realised we would need them and went back in time and built them, maybe as a navigation system to get from the Orion's Belt. Or maybe the hieroglyphics are actually how we write in the future, I mean really they're just big emojis. Who even writes "I'm laughing" in a text any more? You don't, you just put the laughing face emoji.'

Lisa was really confused, not about my theory but how I managed to find Stephen Hawking's details. 'But how did you manage to find out how to get in touch with him?'

'Well, after spending most of my day trying to find his contact details I found an email address on Google: *stephenhawking@ hotmail.co.uk*. So to be honest, on reflection, I don't think it was his account. I can't really imagine him having hotmail.'

So after the show during *Extra Camp*, Ant and Dec announced, 'We got an email from Stephen Hawking after that about Scarlett's theory. He said he enjoyed her thoughts on the pyramids.'

Now I know this doesn't mean he's going to be inviting me to do any work with him at Cambridge University any time soon but it does mean he knows I exist and I'm one step closer to that call: 'Do you want to meet up for a coffee, Scarlett, and become my assistant in some time-travel shizz I've got going on?'

As well as my predictions, I also sometimes have premonitions – well, more like coincidences really. I was helping my dad paint my Harry Potter cupboard, sorry I mean my room, about four years ago. 'Do you know what I could do with, Dad? A new mattress. Like I would love one of those memory foam mattresses.' No quicker had the words come out my mouth than there was a knock at the door. Me dad ran down the stairs and about two minutes later shouted up for me. 'Scarlett, quick, you are never going to believe this.'

There were two men stood there selling memory foam mattresses. 'You have got to be kidding. Are there cameras in this house?' we laughed. We purchased the mattress from the back of a van for a bargain price of eighty quid and it is honestly the comfiest bed I've ever had. Weird or what?

Go back to 2007 when I was seventeen, I had just started at Queen Elizabeth Sixth Form College, which I loved. You were supposed to go to these compulsory classes called General

Studies. Why, I do not know. They didn't count towards your UCAS points for university, they were always super early on a morning and in my opinion they weren't really needed. You would learn snippets of information about politics, ethics, science, technology and mathematics. Now in all honesty I didn't enjoy that class, I thought it was a waste of time, and so did my mate Katie. So we would spend the time that we should have been at that class doing productive stuff like shopping or going for breakfast.

Now on one of these days we spotted an old lady struggling with her shopping bags. She looked quite lost and everyone was just walking past her. We approached her.

'Are you OK?' I asked.

'Not really, dear. I have forgotten how to get home.'

'It's OK, we will help you. Whenever I forget something I always ring someone in my family. Is there anyone we can call who will be able to help?'

'Well, yes, I have daughters. One of them works at the college just up by the bank.'

'Great, have you got her mobile number or name and we can call her?' She didn't have her number but we called the college and asked for Mrs Beath.

'Hi, is Mrs Beath there please? It's very important. We have her mam with us wanting to speak to her.'

'Yes, putting you through now.'

Mrs Beath came and collected her and took the lovely lady home. We were so happy she got back safe. Right now, fast-forward two weeks and another two missed General Studies classes, I received a letter explaining I had a meeting with the head teacher about my attendance.

I walked into the office wondering what repercussions were heading my way. Well, guess who was the head? Only Mrs Beath. She giggled when I walked in. 'Well, Scarlett, firstly thank you so much for making sure my mam got home safely, it was very kind of you. I was going to be telling you what was going to happen due to you missing eight classes which is the maximum you can miss, but I understand that you missed one due to helping my mam, so if you can make sure you don't miss any more classes we will leave it at that.'

I mean, if that isn't karma I don't know what is.

So with all these crazy premonitions and coincidences I thought I would try and predict what the future has in store for me (or more to the point what I would love to happen to me). So here are my dream jobs that I would love to get by 2020.

2020 Top Five Dream Jobs

To have a part in a West End musical
Imagine having a job where you get to sing, dance, act and play dress-up all day. Ideally I would love to play my childhood heroine Belle in *Beauty and the Beast* but I'd settle for Mrs Potts, to be fair.

To be a part of *Strictly Come Dancing*
With eighteen years of ballroom and Latin knowledge up my sleeve I would love to dive headfirst back into all that glitter, fake tan and snakehips action. To be honest, in an ideal world (I mean this is my dreams page, after all), I would

love to be a judge or presenter. But if I can't achieve that I'd happily pull the rope that lifts the curtain up for them at Blackpool Tower ballroom.

To write a children's book
I'd love to be a little Pied Piper of literature. I feel pure joy and happiness when I watch my little sister get lost in a book and I would love to bring this happiness to other children too.

To be a chocolate tester
I feel like this needs no explanation other than the fact you would actually get paid to eat chocolate (plus no one could ever make you feel guilty about eating three family-sized bars of Cadburys as you could reply, 'Well, I'm just doing my job').

To carry on doing what I'm doing now
To be perfectly honest I am living my dream now. I get to work with legends like Ant and Dec, meet amazing people every day and get to present on shows I have watched for years.

I am so grateful I get to do a job I love. I realise how lucky I am. I mean I get to do things like chat to you through this book and it's made me reflect on my life so far. I have learnt so much. I have learnt that despite my parents being the most sarcastic people I know, despite them choosing my name over a game of Scrabble and them 'character-building' me – well, taking the piss out of my monobrow – for most of my life, it is their way of showing me they love me. I know I am very lucky to have two people that are always there for me no matter what.

I have learnt that I am lucky enough to have a sister who loves me enough to always tell me the truth if she thinks my fake tan is streaky and my hair looks like, and I quote, 'a hot mess'.

I have learnt that the gaggle of girls who tried to make my life hell at school made me a stronger person and they may have won a few battles but they did not win the war.

I have learnt to finally love my face despite trying to hide it for so long after the Bell's palsy and the accident. In fact I love it so much I now take selfies of it and post them online for everyone to see.

And I have learnt that life is fucking crazy and by saying yes to just one opportunity, in my case *Gogglebox*, your life can change overnight. So after experiencing what feels like a million things in just twenty-seven years I have learnt that life is full of ups and downs. And even though I've had some rough times, I can't complain because:

'Me life is sofa so good.'

THE YOUNG GIRL AND HER PLAITS FABLE

Once upon a time there was a young girl who always said and did things that others around her said were strange. She would sing aloud whilst wearing her hair in two plaits. She would go metal-detecting whilst asking questions about pyramids and aliens. And she was forever telling people facts about everything.

'Why are you so weird, why don't you just act like a normal, ordinary person?' said a classmate to the young girl. 'Don't you want to fit in?'

So that's exactly what the young girl did. She let down her plaits that night and the next day she acted like the other girls around her. She tried to fit in. She managed it for a whole six hours.

'How are you enjoying acting normal for a change?' said the classmate.

'Well,' replied the young girl, 'I am bored.'

'I don't understand,' said the classmate.

'See, I have come to realise I don't mind not fitting in. I have realised I don't want to be ordinary. I got bored acting like everybody else. I don't want to change myself just to blend in with everybody else. I have decided to go back to being me.'

And with that, the young girl smiled to her classmate and skipped off, singing out loud whilst plaiting her hair.

Moral of Scarlett's Fable: '*Stay true to who you are even if people try to change you and you will live a happy life.*'

ACKNOWLEDGEMENTS

I would like to thank every single person that has supported me, just by watching me on the TV, by reading this book, by following me on Twitter, Instagram and Facebook, or by coming up to me in the street and simply having a chat or a selfie. To everyone who voted for me in *I'm a Celebrity*, I wish I could give every single one of you a huge cuddle and a kiss. Seriously, each and every one of you (if I could name you all, I would) have helped me to become a more confident person and allowed me to live out my dream in real life.

A mahoosive thank you to the greatest parents in the world (I know everyone says that but my parents 'in my opinion' really are the greatest) – my mam and dad. I am so grateful to have you in my life, and not just because you taught me how to robot dance and allow me to sing like a Disney princess in your house even though it annoys you, but also because you have always given me your full love and support. You guide me through life and I wouldn't be writing this book without you both.

To my little sister Ava, my favourite person in the whole wide world and back again. Thank you for making me laugh every single day, you beautiful human being.

To my family that are always there for me: my nanny and pappy (for being my second set of parents) and Kirsty, the best auntie a girl could ask for (thanks for letting me pinch your lipstick when I was little and always being there when I need to talk).

To my uncle Daniel (I know if I ever needed you I could rely on you and thank you for giving me some of my best memories at Nanny's parties including those shaved eyebrows) and my uncle Karl (I love you for introducing me to great comedies, but it does not let you off for the time you microwaved my dolls' heads when I was seven).

To my amazing cousins, you two are like the brothers I never had: Josh (I know you've probably read this book in less than ten minutes, you genius) and Noah (you are an amazing kid and I hope your love of Hoovers evolves into you becoming the next Mr Dyson; you're going to be a top vacuum inventor). Also to my cousin Keegan (I hope you let Luca play in a dog kennel one day like we used to).

To all my forever friends: Sarah (you are my best friend, thank you for always looking after me, you've saved my life at least twice. Thank you for giving me advice and the confidence to be myself. And of course for giving me the best gift a friend could ask for, Jacob, to be a part of my life as my godson); Billie (for always being there for me, for coming to watch me on *Saturday Night Takeaway* and never saying no to 'Should we have another drink?'); Ivo (for all our car trips where we laughed so hard it would hurt and for you and your family always supporting me in everything I do); Nicola Morris (for all your support and love, my girl); Bam; Kelly (for asking me to Crookfest that day; it's the first time I had ever felt like I was part of a friendship group); and Sam and Hannah (for upping my sarcasm game to a whole other level).

To my queens, Tess Tickle, Mr Mark Tickle, Emma Royd and Cara O'Hara, for always making me smile, the advice and support (and the greatest holiday to Vegas ever: Cher, Britney, Dick's Bar, the Fruit Loop and watching a woman ride a unicorn would not have been the same if it wasn't done with you lot).

To my university girls for sticking by me through my bad eyebrow stage and giving me so many amazing memories (some that don't even involve alcohol), for true friendship and for being my forever friends: Zoe, Jess and Siân.

Massive thanks to Dianne Howe – I class you as an auntie, your dance school gave me a place to be myself and a safe haven from the bullying. You encouraged my love of dance and helped build my confidence.

To Ant and Dec for believing in me and giving me opportunities and guidance that has changed my life forever.

Of course a huge thank you to ITV for giving me so many amazing and overwhelming opportunities. Thank you Shu, Angela, Richard, Pete (my fellow Victoria Wood lover), Micky, Daisy, Diego, Saul, director Chris, Andy Milligan, Mike Spencer (my lovely producer), and the hair and make-up team for making me look decent for a change, especially Alice with her wispy eyelashes.

And of course a huge thank you to everyone at Channel 4: without you I wouldn't be writing this book, you have given me so many amazing opportunities and I am so grateful. Thanks to everyone at Studio Lambert, especially Tania Alexander and Tommy Turnbull and to everyone who worked on *Gogglebox*. To Tiger Aspect – can't believe we brought back *Streetmate* – every single one of you put your heart and soul into making the best show we could.

Thank you to Jadeen (for literally organising my life for the last year and for all your support), to John for believing in me, to Dave for making me laugh throughout *Streetmate* and to Jess (for all the times I got confused at the train station).

ACKNOWLEDGEMENTS

And a huge, huge thank you to everybody at Blink Publishing for making my dream book a reality. A special thank you to Natalie Jerome for believing in me (and for putting up with my endless run of emails).